Abstracts of the
TESTAMENTARY PROCEEDINGS
of the
PREROGATIVE COURT OF MARYLAND

Volume II: 1670–1674

Libers: 5, 6

by
V. L. Skinner, Jr.

CLEARFIELD

Printed for
Clearfield Company, Inc. by
Genealogical Publishing Co., Inc.
Baltimore, Maryland
2005

International Standard Book Number 0-8063-5283-3

Made in the United States of America

Dedication to
Vernon L. Skinner, Sr.
1907–1975
and
Frances D. Skinner
1920–2003

"If it is worth doing, it is worth doing right."
Frances D. Skinner

INTRODUCTION

Purpose of the Prerogative Court.

The Prerogative Court was the central point for probate for Provincial Maryland. It was mirrored after the Prerogative Court of Canterbury. There was a judge as well as clerk(s) of the court. Initially, all probate was brought directly to the Prerogative Court, located in the Provincial Capital. As the Province became more populous, all documents were still to be filed with the Prerogative Court; however, administration of probate was delegated to the various county courts. Even so, there are documents only in the Prerogative Court and not in the appropriate county, and vice versa.

Documents filed in the Prerogative Court.

The following documents were filed in the Prerogative Court: administration bond, will, inventory, administration accounts, and final balances. The testamentary proceedings contain the administration bond and the docket for the court. If the administrator is lax in filing documents, then a summons is also recorded.

Equity Court

The Prerogative Court was also the court for equity cases--resolution of disputes over the settlement and distribution of an estate. The case was brought before the judge and could take several years to resolve. Often depositions were taken and recorded in the minutes.

Notes on the Abstraction.

1. The left hand column contains the liber/folio number. The folio numbers are presented just as they appear in the actual document, e.g., 32a, 78½.

2. The right hand column contains the abstraction text.

3. Various libers specify a particular session for the Prerogative Court, e.g., 1678; or, September Court 1742. This information is presented as "Court Session:" followed by the

appropriate session. Should no session have
been specified, then the phrase "no date" is
used.

4. An ellipsis (...) is used to indicate a
continuation of the previous information, but no
relevant genealogical information is present.

5. The following symbols are used in the
abstraction:
```
?    difficult to read.
#    pounds of tobacco.
!    [sic].
```

<u>Abbreviations</u>.

The following abbreviations have been used
throughout this abstraction:

AA - Anne Arundel Co.
BA - Baltimore Co.
CE - Cecil Co.
CH - Charles Co.
CR - Caroline Co.
CV - Calvert Co.
DE - Delaware
DO - Dorchester Co.
ENG - England
FR - Frederick Co.
g - gentleman
HA - Harford Co.
IRE - Ireland
KE - Kent Co. MD
KEDE - Kent Co. DE
LoA - letters of
    administration
MA - Massachusetts
MD - Maryland

MO - Montgomery Co.
NE - New England
NY - New York
NYC - New York City
p - planter
PA - Pennsylvania
PG - Prince George's
    Co.
PoA - power of
    attorney
QA - Queen Anne's Co.
SM - St. Mary's Co.
SMC - St. Mary's City
SO - Somerset Co.
TA - Talbot Co.
VA - Virginia
WA - Washington Co.
WO - Worcester Co.

5:1   6 November 1670. Inventory of William
        Beson. List of debts: Edward Cowdries,
        Mr. Francis Brookes, Francis Spencer,
        George Hinson. Amount: #1870.

        Inventory of Marke Phepo. Date: 20
        February 1669.
5:2   Amount: #1685. Appraisers: Thomas Doxe,
        George Marshall.

        Daniell Jenifer (g, SM) was granted
        administration on estate of Capt.
        William Smith (inholder, SM). Estate
        was unadministered by Mary Jenifer (his
        wife) lately Mary Smith (wife &
        executrix of said William).

5:3   Daniell Jenifer (g, SM) was granted
        administration on estate of his wife
        Mary Jenifer (late Mary Smith).

5:4   21 December 1670. Capt. John Collier
        (g, BA) to prove will of Henry
        Broadwater.

        15 December 1670. John Vanheck & Thomas
        Salmon were granted administration on
        estate of Godfrey Bayley (BA), for the
        orphans during their minority. Capt.
        Thomas Howell to prove said will.
5:5   Appraisers: John James, William
        Salisbury.

        28 December 1670. Richard Gould (TA)
        was granted administration on estate of
        William Maddox (TA). Bondsman: Robert
        Knapp. Appraisers: Robert Knapp,
        Richard Royston. John Foster (g) to
        administer oath.

        Inventory of Walter Beane (CH).
        Executor: Elinor (widow). Appraisers:
        James Walker, John Dent.
5:6-7   ...
5:8   Servants mentioned: Edward Nibbs, Thomas
        Ellis, John Boswell, Richard Bell,
        William Streete, Elisabeth Munday. Also
        lists items in SM. Amount: #79955.

        Inventory of Patrick Cammell.
5:9   Aount: #14340. Date: 14 June 1670.

Court Session: <no date>

Appraisers: John Biger, William Mills.

5:10   Inventory of Alexander Toulson (KI).
Appraisers: Thomas Ringold, Arthur
Wright.

5:11   Amount: #20077. Signed: Thomas
Ringould, Arthur Wright. Witnesses:
Solomon Blackleach, Nicholas Wyat.

5:12   Inventory of William Tettershall (New
Towne). Servants mentioned: Tho.
Holland, Tho. Brookes, James Pencoate,
Ellinor Harvey.

5:13   Amount: #29530. Date: 28 November 1670.
Appraisers: Walter Hall, Edward Clarke.
List of debts: Mr. Henry Phipps, Mr.
George Manwaring, Peter Mill, James
Greeneaway. Amount: #9800. Further
list of debts: Thomas Marshall, John
Jeffs, Gregory Rowse. Amount: #8300.
Proved by Henry Neale.

5:14   Inventory of John Minter. Date: 15
October 1670. Appraisers: Morrice
Baker, Peter Band.

Inventory of Hopkin Davis. Date: 21
March 1669.

5:15   List of debts: Mr. Thomas Stockett, Mr.
Nathaniell Styles, Richard White.
Amount: #9975. Appraisers: Tho.
Vaughan, Hugh Sherwood.

8 December 1670. Daniell Jenifer (SM)
was granted administration on estate of
Thomas Jones (SM). Bondsman: Robert
Ridgely. Appraisers: Robert Ridgely,
Richard Moy (g).

5:16   Samuell Cressy, age 27, deposed that
last June, Michaell Jefferson was at the
house of the deponent & declared all of
his estate to go to the Catholique
Church. Date: 30 November 1670.
Before: Henry Adams.

Susanna Cressy, age 29, deposed the
same. Date: 30 November 1670. Before:
Henry Adams.

Inventory of Michaell Jefferson.
Appraisers: Ignatius Causin, George

Manwaring. Henry Adams (g) gave oath.
5:17 Exhibited by: Henry Warren, Esq. Date:
3 December 1670. List of debts: Amos
Short, Richard Dodd, Abell James, Thomas
Becker. Amount: #4448.

28 November 1670. Barbara Cooke relict
of Henry Cooke (merchant, London) was
granted administration on his estate.
Security: John Waghob. Appraisers: John
Waghob, George Macall. Henry Hyde (SM)
to administer oath.
5:18 Inventory of Henry Cooke (merchant,
London) by Barbara Cooke (widow). Date:
27 December 1670.
5:19 Amount: #52887. Appraisers: George
Macall, John Wahob.

5:20 19 December 1670. Will of Edward
Pomfret (AA). Bequests: John Boulton
(James Rigby's man), Mr. Samuell
Withers chattel at Robert Neave, Mr.
Samuell Withers & James Rigby. Date: 15
December 1670. Witnesses: John Harris,
Charles Haynes. Will proved 12 January
1670.

12 January 1670. Samuell Withers (g)
was granted administration on said
estate. Appraisers: Robert Lusby,
Robert Dabridge. Robert Burle (g) to
administer oath.

21 January 1670. Elisabeth Johnson
widow of Daniell Johnson (CH) was
granted administration on his estate on
behalf of Daniell Johnson (orphan of
said dec'd).
5:21 Bondsmen: George Manwaring, Thomas
Hussey (merchants, CH). Appraisers:
John Coates, Bartholomew Coates. Henry
Adams (g) to administer oath.

11 January 1670. Joseph Weeks (g, TA)
to take possession of the estate of
Thomas Hill (TA) for use of Penelope
orphan of said Hill. (Estate is too
small for administration.)

Inventory of David Boughen (CV).
Appraisers: Thomas Sedgewick, William
Harbert. Date: 3 November 1670.

Court Session: <no date>

Servants mentioned: Thomas Skillton (age 17), Honour Dowdle, Thomas Sterrick.

5:22 List of debts: William Bold, John Miller,

5:23 William Meere, John Merwheere. Amount: #7547. Signed: Tho. Sedgewick, William Herbert.

Inventory of Thomas Walley (chirurgeon, St. Leonard's, CV). Date: 15 January 1670.

5:24 List of debts: Dr. Henry Hough, George Sealy, James More, Patrick Macane. Amount: #8181. Appraisers: Richard Hooper, James Price.

Will of Andrew Robinson. Date: 12 September 1666. Executrix: wife Jane Robinson. Bequests: wife Jane Robinson plantation,

5:25 goddaughter Jane Johnson then to Judeth Johnson, William Innes, Jr. (under age), William Huninton the younger (under age), Jonathon Prater the younger (under age). Overseers: William Innes, Jone Gant. Witnesses: Thomas Gantt, William Innes. Will proved by Thomas Gant & William Innes on 23 January 1670.

5:26 27 Janaury 1670. Jane Robinson was granted administration on said estate. Appraisers: Robert Tyler, Thomas Carleton.

Accounts of Mr. John Lugor. Amount of inventory: #4800. Payments to: John Hill. Signed: Martha Lugor. Amount: #5880.

Accounts of James Adams (CV). Administrator: Thomas Bowdell for use of orphans. Amount of inventory: #6257.

5:27 Payments to: Richard Keen, diet of Isabell Adams, diet of Georg Adams, diet of Margarett Adams, nursing of Elisabeth Adams, John Cary, John Gramm, diet of John Adams. Legatees: George, Margarett, Elisabeth. Amount: #1655. Signed: Thomas Bowdle.

5:28 Isaack Winchester (KE) administrator of John Winchester (KE) was granted

Court Session: <no date>

discharge. Date: 18 February 1670.

5:29 Richard Windley (BA), age 24, before
John Collier (BA) deposed that 3 years
ago the deponent was with Hugh
Broadwater at the house of John Dixon,
who bequeathed to Michaell Shadwell
brother to John Shadwell. Michael
Shadwell has drowned. Date: 4 January
1670.

Henry Inloes (BA), age 38, before John
Collier (BA) deposed that he was at the
house of Mr. John Dixon (Back River),
where (N) Broadwater was ill & he
bequeathed to Mr. John Dixon & Michaell
Shadwell (since dec'd) & his brother
John Shadwell. Signed: Hendrick Enloes.
Date: 4 January 1670.

4 March 1670. Mary Burton relict of
Edward Burton (KI) was granted
administration on his estate. Bondsman:
John Wright. Appraisers: William
Lawrence, John Browne.

5:30 Will of Thomas Mannyng (CV). Executrix:
wife Grace Manning. Bequests: sons
Thomas Manning & Nathaniell Manning
"Manning's Resolution" 800 a., eldest
son John Mannyng "Elton's Plantation" &
300 a., wife Grace Mannyng part of
"Theabush". Date: 9 October 1666.
Witnesses: Christopher Rowsby, And.
Cooke. Codicil: bequests: son John
Mannyng chattel bought of Henry Michard.
Date: 5 October 1670. Will proved by
Christopher Rowsby.

5:31 4 March 1670. John Manning (orphan of
Thomas Manning (g, CV)) chose Richard
Smith (St. Leonard's, CV) as his
guardian. Said Richard was granted
administration on the estate. Bondsman:
Michael Higgins. Appraisers: William
Evans, William Dare, John Hollins.
George Peake (g) to administer oath.

Will of Samson Wareing. Executrix: wife
Sarah Wareing. Bequests: said Sarah &
son Bassill Wareing (under age 20),
Thomas Prichard (my countryman). Date:

18 January 1663. Witnesses: Stephen
Benson, Thomas Elior, Francis Riggs,
Henry Hosier, Rich. Johns, Frances
Backstone, John Vahan. Will proved by
Henry Hosier & Richard Johns on 18 March
1670.

5:32   18 March 1670. Sarah Warring widow &
executrix of Samson Warring (CV) was
granted administration on his estate.
Appraisers: John Throster, James Veitch.
George Peake (g) to administer oath.

Charles James (g, BA) who married
Elisabeth sole daughter & heir of
Leonard Stronge (merchant, AA) was
granted administration on said estate.
Appraisers: Robert Lusby, Robert
Dabridge. Samuell Withers (g) to
administer oath.

Will of Robert Slye (merchant, Bushwood,
St. Clement's Mannor, SM).
5:33   Bequests: little daughters Elisabeth
(under age 16) & Frances (under age 16)
"Rich Neck" 500 a. between Matepony &
Bushwood
5:34   & chattel to be in the hands of Col.
Henry Meese & my kinsman Mr.
Strangwaies Mudd (London), youngest son
Robert (under age 18) plantation
"Lapworth" & "Norwood Lapworth Lodge" &
"Cleare",
5:35   wife Susanna Slye chattel, eldest son
Gerard Slye (under age 18) residue.
5:36   Executor: son Gerard Slye. Overseers:
Mr. Thomas Notley, brother Mr.
Justinian Gerard, brother Mr. Nehemiah
Blackiston, Mr. Benjamin Solly.
5:37   On death of all my children:
brother-in-law Thomas Gerard &
brother-in-law John Gerard &
sister-in-law Mary Gerard "Bushwood"
1000 a.,
5:38   eldest son of sister Mrs. Elisabeth
Russell (London) "Rich Neck" (St.
Clement's Mannor), nephew Timothy Cooper
(Springfield, NE) "Lapworth", nephew
Thomas Cooper (Springfield, NE) "Norwood
Lapworth Lodge" & "Cleare". Date: 18
January 1670. Witnesses: John
Blackiston, Ebenezar Blackiston, John

Court Session: <no date>

Bullocke, Mary Gerard. Will proved by
Mr. John Blackiston & Mrs. Mary Gerard
on 13 March 1670.

5:39   Will of Adam Delap (p, South River, AA).
Bequests: wife Ann Delap & son Abraham
Delap plantation, 5 children (under
age): Abraham Delap, Mathew Delap, Sarah
Delap, John Delap, Deborah Delap.
Executrix: wife. Date: 15 February
1670. Witnesses: John Groome, Nicholas
Gasaway, Francis Johnson, David Howard.
Will proved by John Groome, Nicholas
Gasaway, & Frances Johnson on 14 May
1671.

29 March 1671. Ann Dulap was granted
administration on said estate. George
Puddington to administer oath.

5:40   Thomas Notley, Justinan Gerard, Nehemiah
Blackiston, & Benjamin Solly (gentlemen,
SM) were granted administration on
estate of Robert Slye (g, SM)

5:41   during the minority of Gerard Slye.

last March 1671. Jesse Wharton (g, SM)
to obtain bond on said estate.
Appraisers: John Jordaine, Thomas Lomax.

5:42   Ann Coperthwayte relict of Robert
Coperthwayte (CV) was granted
administration on his estate. Bondsmen:
Morcecai Hunton, John Anderson.
Appraisers: Charles Ashcombe, Michaell
Farmer. William Groome (g) to
administer oath.

Richard Bayly was granted administration
on estate of George Aldridge (CV).
Bondsman: William Thompson. Appraisers:
William King, William Innes. Robert
Tyle (g) to administer oath.

5 April 1671. William Hemsley (TA) was
granted administration on estate of
William Bennet (TA). Appraisers:
Daniell Walker, John Warner. Edward Roe
(g) to administer oath.

5:43   John Browne (TA) was granted
administration on estate of Warner
Shudall (BA). Appraisers: Philip

Page 7

Court Session: <no date>

Stevenson, Thomas Emerson. Richard Ball
(g) to administer oath.

George Peake was to administer the oath
to Sarah Warring executrix of Samson
Warring & said George is now dec'd.
Edward Keene (CV) to administer the
oath. Date: 11 April 1671. Appraisers:
John Throster, Robert Heigh. Edward
Keene to administer oath.

10 April 1671. Charles Brooke was
granted administration on estate of
Francis Brooke (CV). Bondsman: Major
Thomas Brooke. Appraisers: Thomas
Sedgewick, William Harbert. Maj.
Thomas Brooke to administer oath.

11 April 1671. Henry Parker (g) was
granted administration on estate of John
Barnes (TA).
5:44   Security: Samuell Winslow. Appraisers:
James Scot, Andrew Skinner. Richard
Woolman (g) to administer oath.

11 April 1671. Samuell Winslow (TA) was
granted administration on estate of
Samuell Sleydon (TA). Security: Henry
Parker. Appraisers: Andrew Skinner,
James Scot. Richard Woolman (g) to
administer oath.

Elisabeth Benson widow of Stephen Benson
(CV) was granted administration on his
estate. Securities: George Beckwith,
Charles Botler. Appraisers: Patrick
Allen, John Hollins. Edward Keene (g)
to administer oath.

5:45   17 April 1671. John Currer the younger
(KE) was granted administration on
estate of John Currer the elder (grocer,
London). Bondsmen: Robert Dunn, William
Bishop. Appraisers: John Wright, Thomas
Bright. Mathew Reade (g) to administer
oath.

24 April 1671. Ellinor Warren widow of
Humphrey Warren (CH) was granted
administration on his estate. Bondsmen:
James Walker, Richard Smoote.
Appraisers: Capt. Josias Fendall, Mr.

Court Session: <no date>

Robert Henly. Henry Adams (g) to administer oath.

Will of John Tawney (Patuxent River, CV).

5:46   Executors: brother Michaell Tawney & John Hawes, then Mr. Tho. Trueman & Alexander Magrooder. Mentions: children (under age).

5:47   Bequests: brother Michaell Tawney, John Hawse, Francis Lee (servant). Date: 11 March 1670. Witnesses: Henry Hough, Margarett Goosey. Will proved 7 April 1671. Michaell Tawney & John Hause were granted administration on said estate. Appraisers: Francis Hutchings, Tymothy Hunton. Edward Keene (g) to administer oath.

5:48   Will of George Peake. Bequests: wife Mary Peake & children, son George Peake, son Joseph Peake 300 a. on Choptank, daughter Johanna Peake, John Cable. Date: 27 March 1671. Witnesses: John Troster, Robert Heighe.

5:49   Codicil: executrix: Mary Peake. Date: 27 March 1671. Mary Peake was granted administration on said estate. Date: 7 April 1671. Henry Keene (g, CV) to prove the will. Appraisers: John Cobreth, Marke Clare. Edward Keene (g) to administer oath.

Will of Joseph Riggs (inholder, CV). Executrix: wife Jane Riggs. Bequests: wife Jane Riggs "Lower Bennett" in Clifts.

5:50   Date: 8 April 1671. Witnesses: Richard Johns, Henry Hosier. Will proved 20 April 1671.

Will of Joseph Horsley (CV). Executrix: wife Rosamond Horsley. Bequests: John Collman, Mr. Richard Bayley, Judith Cooper. Date: 25 February 1670. Witnesses: John Collman, George Foxwell, Richard Bayley, William King.

William King (CV), age 27, deposed that on 25 February

5:51   he was at the house of Richard Bayley (inholder, Patuxent River) with Joseph

Court Session: <no date>

Horsley. The deponent & Mr. George
Foxwell urged the said Horsley to make
his will. Said Horsley did--indicating
that his wife was to have all. Date: 28
April 1671.

28 April 1671. Rosamond Horsley widow &
executrix of Joseph Horsley (g, CV) was
granted administration on his estate.
Appraisers: George Beckwith, Richard
Keene. Robert Tyler (g) to administer
oath.

5:52   Will of Thomas Stocket (AA). Date: 23
        April 1671.
5:53   Bequests: wife Mary (pregnant) then to
        my daughters, son Thomas, brother
        Francis Stocket, brother Henry, brother
        Mr. Richard Wells, cousin Henry White.
5:54   Executors: brothers Francis Stocket,
        Henry Stocket, Richard Wells.
        Witnesses: Tho. Besson, Tho. Hedge.
        Will proved by Thomas Hedge on 4 May
        1671. Will proved by Thomas Beson, Jr.
        on 15 May 1671.

5:55   Will of James Lindsey (St. Thomas'
        Mannor, CH). Bequests: Roman Catholic
        Priest at Portobacco, wife Mary &
        children. Executrix: wife. Overseers:
        Benedict Merchayes, Ralph Courts. Date
        21 April 1671. Witnesses: Will.
        Bretton, Nicholas Solby, John Sherman.
        Will proved by William Bretton & John
        Cherman on 3 May 1671.

5:56   4 May 1671. Mary executrix of James
        Lindsey was granted administration on
        his estate. Appraisers: Thomas Mathewes
        (g), Bartholomew Coates (g). Henry
        Adams (g) to administer oath.

        Francis Stocket, Henry Stocket, &
        Richard Wells were granted
        administration on estate of Capt.
        Thomas Stocket. Appraisers: Capt.
        William Burgess, Robert Franklyn, John
        Welch. Samuel Chew, Esq. to administer
        oath.

        Will of Georg Manwaring (g, Portobacco,
        CH).

Court Session: <no date>

5:57   Bequests: Mr. Henry Warren
(Portobacco), Mr. Michaell Foster (St.
Inigoes), Mr. Bernard Haines, Mr.
Will. Turberville, wife Ann 880 a. in SM
& plantation in CH. Executors: Mr.
Henry Adams, Mr. Thomas Mathews.
Overseer: Mr. (Portobacco). Date: 11
April 1671. Witnesses: Will. Bretton,
Temperance Bretton, William Guither.
Will proved by William Bretton & William
Guyther on 5 May 1671.

5:58   5 May 1671. Mr. Henry Adams & Mr.
Thomas Mathews were granted
administration on said estate.
Appraisers: Ignatius Courseene, Thomas
Hursey (g). Mr. Benjamin Rozer to
administer oath.

Thomas Paget was granted administration
on estate of Robert Kingsbury (CV).
Appraisers: William Singleton, William
Turner. Richard Pery (g) to administer
oath.

Sarah Hawkins (NYC) widow & relict of
John Hawkins (Elke River), who was
granted administration on said estate by
Gov. Francis Lovelace, appointed John
Damrell as her attorney.
5:59   Date: 4 April 1671. Witness: Jo.
Clarke.

10 May 1671. Per PoA, John Damrell was
granted administration on estate of John
Hawkins (BA). Appraisers: Thomas
Salmon, Abraham Wilde. Capt. Thomas
Howell to administer oath.

Will of Lyonell Paully (p, AA). Date:
18 March 1670/1.
5:60   Bequests: Nathan Smith "Bersheba" at
back of Jerico, my man William Anderson
100 a. at back of Richard Deavor, Grace
Deavor. Executor: Charles Beanen.
Witnesses: Samuell Lane, Richard Deavor.
Will proved 20 May 1671.

5:61   12 May 1671. Charles Benen was granted
administration on said estate.
Appraisers: Thomas Morgan, Henry Benitt.
Samuell Chew, Esq. to administer oath.

Court Session: <no date>

Will of George Peake (Clifts, CV) was proved by John Troster & Robert Heigh on 29 April 1671. Signed: Edward Keene.

15 May 1671. John Wright was granted administration on estate of John Lawrence (KE). Appraisers: Francis Pyne, Charles Delaroch. Tobias Wells (g) to administer oath.

5:62 19 May 1671. John Fitzharbert (g) was granted administration on estate of Margaret Brent (VA). Bondsman: Edward Fitzharbert, Esq. Appraisers: John Browne, William Lawrence. John Wright (g) to administer oath.

Will of Samuell Withers (Durant's Point, AA). Bequests: wife Elisabeth Withers,
5:63 son Samuell Withers, Capt. William Burges & Richard Hill to receive custody of William & Thomas Pennington (orphans of William Pennington (AA, dec'd)) & for them 600 a. "Suffolk" on Tuckahoe Creek on Choptanke.
5:64 Overseers: Capt. William Burges, Richard Hill. Executor: son Samuell Withers. Date: 23 March 1670. Witnesses: Thomas Marsh, Robert Lusbe, Richard Hill. Elisabeth Withers widow & relict of Samuell Withers was granted administration on his estate, during the minority of Samuell Withers, Jr. Date: 2 June 1671.
5:65 Appraisers: Robert Davidg, Robert Lusby. Robert Burlt (g) to administer oath.

Will of George Collings (AA). Bequests: John Clerk. Executor: said John. Date: 17 November 1670. Witnesses: Henry Lewis, Oliver Holloway. John Clerke was granted administration on said estate. Date: 8 June 1671.
5:66 Appraisers: Robert Tyler, Abraham Dawson. Robert Burl (g) to administer oath.

15 June 1671. Charles Boteler & John Hollins appointed to appraise the estate of Stephen Benson. Patrick Allen refused to take the oath. Edward Keene (g) to administer oath.

Court Session: <no date>

Will of Richard Wells (Herrin Creek,
AA). Bequests: wife Sophia "Wells Cont"
600 a. & "Wells Hills" 430 a.

5:67 adjoining Anthony Solloway then to heirs
of my brother George Wells then to heirs
of my brother Benjamin, Samuell Lane
"Brosty Hall" 800 a. Executrix: wife.
Date: 11 May 1671. Witnesses: Richard
Ewens, John Jeffryes. Will proved 9
June 1671. was granted administration
on said estate. Appraisers: William
Burggess, Anthony Salloway, Robert
Franklin (g). Samuell Chew (g) to
administer oath.

5:68 Inventory of Robert Coberthwayt.
Amount: #6570. Date: 8 April 1671.
Appraisers: Charles Ashcom, Michael
Farmer.

19 June 1671. Richard Mascall who
married Katherine widow & relict of
Henry Gutterick (AA) was granted
administration on said estate.
Bondsmen: Richard Ewen, William Head.
Appraisers: William Head, Mathew Howard.
Richard Ewen (g) to administer oath.

17 July 1671. Mary Bramble widow &
relict of Thomas Bramble (DO) was
granted administration on his estate.
5:69 Bondsmen: James Selby, Francis Swinfen.
Appraisers: William Thomas, Thomas
Newton. Daniel Clerke (g) to administer
oath.

Will of George Collings (AA) proved by
Mr. Henry Lewis & Oliver Holloway.
Date: 10 July 1671.

Will of Samuell Withers (g, AA) proved
by Thomas Marsh (g), Robert Lusbie, Mr.
Richard Hill.
5:70 Elisabeth Withers relict &
administratrix took oath. Appraisers:
Robert Davidg, Robert Lusbie. Date: 26
June 1671. Inventory of Samuell Withers
(g, AA). Date: 26 June 1671.
5:71-73 ...
5:74 Amount: #79158. Signed: Robert Davidg,
Robert Lusby.

5:75   Inventory of Richard Rider, Jr. by
        William Harris. Date: 21 September
        1671.
5:76   Appraisers: John Boothe, Philip Jones.
        John Warren administered the oath.

        <u>29 September 1671</u>. William Hemsley (TA)
        was granted administration on estate of
        John Whaley (TA). Appraisers: Charles
        Masters, John Segivant. Richard Woolman
        (g) to administer oath.

        Inventory of John Barnes (TA).
5:77   Amount: #2980. Date: 8 May 1671.
        Appraisers: A. Skinner, James Scott.
        Mr. Henry Parker administrator of said
        estate was granted continuance for an
        additional inventory. Date: 2 October
        1671.

        Inventory of Samuell Sleydon (TA).
        Appraisers: Andrew Skinner, James Scott.
        Date: 6 May 1671. List of debts:
        Abraham Bishopp, John Mitchell, Henry
        Taylor, Will. Pollard. Amount: #1674.
        Filed: 8 May 1671.

        Inventory of Mr. John Dixon.
        Appraisers: Capt. John Collier, Mr.
        Godrey Harman. Date: 31 December 1670.
5:78   ...

5:79   Inventory of Henry Gutrick (AA). Date:
        12 July 1671.
5:80   ...
5:81   Land mentioned: "The Range" 100 a. on
        Patapsco River, "Midle Neck" 150 a.,
        "Kinseys Cheird" 150 a., "Rich Neck" 100
        a., "West Humphreiss" 300 a.
        Appraisers: William Slade, Mathew
        Howard.

5:82   John Hollins & Charles Boteler took oath
        as appraisers of estate of Stephen
        Benson (CV). Date: 1 August 1671.
        Inventory of Stephen Benson (Clifts,
        CV). Date: 15 June. Amount: #10462.

5:83   Will of Tobias Apelford (KI). Bequests:
        Henry Davis, John More, Richard Nash.
        Executor: said Richard Date: 14
        September 1671. Signed: Tobias

Court Session: <no date>

Apellford. Witnesses: John Ereckson, John Bredborne. Richard Nash was granted administration on said estate. Date: October 1671. Appraisers: Isaack Winchester, John More. John Wright (g, KE) to administer oath.

5:84 Inventory of Mr. Simon Carpenter (TA). Appraisers: Joseph Weekes, Philemon Loyd. Date: 2 January 1670.
5:85-86 ...
5:87 List of debts: Thomas Vaughen, Richard Cookeman, Richard Jones. Amount: #68728. Filed: 17 August 1671. Signed: Josh. Wickes, Phil. Loyd. Reviewed by Henry Coursey, Esq. on 3 October 1671.

Inventory of Edward Burton (KE). Date: 1 April 1671.
5:88 ...
5:89 Amount: #22184. Appraisers: William Lawrence, John Browne. List of debts: Lucus Abell (BA), Henry Williams (TA), Mr. Hemsley, Mathew Smithe, Ceaser Sutton,
5:90 Ralph Elstone, John Madbery, George Lancaster (KE), Edward Hull, Maier Ingram, Edward Lakeby, John Browne, John Tassell, William Grace, Mr. Wright (dec'd), Robert Kent, James Thompson (CV), Robert Davigi, Mr. Jerome Catton. Amount: #16182.

Accounts of Hopkin Davis. Payments to: Mr. Richard Gorsuch, Henry Lambert, John Pitt, William Hinsley, John Wheeler, Francis Pine, Stephen Benson, Hanry Wharton, Dr. Tilghman. Amount: #18262.
5:91 Amount of inventory: #9975. Appraisers: Thomas Vaughen, Hugh Sherwood. Administratrix: Elisabeth Smith (late Elisabeth Davis) now wife of William Smith (TA). Date: 28 September 1671.

5 October 1671. Michaell Miller who married the widow of John Steveens (KE) was granted administration on his estate. Bondsman: Jonathon Dickinson. Appraisers: John Ingram, Tobias Wells. John Wright (g, KE) to administer oath.

Thomas Hinson (g) to summon Susanna Lamb
widow & relict of Henry Lamb (KE) to
determine if she will administer the
estate. Michaell Miller is demanding
administration, as greatest creditor.

5:92   Will of Samuell Gouldsmith (g, BA).
        Date: 12 October 1670. Bequests: my
        son-in-law Capt. George Wells, wife
        Johanna Gouldsmith,
5:93   daughter Susanna Uty who married Mr.
        George Utie, daughter Hannah Wells,
        son-in-law Mr. George Utie, godson
        Georg Gouldsmith, Mrs. Mary Gouldsmith.
        Executors: wife Johann Gouldsmith,
        son-in-law Capt. Georg Wells.
5:94   Witnesses: Mathias Stevenson, Nicho.
        Banckes. Will proved 6 October 1671.
        Mr. Georg Utie or Capt. John Collier
        to swear executors. Appraisers: Thomas
        Salmon, Henry Haselwood.

        7 October 1671. John Lawes who married
        Katherine widow & relict of John Nelson
        (SO) was granted administration on his
        estate. Appraisers: Philip Shapleigh,
        Richard Whittey. William Stevens (g) to
        administer oath.

5:95   Robert Lusbie & Robert Davidge appointed
        appraisers of estate of Mr. Leonard
        Strong (AA). Robert Burle (g)
        administered oath. Date: 22 May 1671.
        Inventory of Leonard Strong (g). Date:
        23 May 1671. Amount: #5315.

        Samuell Bowen (BA), age 31, deposed that
        he was a servant to Henry Jones last
        January & was with said Jones & Samuell
        Hewes & said Jones made his will.
        Bequests: wife Ann & 2 daughters Sarah &
        Mary. [Cites an inventory of assets,
        including 100 a.] Signed: Sa. Bowen.
        Date: 13 October 1671. Before: Robert
        Ridgely.

5:96   13 October 1671. John West (BA) who
        married Ann widow & relict of Henry
        Jones was granted administration on his
        estate. Capt. Thomas Howell to take
        deposition of Samuell Hewes.
        Appraisers: William Dunkerton, Richard

Court Session: <no date>

Leake. Capt. Thomas Howell to
administer oath.

Will of James Selby (DO). Date: 26
August 1671.
5:97   Bequests: Thomas Newton & Samuell
Pritchet, Thomas Kendall, Mr. Daniell
Clerke "Perith" on the Blackwater,
executors. Executors: William Worgan &
his wife Alice. Witnesses: Thomas
Kendall, Samuell Pritcherd. Will proved
13 October 1671. William Worgan was
granted administration on said estate.
Appraisers: Thomas Skinner, John
Rawlings. Daniell Clerke (g) to
administer oath.

5:98   Will of Mrs. Barbara Wright (widow, BA,
late of Bovill Parish of St. Andrew's
Glamorganshire). Bequests: niece
Margaret Penry (said Parish) "Bovill",
maidservant Dorothy Thomas. Executrix:
said niece. Witnesses: Thomas Howell,
John Owen, Tho. Scott. Will proved by
Thomas Howell & Thomas Scot on 16
October 1671. Margaret Penry was
granted administration on said estate.
Appraisers: Edward Beetle, William
Salisbury. Capt. Thomas Howell to
administer oath.

5:99   Will of Edward Deane (CH). Bequests:
Elisabeth Lindsey daughter of Mr. James
Lindsey & his wife Mary. Mentions: John
Wheeler. Witnesses: Coates Ralph, John
Colling, Richard Wall.
5:100 Will proved by Ralph Coates & Richard
Wall on 14 September 1671.

Will of William Allen (CH). Date: 3
January 1669.
5:101 Bequests: daughter Elisabeth Allen, wife
Martha Allen, goddaughter Mary Harrison
(under age) daughter of Joseph Harrison
chattel at John Wheeler, Luke Greene
(CH) chattel at John Ashbrook, John Munn
(son of John Munn), Roger Dickison.
Executor: brother-in-law John Munn.
Witnesses: Walter Cooper, Charles
Woolen. John Munn relinquishes
administration to Gerrard Browne. Date:
18 July. Witnesses: Mary Allenson,

5:102   Peter Dosson.
Will proved by Charles Wooley on 13
September 1671.

5:103   Will of Nicholas Emanson (CH). Date: 20
March 1670.
Bequests: daughter Phebe, wife Elisabeth
& daughter Mary Emanson (minor).
Executrix: wife. Witnesses: James
Martin, Steeven Mountgue, William
Marritt.

5:104   Will proved by James Martin. Date: 8
September 1671. Will proved by Steeven
Mountagu & William Marritt. Date: 14
September 1671.

5:105   Ignatius Causeene & Thomas Hussey were
sworn as appraisers of estate of Georg
Manwaring (CH). Date: 16 May 1671.

Thomas Allanson & Henry More were sworn
as appraisers of estate of William Allen
(CH). Date: 13 September 1671.

5:106   Mr. Henry Adams & Mr. Thomas Mathewes
took oath as administrators. Date: 11
April 1671.

Inventory of George Aldridge. Date: 7
August 1671. List of debts: William
King, Charles Ashcomb, Hen. Darnall,

5:107   William Dare, Fran. Bennett, James
Williams, Roger Baker, Peter Bayard,
William Wood, Tho. How, Jesper Allen,
Henry Hooper, Jr., Nath. Ashcombe, Guy
White, Geo. Beckwith, C. Boteler.
Amount: #4501. Appraisers: William
King, William James.

Will of Daniell Silvaine (BA).
Bequests: John Ryland & John Brisco
"Daniell's Denn" 400 a. on Sasafras
River, William Dumberton "Daniell's
Hope" 200 a. on Sasafras River & chattel
at Nicholas Allonie & chattel left me by
Lancellot Hallet,

5:108   John Bromfeild 150 a. on Wharton Creek
(BA) then to Nathaniell Howell then to
Thomas Howell, Jr., Mr. Mr. Nicholett
(Minister of God's Word), servant Morgan
Pennery, Jeremiah Silvane, Philip
Conyer, Nicholas Allonie, Nicholas
Allonie & his wife Margaret, Robert

Court Session: <no date>

5:109   Saunders, Frances Williams, Elisabeth &
Rosamond Bayly 2 daughters of Mr. Bayly
chattel bought of Richard Leake, William
Johnson, Roger Roberts, Gidion Gundry,
Ralph Cassell, Thomas Howell, Jr.,
William White, Richard Leake, Thomas
Salmon to pay the sheriff, William
Dunkerton 150 a. on Norton Creek,
William Dunkerton & Nicholas Allonie to
take acknowledgement from William
Salsbury for said John Bromfeild.
Executors: William Dunkerton, Nicholas
Allonie. Date: 26 September 1671.
Witnesses: Benj. Gundry, John
Richardson. William Dunberton &
Nicholas Allonie were granted
administration on said estate. Date: 20
October 1672. Appraisers: Tho. Overton,
Joseph Langley. Thomas Howell (g) to
administer oath.

5:110   Inventory of Capt. Lyonell Pawly (AA).
Date: 2 October 1671. Appraisers:
Thomas Morgan, Henry Bennett.
5:111   Amount: #6639. Signed: Thomas Morgan,
Henry Benett.

17 October 1671. Elisabeth Davis widow
of Hopkin Davis was granted discharge.
Elisabeth Smith administratrix of Hopkin
Davis (TA) was granted discharge.

5:112   Inventory of Thomas Bramble (DO).
Appraisers: William Thomas, Thomas
Newton. Date: 22 July 1671. Amount:
#2459.
5:113   Accounts of Thomas Bramble. Payments
to: John Peerce, James Selby, Joseph
Sargent. Amount: #2626.

18 October 1671. Mary Bramble
administratrix of Thomas Bramble was
granted discharge. Date: 17 October
1671.

5:114   Accounts of John Tinker. Payments to:
Garret Vanswaringen, James Williams,
Thomas Paget, Thomas Plat, Marck Cordea,
Thomas Bowdle. Amount: #9918. Widow &
administratrix: Amy Burges. Amount of
inventory: #7253.

Court Session: <no date>

20 October 1671. John Burges who
married Amy aforesaid was granted
discharge.

5:115   Inventory of Thomas Jones. Appraisers:
Richard Moy, Robert Ridgely. Date: 25
May 1671. Amount: #742. Date: 20
October 1671.

5:116   Thomas Greene (Patapsco) acknowledged
receipt of items to be delivered to
Winifred Jones. Date: 21 February 1670.
Witnesses: Bru. Vawghan, Richard
Thussell.

26 October 1671. Curtis Fletcher (SM)
was granted administration on estate of
John Lewis (merchant, Bristoll).
Bondsmen: Garret Vanswaringen, Vincent
Atchinson. Appraisers: Thomas Spinke,
Thomas Perce. Thomas Dent (g) to
administer oath.

5:117   Susanna King widow of Robert King (SM)
was granted administration on his
estate. Bondsman: John Barnes.
Appraisers: Walter Waterling, Thomas
Perce. William Calvert, Esq. to
administer oath.

18 October 1671. Henry Bonner (CH) was
granted administration on estate of
Thomas Burston (CH). Bondsman: Thomas
Lomax. Appraisers: William Marshall,
Robert Ingolsby. Francis Pope (g) to
administer oath.

Ellen Reade widow & relict of William
Reade (TA) was granted administration on
his estate. Bondsmen: John Richardson,
John Anderson. Appraisers: Thomas
Vaughan, John Marckes. Edward Roe (g)
to administer oath.

16 October 1671. Benjamin Rozer (CH)
was granted administration on estate of
Samuell Burford (CH). Bondsman: Robert
Ridgely.

5:118   21 October 1671. Margaret Penry was
granted administration on estate of
Francis Wright (BA). Bondsman: Jacob
Young. Appraisers: Edward Beetle,

Court Session: <no date>

William Salisbury. Capt. Thomas Howell
to administer oath.

Inventory of Joseph Horsley.
5:119-120 ...
5:121   List of debts: Will. Smith, James
Morgan, John Neavill, Henry Tasterling.
Amount: #34481. Date: 13 June 1671.
Appraisers: Geo. Beckwith, Ric. Keene.

Inventory of John Sterrill. Appraisers:
Thomas Basset, Richard Bennet. Date: 30
October 1671. List of debts: Walter
Green, Arthur Thomson, Thomas Bennet,
Robert Beard, Ebrius Rowlin, John
Medbry. Amount: #4230.

Inventory of Richard Johnson.
5:122   ...
5:123   Amount: #9343. Appraisers: Henry
Andrews, Richard Stotting.

3 November 1671. James Munkister who
married Elisabeth widow & relict of John
Chagreman (p, CH). Bondsman: Kenelm
Mackloughlyn. Appraisers: Stephen
Mountague, John Elmes. Henry Adams (g)
to administer oath.

5:124   10 November 1671. Thomas Carleton was
granted administration on estate of John
Webster (TA). Bondsman: Richard Keene.
Appraisers: Richard Royston, Seth Foster
(g). Edward Roe (g) to administer oath.

Inventory of John Hawkins. Date: 18
August 1671.
5:125   Servants mentioned: Ja. Robinson (boy),
Francis Collins (boy). Amount: #52995.
Appraisers: T. Salmon, Abraham Wilde.

5:126   Inventory of Thomas Thomas. Date: 12
August 1671.
5:127   Amount #7140. Appraisers: Robert Drury,
John Deane. William Boswell
administered the oath.

23 November 1671. Jane Riggs widow &
executrix of Joseph Riggs was granted
administration on his estate.
Appraisers: Robert Heigh, Thomas
Billingsley. Edward Keene (g) to

administer oath.

Will of Richard Howard (TA), age 43.
Bequests: Robert Wolderton & his wife
Micaell all land on Tredavon Creek &
after their death to Elisabeth Todd now
wife of Nathaniell Teagle,
5:128 said Elisabeth Teagle, Robert Harding,
John Dolby, Ant. Meale (also Ant.
Mayle), Rachell Hacker (daughter of
Richard Hacker (VA)) "Batchelor's Range"
250 a. on Choptank River. Executor:
Micaell Woolderton. Date: 13 July 1671.
Witnesses: Anto. Mayle, John Dolby, Edw.
Roe, Will. Sheires.
5:129 24 November 1671. Robert Woolderton who
married Michaell was granted
administration on said estate.
Appraisers: Edward Roe, Anthony Meale.
Seth Foster (g) to administer oath.

Will of Nicholas Waterman (AA). Date: 8
March 1670.
5:130 Bequests: son Nicholas Waterman (under
age 18), unborn child, wife plantation
on West River toward Anthony Holland.
Executrix: wife Ellinor Waterman.
Witnesses: Robert Francklin, Samuell
Lane.

5:131 27 November 1671. Robert Lockwood who
married Ellinor executrix of Nicholas
Waterman was granted administration on
his estate. Appraisers: Robert
Francklin, James White. Samuell Chew,
Esq. to administer oath.

Will of Samuell Neale. Bequests: son
Samuell Neale (under age 20), Everart
Robert, 3 children, Thomas Seekings,
daughter Margret Neale (under age 18) to
Henry Smith & his wife, daughter Rebecka
(under age 18) to John Barnes.
5:132 Witnesses: Evan Caricio, John Ashcombe.
Date: 1671. Will proved 25 November
1671. Thomas Spinke (SM) was granted
administration on said estate.
Bondsmen: John Barnes, Henry Smith.
Appraisers: Thomas Peerce, Walter
Waterling. Thomas Dent (g) to
administer oath.

Court Session: <no date>

Will of Stephen Horsy, Sr. Bequests: 3
youngest sons Samuell & Nathaniell &
Isaack (all under age 21) land I live on
to be equally divided,
5:133   children Stephen Horsy & John Horsy &
Samuell & Nathaniell & Isaack & Mary &
Abigale Horsy. Executors: 2 oldest sons
Stephen, John. Overseers: Michael
Williams, Alexander Draper, Benjamin
Sumner. Date: 10 April 1671.
Witnesses: John Wallop, Henry Powell.
William Stephens to prove the will.
Date: 28 November 1671.

Inventory of William Allen. Date: 23
November 1671.
5:134   List of debts: Henry More, Thomas
Allenson, John Royden, Thomas Benet
(SM). Appraisers: Tho. Allanson, Henry
More.

5:135   Will of Charles Brooke (g, "Brooke
Place", CV). Bequests: brother John
Brooke pt. Mannor, brother Henry Brooke
(under age 21), nephew Robert Brooke
(son of brother Robert Brooke) pt.
Mannor,
5:136   William Brooke (under age 21, son of
brother Robert Brooke) pt. Mannor
between his brother Robert & land of
Roger Brooke until he comes of age to
his mother & father-in-law Thomas
Cosden, brother Henry Brooke pt. Mannor,
5:137   sisters Ann Brooke & Elisabeth Brooke to
live on my plantation as long as they
are unmarried, brother Roger Brooke
"Battle Creek Neck", brother Henry
Brooke (under age 21) "Island Creek
Neck" if he died before age 21 & after
death of my sisters Ann & Elisabeth then
to brother John Brooke,
5:138   sisters Ann & Elisabeth "Brooke Ridge"
1000 a. on Patuxent River, nephew Robert
Brooke (son of brother Robert Brooke)
land on
5:139   St. Charles Branch if he died under age
21 then to Baker Brooke (son of brother
Baker Brooke), niece Mary Brooke
(daughter of brother Robert Brooke), Mr.
Warren, Mr. Foster. Overseers: brothers
Roger Brooke, John Brooke. Executors:
said brothers Roger & John with sister

Page 23

Court Session: <no date>

5:140　Ann.　Date: 29 May 1671.
Witnesses: Joseph Newman, William
Andrews.

15 December 1671. Said will proved on
this date. Roger Brooke, John Brooke, &
Ann Brooke were granted administration
on said estate. Appraisers: Charles
Boteler, Cuthbert Fenwick (g). Baker
Brooke, Esq. to administer oath.

5:141　Will of George Gouldhawke (KE).
Bequests: wife Mary Gouldhawke.
Executrix: wife. Mentions: maidservant
Martha Robertson.
5:142　Date: 11 March 1671. Witnesses: Joseph
Wickes, Amy Williams.

Will of Mary Gouldhawke (KE). Bequests:
Mary Cammel,
5:143　Sarah Nash daughter of Alexander Nash,
manservant Richard Hill, sister Rachell
Wickes, manservant Henry Vizard,
Michaell Miller, maidservant Martha
Robertson, unborn child, brother &
sister Joseph & Rachell Wickes.
Overseer: father Mr. Joseph Wickes.
5:144　Date: 27 April 1671. Witnesses: Mi.
Miller, Mary Cammel. Codicil: Executor:
father Joseph Weekes. Date: 10 may
1671. Witnesses: John Hodgson, Sr.,
Jer. Eaton.

19 December 1671. Joseph Weekes was
granted administration on estate of Mary
Gouldhawke (widow).
5:145　Appraisers: John Ingram, John
Winchester.

4 January 1671. Richard Beck (CH) was
granted administration on estate of
Elisabeth Emanson (widow, CH).
Appraisers: John Lambert, Thomas Kinge.
Benjamin Rozer (g) to administer oath.

Additional inventory of Richard Rider.
Appraisers: John Booth, Philip Jones.
Amount: #1000.

5:146　Inventory of William Greene (taylor,
CV). Date: 12 August 1671.
5:147　...

5:148   Amount: #7760. Appraisers: Richard
Wadsworth, Richard Marsham. Mr. Tobias
Norton administered oath.

5:149   Inventory of Robert King.
Appraisers: Thomas Perce, Walter
Waterling.

5:150   Will of Robert Smith (TA).
Bequests: grandchild Mary Waterlin, Ann
Walters daughter of Christopher Walters
(dec'd), Elisabeth King daughter of
Marck Kinge (dec'd), Robert King eldest
son of said Marck Kinge plantation 200
a., Robert Walters plantation that his
father Christopher Walters lived on,
daughter Ann Emory plantation she lives
on

5:151   then to John Kinge youngest son of said
Marck Kinge. Residue of land in 3
parts: Robert Walters (under age 18),
John Kinge (under age 18), James Symonds
(under age 18) son of Thomas Symonds.
Residue to: Ann Walters, Mary Waterlin,
Elisabeth Kinge. Executor: William
Coursey, Trustram Thomas. Date: May
1671. Witnesses: Thomas Jackson, Edward
Tomlim. Will proved 9 December 1671.

5:152   20 December 1671. William Coursey &
Trustram Thomas were granted
administration on said estate.
Appraisers: Jonathon Sybery, Philip
Stevens. Capt. Philemon Lloyd to
administer oath.

Will of Mr. Robert Slye (SM) was proved
by John Bullock on 19 December 1671.
Former administration to Thomas Notley,
Justinian Gerard, Nehemiah Blackiston, &
Benjamin Solly declared void. Gerard
Slye was granted administration on said
estate. Inventory of Mr. Robert Slye
(merchant, SM). Appraisers: Benjamin
Solly, Thomas Lomax. Date: 1 September
1671.

5:153-163 ...

5:164   Mentions: Capt. Benjamin Cooper
(commander from London).

5:165-178 ...

5:179   White servants: Humphrey Willey, John
Slye, James Needles, John Merry, Thomas
Elliott, Ralph Wilkenson, James Kershaw,

Court Session: <no date>

Margaret Sturges, Mary Starbruck. Negro
men: Negro Clauser, Negro Bambo, Negro
Dockay, Negro Tony, Negro Tom. Negro
women: Negro Bess, Negro Alce, Negro
Hannah, Negro Love, Negro Joane, Negro
Sue, Negro Maria. Negro children: Negro
Pegge, Negro Nanny, Negro Mingo.

5:180 List of debts: James Bowling, Edward
Turner, Ellinor Beane, William
Hollingsworth, William Breton, Sr.,
Thomas Carvile, Gyles Tomkins, John
Kingly, Allexander Smith, Thomas
Jourdaine, Tho. Warne (Plymouth), Robert
Rowland, Edw. Donnman (Plymouth), Thomas
Miles, Edward Solley, Joane Mitchell,
Robert Joyner, William Summerhill, Hugh
Macknemarry, Joshua Guibert, Richard
Otame, Robert Farra, Tho. Hussey, Lt.
Col. John Jarbo, Capt. Hugh Oneal,
Tho. Dewberry, Gregory Rowse, Tho.
Beamont,

5:181 Mathew Hill, Francis Pope, John
Abbington, Archibold Wahobb, Philip
Calvert, Esq. (Chancellor), Hugh
Mathews, Col. Gerard Fowke, Edmond
Lindsey, Richard Shippey, Ebenezar
Blackiston, Samuell Harris, Tho. Melton,
William Smoote, Thomas Baker, Capt.
Josias Fendall, Richard Dodd, John
Newton, John Foxall (VA), William
Perfit, James Greene, Capt. James
Neale, Vincent Mansell, Benj. Rozer,
John Warren, Capt. Tho. Cornwallis,
John Tennisson, Arthur Thompson, Samuell
Dobson, Ellinor Warren, Edward Swann,
Garrett Vanswaringen, John Farsen,

5:182 Gilbert Cropper, Thomas Ward, Robert
Englesby, William Marshall, John Morris,
Michaell Thompson, Andrew Ward, Thomas
Speake, Symon Reddor, John Appleton
(VA), John Smith, Richard Boughton, Tho.
Stonestreet, William Roswell, Peter
Mills, Ann Shirtclife, Edward Clerke,
Henry Neall, Samuell Cressey, Peter
Roberts, William Miles, John Compton,
John Stanley, Henry Taylor (NE), John
Pyper, Robert Atkins, Thomas Reves, John
Hauskins,

5:183 Justinian Tennison, John Heard, Jenken
Joannes, Thomas Evans, Francis Knott,
John Long, Clement Haley, Robert Browne,
John Courte, Marmaduke Snow, John Pile,

Court Session: <no date>

Richard Preston, Henry Shadock, Thomas
Gibson, Robert Hutcheson, Thomas
Simpson, Richard Edelen, John Gee, John
Medley, John Jordaine, George Newman,
John Walton, John Poppin (NY), Richard
Upgate, Edward Connore, John Harrison,
Marmaduke Simpson, John Blackistone,
5:184   Thomas Cosden, Richard Morris, Capt.
Luke Gardner, Robert Downes, John Grace,
George Bankes, Thomas Notley,
Elliphellet Hett (NE), John Shanker,
Rowland White, George Diamond, James
Walker, John Gouldsmith, Benjamin Solly,
Robert Hunt, Richard Foster, John Cock,
Bryan Cummin, John Sheppard, John
Turner, John Hilton, Thomas Gerard,
Esq., Humphry Jones, Thomas Gerard, Jr.,
Henry Hardy, Justinian Gerard, Robert
Cooper, Nehemiah Blackistone, William
West,
5:185   Thomas Lomax, Charles Ducres, Capt.
Benjamin Cooper, John Hatch, Robert
Carey, Lt. Col. John Washington (VA),
James Traske, Edward Applebe,
Bartholomew Slaughter, John Gooch,
Anthony Watts (VA), John Dobbs, William
Barton, Jr., Tho. Bellerbe, John Gillam,
Ann Martin, John Thomas (VA), James
Hayes, John Harvey, John Frodshall (VA),
George Homes, John Allen, John
Morecraft, his Excellency Capt.
Generall, James Sean, James Seager,
5:186   Gyles Cole, Samuell Maddox, William
Goddard, Henry Bonner, Dennis White,
Verlinda Stone, Thomas Stauly, William
Hawton, Abraham Comes, Thomas Oakely,
John Stone, Richard Saunderson. Amount:
#239518. Further list of debts: Isaack
Bedloe, James Lindsey, John Ashbrooke,
William Gaudy, Zachary Gillam, Richard
Hill, George Thompson, Jenkin Morgan,
Robert Ford, James Pattyson, John
Camell, James Johnson, John Pheesey,
Eliz. Johnson, John Farrell,
5:187   Jacob Peterson, William Simpson, Gerard
Breedon, William Felstead, Roger
Dwiggen, Robert Sampson, Tho. Covant
(dec'd), Richard Cole (VA), Elisabeth
Barber (dec'd), Thomas Cager, Tho.
Casey, Dr. Robert Peirce, Joseph Alvey,
George Hinksman, Joseph Peirce (Lime),
William Cheshire, James Cougdon.

Amount: #32461. Further list of debts:
(runaway & dead insolvent): John
Andrews, Thomas James, John Symonds,
Robert Davisson, William Browne (dec'd),
Capt. William Lewis (dec'd), Francis
Gray (VA), Jacob Baker (NY),
5:188 Nathaniell Mucert (VA), Anthony
Marckham, Thomas Harper, Michaell Abbot,
Mathew Rowse (dec'd), Thomas Steed
(dec'd), Samuell Osborne (B.B.), Arthur
Turner (dec'd), Edward Cole & John Berry
(B.B.), Jacob Johnson (Norway),
Nathaniell Rudd (dec'd), Jacob Johnson
(MD), Robert Ratcliffe (dec'd), Joshua
Lee, John Ray (dec'd), Anthony Howd,
Walter Peake (dec'd), Thomas Kirkley,
William Coulson, Joseph Edmunds (VA),
Robert Lunn, Tho. Ball (dec'd), John
Dyne, Thomas Phillips, Jeffery Fish
(dec'd), William Shrewes, Thomas Brewer,
John Selby. Amount: #23213.
5:189 Further list of debts: Thomas Gerard,
Esq., Tho. Underwood (Boston, NE),
Vincent Mansell, Lt. Col. John
Washington (VA), Peter Evars, John
Appleton (VA), Tho. Philpot (VA),
Justinian. Gerard. Amount: £25.14.17.
Further inventory at Lapworth
Plantation.
5:190 White servants: John Ware, Mary Smith.
Negro men: Negro Tom, Negro Caffee.
Appraisers: Benjamin Solley, Thomas
Lomax.

5 January 1671/2. Inventory of John
Charnam (CH).
5:191 Amount: #5030. Appraisers: Stephen
Mountague, John Irelire.

Date: 30 December 1671. Inventory of
Mr. James Lindsey (CH).
5:192 Amount: #14010. Appraisers: Thomas
Mathews, Bartholos Coates.

Will of William Hattoft (merchant).
5:193 Bequests: goods from England at Patuxent
on board ship Francis & Mary at anchor
in St. Mary's River to be taken by Caleb
Baker & Maier Edward Fitzherbert &
residue to be shipped to Bristol for use
of Mr. William Dunning & Mr. Thomas
Smart, said Caleb Baker, said Maier

Court Session: <no date>

5:194
Fitzherbert, Mr. Curtis Fletcher & Clement Chevirall, John Thompson & his son John Thompson, Patrick Forrest & George Dundas, Elisabeth Spinck daughter of Thomas Spinck, George Dundas, Ellinor Forrest wife of Patrick Forrest, Eliz. Forrest & their other children, Clement Chivrall daughter [sic] of John Chivrall, Mrs. Smart wife of said Thomas Smart, brother Richard.

5:195
Executors: Caleb Baker, Maier Edward Fitzherbert. Date: 19 December 1671. Witnesses: Abell James, Geo. Dundas. Will proved by Abell James & George Dundas on 30 December 1671. Edward Fitzherbert & Caleb Baker were granted administration. Date: 4 January 1671. Bondsmen: Garret Vanswaringen, Walter Waterling. Appraisers: Walter Hall, Thomas Innis.

5:196
Rebecka Painter relinquished her administration on estate of her husband George Painter to Samuell Goosey, as greatest creditor. Date: 10 January 1671. Witnesses: Thomas West, John Kinge.

12 January 1671. Samuell Goosey (CV) was granted administration on estate of George Painter (CV). Appraisers: Thomas Clabone, Robert Dove. Edward Kane (g) to administer oath.

5:197
15 January 1671. John Grammer (CV) was granted administration on estate of John Milner (CV). Bondsman: Edward Armstrong. Appraisers: Roger Brooke, John Parish. Maier Thomas Brookes to administer oath.

19 January 1671. Jarret Hopkins (AA) who married Tomasine widow of Andrew Baker (AA) was granted administration on his estate. Appraisers: Robert Peaca, Jeremiah Swillivant. Samuell Chew, Esq. to administer oath.

5:198
Will of Mrs. Mary Peake. Executors: Robert Heigh, Joseph Tilly, Dr. John Stansbey. Bequests: son Joseph (under age 18),

daughter Katharine Peake (under age 18),
son George Peake (under age 18), Jane
Merret chattel due from Thomas Padget.
Date: 15 May 1671. Witnesses: John
Troster, Will. Stanesby, Abraham Parke.
Robert Heigh & Joseph Tilly renounce
administration. Date: 9 January 1671.
Witnesses: Robert Rouse, Richard Pelly.

23 January 1671. Said Mary Peake is
executrix of George Peake. Edward Keene
(g) to prove the will.

5:199   Elisabeth widow & relict of John Knap
(CV) was granted administration on his
estate. Bondsman: Thomas Trueman, Esq.
Appraisers: Philip Cox, John Sinker.
Tho. Trueman, Esq. to administer oath.

Will of Francis Pope (CH). Date: 7
August 1671.
5:200   Executors: sons Thomas, Francis Pope.
5:201   Bequests: sons Thomas & Francis Pope
"Bryan's Clift" 400 a. & "Battens Clift"
350 a., sons Richard & John Pope (2
younger sons, both under 21, John is the
elder) "Roome" 400 a.,
5:202   ...
5:203   Mentions: William Marshall, John
Worland. Date: 1 October. Witnesses:
Thomas Harris, John Bayly, James Tier.

25 January 1671. Will proved by Thomas
Harris & John Bayly.
5:204   Thomas Pope & Francis Pope were granted
administration on said estate.
Appraisers: Robert Henly, John Dowglas.
Henry Adams (g) to administer oath.

27 January 1671. Will of Ann Peake
[sic] proved by John Troster & Abraham
Clerke. Signed: Edw. Kene.

30 January 1671. Dr. John Stansby was
granted administration on estate of said
Mrs. Mary Peake. Bondsman: Richard
Moy. Appraisers: Tho. Billingsly, John
Russell. Edward Keene (g) to administer
oath.

5:205   Will of Mordecay Hamon (p, Brittans Bay,
SM). Bequests: wife Margaret Hamon "St.
Margaret's" 300 a. behind plantation of

Court Session: <no date>

James Greenewood & chattel to be
delivered by Daniel Hamond, brother
Daniell Hamon, Ann Peake wife of Peter
Peake chattel in possession of my
father-in-law Pope Alvy, William Styles,
Martha Tossey sister to William Stiles,
Edward Rookwood, Pope Alvy & Ann wife of
Pope Alvy, Elisabeth Peake.
5:206 Date: 12 January 1671. Signed: Mordecay
Hamond. Witnesses: George Cox, Francis
Fitzherbert. Will proved 24 January
1671. Pope Alvy to administer said
estate. Signed: Margaret Hamond. Date:
3 February 1671.

5 February 1671. Pope Alvy was granted
administration on said estate.
Bondsman: Stephen Merty.
5:207 Appraisers: James Pattyson, Henry Neale.
John Warren (g) to administer oath.

8 February 1671. Capt. William Burges
& Richard Hill were granted
administration on estate of Elisabeth
Withers (AA). Appraisers: George
Puddington, Robert Burle, Thomas Marsh
(gentlemen). Thomas Taylor (g) to
administer oath.

Richard Keene (CV) was granted
administration on estate of Henry Keene
(CV). Bondsman: John Griggs.
5:208 Appraisers: Thomas Bowdle, Demetrius
Cartwright. Thomas Sprigg (g) to
administer oath.

Will of Francis Parrot. Date: 26 July
1669. Bequests: wife Sarah (pregnant).
Witnesses: William Wood, Clement Sale,
John Brobant, Ralph Nicholson.
5:209 Will proved by Clement Sale & John
Brobant on 10 February 1671.

10 February 1671. Sarah Parrat widow &
relict of Francis Parrat (TA) was
granted administration on his estate.
Bondsman: Isaack Abraham. Appraisers:
Edward Roe, Anthony Male. Richard
Gorsuch to administer oath.

Will of John Paine. Bequests: son John
Paine "Much Haddum" 50 a. & "Rally" 100

5:210
a., wife Mary Paine land then to her son John Paine, George Clerke, wife to set servant Thomas Bradshaw. Overseers: John Hanson, Robert Robins. Date: 3 January 1671. Witnesses: Thomas Mathews, Robert Masters.

10 February 1671. Mary Paine widow of said John Paine (CH) was granted administration on his estate. Appraisers: Archiball Wahob, Owen Jones. Henry Adams (g) to administer oath.

5:211
Will of William Grannt (South River, AA). Bequests: Thomas Roper. Executor: said Thomas. Date: 19 December 1671. Witnesses: Robert Francklin, William Roper.

13 February 1671. Thomas Roper was granted administration on said estate. Appraisers: George Puddington, Henry Ridgely. Samuell Chew, Esq. to administer oath.

5:212
5:213
Will of William Stanley (p, Swan Creek, KE). Bequests: wife Mary Standly then (if she marry) to children when they come of age. Date: 14 January 1671. Signed: William Standly. Witnesses: Christopher Andrews, John Hodgson, Jr., Edward Best.

16 February 1671. Mary Stanly (widow) was granted administration on said estate. Appraisers: Robert Parkes, Robert Nese. James Ringold (g) to administer oath.

Inventory of Robert Kingsbury. Date: 2 June 1671.
5:214
5:215
...
Amount: #12387. Appraisers: William Singleton, William Turner.

Inventory of Nicholas Waterman (AA). Date: 5 February 1671.
5:216
Amount: #19177. Appraisers: Robert Francklyn, James Whyte.

5:217
5:218
Inventory of Charles Brooke (CV).
...

Court Session: <no date>

5:219   Amount: #24278. Appraisers: Charles
Boteler, Cuthbert Fenwick. Sworn by
Baker Brooke, Esq. Date: 8 February
1671.

Inventory of Danyell Silvane. Date: 8
November 1671.
5:220-221 ...
5:222   Amount: #9595. Appraisers: Thomas
Overton, Jo. Langley.

Samuell Hews, age 36, deposed concerning
the estate of Henry Jones, that said
Henry desired his estate to be divided
between his wife & his children. This
voided his first will. Mentions:
servant Samuell Bowen. Overseers:
William Peirce, Joseph Hopkins. Signed:
Samuell Hewes. Date: 7 December 1671.
Before: Thomas Howell.

Daniell Silvaine will was proved by John
Richardson & Ben. Gundry on 7 December
1671. Before: Thomas Howell.

5:223   The widow Lamb refused administration.
Administration was granted to Michaell
Miller. [name of deceased not given]
Date: 16 December 1671. Signed: Tho.
Hynson.

17 February 1671. Michaell Miller (KE)
was granted administration on estate of
Henry Lamb (KE) with consent of the
widow. Bondsman: John Wright (KE).
Appraisers: Toby Wells, John Winchester.
Francis Pine to administer oath.

15 February 1671. Tobias Norton (CV)
was granted administration on estate of
John Francklin. Bondsman: Francis
Swinfen. Appraisers: William Watson,
Edward Cooke. Edward Keene to
administer oath.

5:224   20 February 1671. Peter Byard was
granted administration on estate of
George Smithee (CV). Bondsman: William
Muffet. Appraisers: James Trueman,
William Groome. Thomas Trueman, Esq. to
administer oath.

Will of James Weedon (g, Pocomoke).
Bequests: son William (under age 18)
"Nonesuch House" in occupation of Edward
Pitt (draper) located on London Bridge
in Parish of St. Magnus the Martyr

5:225 then to daughter Ann Weedon (under age
18) then to wife Luce Weedon then to my
brother William Weedon (g, London), son
William Weedon, daughter Ann Weedon,
testator to move to Rehoboth Bay by the
sea near Whoarkill Creek near the south
cape of Delaware Bay on tract to my wife
Luce Weedon, son William & daughter Ann
a warrant for 1000 a., brother William
Weedon, Mr. William Steevens
(Pocomoke).

5:226 Executrix: wife. Overseers: brother
William Weedon (g, London), Mr. William
Steevens (Pocomoke). Date: 12 January1
670. Witnesses: John Rhodes, Pier
Piera.

21 February 1671. Luce Weedon executrix
of Mr. James Weedon (SO) was granted
administration on his estate.

5:227 Appraisers: Edward Whaley, John Emet.
William Stevens (g) to administer oath.

Will of Tobyas Apelford was proved by
John Erreckson & John Bredborne on 14
November 1671. Signed: John Wright.

1 March 1671. Will of John Paine was
proved by Thomas Mathews & Robert
Masters. Signed: Hen. Adams.

9 March 1671. George Credwell (CH) was
granted administration on estate of
Francis Jenkins (CH). Appraisers: James
Walker, John Cadge. John Bowles (g) to
administer oath.

5:228 12 March 1671. Will of William Grannt
(AA) was proved by Robert Francklin &
William Roper. Signed: Sam. Chew.

Will of William Robison (p, Bush River,
BA). Bequests: Henerika Robison.
5:229 Date: 24 April 1671. Witnesses: William
Heath, Mary Elinge.

Court Session: <no date>

8 April 1672. Edward Swanstone who
married Henerika widow of William
Robison (BA) was granted administration
on his estate. Appraisers: William
Yorke, William Osbourne. George Utye
(g) to administer oath.

5:230   Inventory of Samuell Gouldsmith (BA).
         Date: 21 March 1671/2.
5:231-232 ...
5:233   Amount: #83826. Appraisers: T. Salmon,
         Henry Haselwood.

5:234   12 April 1672. Arthur Ludford, age 58,
         deposed that he was at the house of
         widow Herring (her husband recently
         dec'd) & she requested that he read his
         will: Bequests: wife Margarett then to
         his child Bartholomew. Overseer:
         William Muffitt.

         John Pott deposed that he was at the
         house of Bartholomew Herring 12-13 years
         ago, when he wished the deponent to
         witness his will.

5:235   Phillip Harrwood deposed that 12-13
         years ago, Bartholomew Herring & his
         wife & William Muffet came to the
         deponent's house, requesting the
         deponent & James Jolley to witness his
         will.

         Administration was granted on the estate
         of Margarett late wife of William Argent
         & relict of Thomas Noales successor to
         Bartholomew Herring (dec'd) for the use
         of Bartholomew Herring (orphan of said
         Bartholomew & Margarett). Said orphan
         is since dec'd. Tobias Norton (g, CV)
         to exhibit an account of the estate.
         Bondsman: William Groome (g).

5:236   Inventory of Elisabeth Emanson (CH).
         Appraisers: John Lambert, Thomas King.
         Sworn by: Mr. Benjamin Rozer. Date: 20
         January 1671.
5:236↓   Amount: #20388.

         Inventory of James Selby (DO). Date: 7
         November 1671.
5:237   List of debts: William Berry, Edward

Hide, Edward Cooke, Stephen Beeson.
Further list of debts: Stephen Beeson,
Francis Taylor, Thomas Browne,
5:238   John Crayly. Amount: #10387.
Appraisers: John Rawlings, Tho. Skinner.

Mary Pine (relict) of Francis Pine (KI)
renounced administration on his estate.
Date: 11 April 1672.
5:239   John Parker (merchant) was granted
administration on estate of Francis
Pyne. Bondsmen: John Edmondson, Richard
Royston. Appraisers: Toby Wells,
William Lawrence. John Wright (g) to
administer oath.

Will of George Stronge (AA). Date: 21
November 1671.
5:240   Bequests: son George Stronge.
Executrix: wife Hannah Strong.
Witnesses: John Beamon, William Jones,
Math. Harden.

14 April 1672. Mary executrix of said
George was granted administration on his
estate. Appraisers: Richard Mosse,
William Slade. Robert Burle to
administer oath.

Katharin Acton widow & relict of Richard
Acton (AA) was granted administration on
his estate.
5:241   Appraisers: Capt. Thomas Beeson,
Richard Beard. Thomas Taylor (g) to
administer oath.

Accounts of John Hawkins (BA).
Administrator: John Damrell. Amount of
inventory: #52995. Payments to: Capt.
Howell, Walter Tucker, & Co., Mr.
Herman, Mr. Henry Ward, Mr. John
Gilbert, Thomas Salmon,
5:242   William Salsbury, Mr. Peter Alricks,
Mr. Nath. Stiles, Mr. Thomas Sprye,
Mr. Harman, Mr. Ward, Richard Foster,
clothing for James Robison & Francis
Collings, John Browning. Amount:
#27417. Date: 12 April 1672.

5:243   Inventory of Geo. Collings. Date: 27
March 1671. Appraisers: Robert Tyler,
Abraham Dawson. List of debts: Geo.

Court Session: <no date>

Abott, John Greene, Edward Lune,
administrator, Patricke Morphew bill
ordered to Stephen Prince. Accounts:
Mr. John Homewood, estate of Samuell
Drue, Francis Smith, Henry Sewell, James
Armstrong, Samuell Alcocke, Will. Slade,
Stephen White, John Pine, Ralph Hawkins,
Will. Hawkins, Robert Barnard,
administrator, Stephen Prince, James
Wells. Amount: #8960. Date: 27 March
1672.

5:244   Inventory of Thomas Covent (Britton's
Bay). Date: 18 November 1671. Amount:
#2052. Appraisers: Edward Clarke, Will.
Asiter.

Will of John Stockes (SM). Bequests:
Humphry Limbrey, Mr. Robert Williams
(merchant), Mr. Bryan Dayly, Constant
O'Keefe, James Lewis,
5:245   carpenter of Mr. Williams, wife
Elisabeth Stockes. Date: 4 March 1671.
Witnesses: Robert Harper, Hum. Limbry,
Constant Daniell. Will proved by
Humphry Limbrey & Constant Daniell on 12
April 1672. Robert Large who married
Elisabeth widow & relict of said John
was granted administration on said
estate. Appraisers: Walter Waterlin,
Tho. Peirce. Tho. Dent (g) to
administer oath.

5:246   Accounts of John Hawkins (BA).
Administrator: John Damrell. Amount of
inventory: #52995. Payments to: Capt.
Howell, Walter Tucker & Co., Mr. Harman,
Mr. Henry Ward, Mr. John Gilbert,
Thomas Salmon, William Salsbury, Mr.
Peter Alricks, Mr. Nathaniell Styles,
Richard Foster,
5:247   clothing for James Robinson & Francis
Collins, John Browning. Amount: #17937.

18 April 1672. Administration on estate
of said John Hawkins was granted to
Robert Hawkins (brother to dec'd).
Bondsman: George Beckwith. Appraisers:
Henry Ward, George Robotham. Thomas
Howell (g) to administer oath.

5:248   Will of Stephen Horsy (SO) was proved by
        John Wallop & Henry Powell on 2 February
        1671. Alexander Draper proved said will
        on 21 February 1671. Before: Will.
        Stevens.

        25 April 1671. Stephen Horsy & John
        Horsy were granted administration on
        said estate. Appraisers: Charles Hall,
        William Planner. William Stevens (g) to
        administer oath.

5:249   Will of Andrew Anderson. Date: 23
        January 1671.
5:250   Executrix: wife Elisabeth Anderson.
        Bequests: wife Elisabeth 100 a., wife's
        son Roger More, Mordecay Hunton.
        Witnesses: Mordecay Hunton, Nicholas
        Buttram. Will proved 24 April 1671.
        Elisabeth Anderson widow & relict was
        granted administration on said estate.
        Appraisers: Francis Hutchins, Edward
        Cawdry. Edward Keene to administer
        oath.

5:251   Will of Thomas Bowth (CV). Date: 15
        February 1671. Bequests: Mary Dewall.
        Executrix: wife. Witnesses: John
        Clarke, George Sealing.

        26 April 1672. Will proved by John
        Clarke & George Sealling on 26 April
        1672. Mary Bowth executrix was granted
        administration on said estate.
        Appraisers: Richard Ladd, Michaell
        Higgins. Robert Tyler (g) to administer
        oath.

5:252   Will of John Elly (p, CV). Date: 20
        February 1671. Executrix: wife Joane
        Elly. Bequests: wife Joane, Catholic
        priest Mr. Michaell Foster, John
        McDunall son of William McDunall,
        servant William Smith,
5:252½ Michaell Higgins the younger, servant
        John Dyer. Witnesses: George Sealing,
        Henry Hariste. Will proved 26 April
        1672. Joane Elly executrix was granted
        administration on said estate.
        Appraisers: Richard Ladd, Michaell
        Higgins. Robert Tyler (g) to administer
        oath.

Court Session: <no date>

5:253   Alice Godscrose widow & relict of James
Godscrose (CV) was granted
administration on his estate. Bondsmen:
Samuell Goosey, Richard Founteine.
Appraisers: Samuell Goosey, Arthur
Ludford. Edward Keene (g) to administer
oath.

Mary Farmer widow & relict of Michaell
Farmer (CV) was granted administration
on his estate. Bondsmen: Samuell
Goosey, Samuell Lester. Appraisers:
Samuell Goosey, Arthur Ludford. Edward
Keene (g) to administer oath.

Inventory of George Painter. Date: 20
January 1671. Appraisers: Thomas
Allibone, Robert Dove.
5:254   Amount: #3296.

Will of Nathaniell Smith (Herring Creek,
AA).
5:255   Bequests: 2 servants Mathias Dring &
Thomas Hobbs "Hunt's Chance" 200 a.,
Edward Mason, Edward Fraye, Roger
Bradly, Richard James, Margaret Holland.
Executor: Humphry Emerton. Date: 10
April 1672. Witnesses: Samuell Lane,
Anthony Kingsland.

5:256   6 May 1672. Humphry Emerton was granted
administration on said estate.
Appraisers: Henry Arther, Jeremy
Swillivant. Samuell Chew, Esq. to
administer oath.

Inventory of Robert Smith. Appraisers:
Jonathon Sybrey, Philip Stevenson.
5:257   Amount: #16843.

5:258   15 May 1672. Francis Swanston (CV) who
married Dorothy widow & executrix of
Hugh Stanly (CV) was granted
administration on his estate. Bondsman:
Christopher Rousby.

Francis Swanston was granted
administration on estate of his wife
Dorothy Swanston (CV). Bondsman:
Christopher Rousby. Appraisers: William
Groome, John Bigger.

5:259   Inventory of John Stoacks.
         Appraisers: Thomas Peirce, Walter
         Waterlin.

         Inventory of Tobias Apelford (KE).
         Appraisers: Isaack Winchester, John
         More. Sworn by: Mr. John Wright.
         Date: 10 October 1671. List of debts:
         Mr. Tho. Osborne, John Every,
5:260   Richard Potter, William Granger, Edward
         Barton, Robert Dunn, Thomas Colins, John
         Wright, Mathias Red, Thomas Bright,
         Charles Steard, John Winchester, Charles
         Delaroch, George Gooldhawke, Thomas
         Ingram, John Webster, Tho. Taylor,
         Philip Thomas, John Lawrence, Mr.
         Francis Pyne, Mr. Jonathon Sybrey, John
         Cooper, Joshua Meriton, Mr. Peter
         Sawyer, William Geater, Storn. Jolley,
         Tho. Shelton, Edward Hall, Mr. John
         Wright, Isaack Winchester. Amount:
         #18450.

5:261   24 May 1672. Ann Collier widow & relict
         of John Collier (BA) was granted
         administration on his estate.
         Appraisers: John Hill, William Yorke.
         Thomas Howell (g) to administer oath.

         Inventory of Samuell Neale (St. Ingroes,
         SM). Administrator: Thomas Spinck.
5:262   Amount: #15952. Appraisers: Thomas
         Peirce, Walter Waterling.

         Inventory of Mr. Richard Wells, Jr.
         (Herring Creek, AA). Date: 19 April
         1672.
5:263-266 ...
5:267   Amount: #3360. Appraisers: Robert
         Francklin, Anthony Saloway. List of
         debts: Thomas Chandler & William
         Russell, James Ogdon, Robert Connitt,
         John Saller, Arinegill Greenewood,
         Anthony Kingsland, Charles Beeven,
         Thomas Morgan, Mrs. Stansby, Walter
         Carr, William Wilkeson, Nicholas Territ,
         William Peirce, John Whips, Jarret
         Hopkins, George Symons, Henry Archer,
5:268   Richard Carver, John Howerton, William
         Richeson, William Russell, Thomas
         Morris, Anthony Stockly, John Larkins,
         Dr. Stansby. Amount: #37379. Further

Court Session: <no date>

list of debts: George Wells. Amount:
#11015. Further debts by Richard Wells
as legatee to 1/5th part of his father
Wells estate bequeathed to him.

Will of James Wilson (p, CV).
5:269 Bequests: wife Margaret Wilson, eldest
son James Wilson 100 a. being part of
200 a. on which I now live beginning at
the corner tree of Mr. Abington, son
John Wilson 100 a. being the other part
of 200 a. & where my dwelling house
stands, son Joseph Wilson 43 a.
5:270 Executrix: wife Margaret Wilson. Date:
3 May 1670. Signed: Jam. Wilson.
Witnesses: Robert Rider, Mary Tilly,
Hen. Cole.

5:271 29 May 1672. Will proved by Robert
Rider & Henry Cole. Margaret Wilson
executrix was granted administration on
said estate. Appraisers: Joseph Tilly,
William Howse. Edward Keene (g) to
administer oath.

Will of Hans de Ringe. Date: 13 April
1672. [Paragraph in Dutch.]
5:272 Mentions: Mattheus de Ringe, Aemilius de
Ringe (cousins). Bequests: Amedes
Vanderminen & his man Richard Leake.
5:273 Witnesses: Hendrick Consturier, Hans
Block, Henrich Jansen. Will proved 18
April 1672. Signed: John Carr, Pieter
Abinsts, Walter Wharton, Ed. Cantabell.
[Translation...
5:274 ...
5:275 by G. V. Sweringen.] Mathias de Ringe
was granted administration on estate of
Hans de Ringe (BA). Bondsman: Garret
Vanswaringen. Appraisers: Jacob Young,
Thomas Salmon. Thomas Howell (g) to
administer oath.

Richard Hallet (merchant, Lyme Regis,
ENG) was granted administration on
estate of Lanncelot Hallet (BA) by
Archbishop of Canterbury on 14 July
1671. Bondsmen: Jacob Young, William
Dunkerton. Appraisers: Capt. Thomas
Howell, Thomas Salmon. James Frisby (g)
to administer oath. Date: 27 May 1672.

5:276   Robert Woolverton who married Michaell executrix of Richard Howard (TA) was granted administration on his estate. Will proved by Mr. Edward Roe & Mr. Anthony Mayle on 4 April 1672. Signed: Seth. Foster. Inventory of Richard Howard.

5:277   Servants: Richard Cozens (runaway), John Fidoe (runaway), William Lupton, Thomas Davis, Ed. Bell. Amount: #23475. Payments to: Cuthbert Philips, Mr. Seth Foster,

5:278   Mr. Augustene, Mr. Ed. Roe, Mr. Miles Taylor, Jonathon Hopkins, Thomas James, Richard Franckes, Mr. Robison, Mr. Cuthbert Potter, Mr. Francis Pine, Capt. Thomas Harwood. Legacies: Anto. Mayle, John Dolby, Robert Harding, Eliz. Teagle. Date: 11 April 1672.

Will of Peter Sharpe (chirurgeon, CV). Date: 23 March 1671.

5:279   Executors: John Gary, William Berry, William Stevens, Jr., William Sharpe.

5:280   Bequests: John Gary 400 a. at Tuckahoe, John Gary & his wife Alice, Robert Harwood & his wife Elisabeth & their 3 children, Judith Harwood, wife

5:281   & children William & Mary, my wife's 2 children John & Elisabeth, daughter Mary & William Stevens, William Stevens 400 a. at Fouling Creek, Friends in the Ministry Alce Gary & William Cole & Sarah Mash then Winlock Christeson & his wife & John Burnit & Daniel Gould,

5:282   cousin Nicholas Oliver (apothecary). Witnesses: John Barker, Mordecay Hunton, Elias Goddard, Julian Foun. Will proved by Mordecay Hunton & John Barker on 28 March 1672.

5:283   Will of John Ringold (Hunting Field, KE). Date: 25 April 1672 [sic]. Bequests: Elisabeth Cooke (unmarried) "Hunting Feild" 300 a. as long as she & any husband be civil toward my brother James Ringold & if not then to my cousin Barbarah Ringold then to my cousin Thomas Ringold, Ann Mungomery, my cousin Barbarah Ringold, my father Thomas Ringold,

5:284   brother James Ringold. Executors:

Court Session: <no date>

brother James Ringold, Richard Hill.
Witnesses: William Toulson, Richard
Hill. James Ringold & Richard Hill were
granted administration on said estate.
Appraisers: John Hinson, Nathaniell
Evet. Thomas South (g) to administer
oath. Date: 11 April 1672.

13 June 1672. Samuell Chew, Esq. to
prove will of Richard Bassell (AA).

Inventory of William Reed. Date: 31
October 1671. Amount: #5300.
Appraisers: Tho. Vaughan, John Marck.

5:285 Inventory of John Knapp. Appraisers:
John Sinckler, Philip Cookesey. Date:
16 February 1671.
5:286 Signed: John Sinckler, John Knap.

Inventory of John Nelson (SO).
Appraisers: Philip Shapleigh, Richard
Whittey. Date: 22 March 1671/2.
5:287 Amount: #8960. Sworn by: John Lawes.

5:288 Accounts of George Smithee (sayler).
Payments to: Joseph Dawkins, widow
Walley, administrator William Muffet,
Richard Bayly, John Sincler, Demetrius
Cartwright, Capt. Baker. Amount: #4100.
Inventory of George Smithee. List of
debts: John Sinckler, Tho. Trueman,
Michaell Catterton. Amount: #4863.
Further list of debts: Michaell
Catterton, Charles Boteler. Date: 5
April 1672. Signed: Peter Bayard.

Accounts of Bartholomew Herring. Date:
15 September 1668. Payments to: Will.
How, Robert Phillips. Amount: #5400.
Amount of inventory: #5400.
Administrator: Tobias Norton. Date
filed: 12 June 1672.

5:289 15 September 1668. CV Court. Present:
Thomas Sprigg, Charles Brooke, George
Peake, William Groome, Tobias Norton
(gentlemen).

Accounts of Bartholomew Herring.
Payments to: fees on administration of
Margaret Argent, rent on 200 a. Amount:

Court Session: <no date>

#1870. Signed: Tobias Norton per Thomas Bankes (clerk).

5:290   19 March 1666/7. CV Court. Present: Thomas Sprigg, Tho. Manning, Hugh Stanley, William Groome, Tobias Norton (gentlemen).

Tobias Norton administrator of Margaret Argent vs. William How, per William Muffet (clerk). Caveat.

Robert Philips vs. estate of Marget Argent, per John Gittings (clerk). Caveat.

14 June 1672. Aforegoing accounts & administration to William Muffet (CV) to whom bequeathed (per nuncupative will of Bartholomew Herring). Appraisers: Arthur Ludford, William Mills. William Groome (g) to administer oath.

17 June 1672. Ann Norwood widow & relict of John Norwood (AA) was granted administration on his estate. Appraisers: Thomas Marsh, John Beamont. Robert Burle (g) to administer oath.

5:291   Will of John Incon (Bristol & MD). Bequests: Mathias DeCosta, uncle Thomas Ward houses on Temple St. in Bristol. Date: 4 May 1672. Witnesses: Henry Rider, Tho. Bayle, John Balley.

18 June 1672. Will proved by Thomas Bayle & John Bayle.

Will of John Godfrey (Petapsco River, BA).
5:292   Bequests: John Malam plantation on Petapsco River, Thomas Cole & Presella his wife, Edward Houghton, Sarah Colle, Ann White (maidservant of Thomas Cole), Richard Kene (formerly Thomas Cole's servant), John Kemp. Executor: said John Mailum. Date: 29 May 1672. Signed: Richard Ball, Richard Gwinn.

19 June 1672. Will was proved by Richard Ball. John Malum was granted administration on said estate.

Page 44

Court Session: <no date>

Appraisers: Charles Gorsuch, Nicholas
Ruckston. Richard Ball to administer
oath.

Will of Maior Thomas Ingram (KE) was
proved by Thomas Cooper (age 24) on 27
July 1671. Walter Thomas & William
Wilson proved said will. Date: 27 July
1671. Signed: John Wright.
5:294 Inventory of Maior Thomas Ingram (KE).
List of debts: Robert Dunn. Date: 28
July 1671.
5:295 Amount: #62028. Appraisers: John
Ingram, Richard Pether.

Inventory of Joseph Riggs (inholder,
Clifts, CV). Appraisers: Robert Heigh,
Thomas Billingsley. Date: 20 March
1671.
5:296 ...
5:297 Amount: #7267.

27 July 1672. Robert Wells was granted
administration on estate of his brother
Benjamin Wells (AA). Appraisers: Robert
Franklyn, Richard Ewens. Thomas Taylour
(g) to administer oath.

5:298 Inventory of Nathaniell Smith (Herring
Creek). Appraisers: Jeremiah Suddivan,
Henry Archer. Date: 7 July 1672.
5:299 ...
5:300 Amount: #21006. Signed: Jeremiah
Sluilivant, Henry Archer. Will of
Nathaniell Smith (AA) was proved by
Samuell Lane & Anthony Kingsland on 20
May 1672.

Will of Ralph Bassell (AA) was proved by
Francis Sandry & Thomas Watkins on 24
June 1672.

Inventory of Francis Pyne (KE).
Appraisers: William Lawrence, Tobias
Wells. Date: <unreadable> May 1672.
5:301 Mentions: estate of Mr. Vicaris.
5:302 Amount: 8202.

Will of Jacob Neale (chirurgeon, AA).
Bequests: Sarah Marsh (under age 16)
daughter of Mr. Thomas Marsh (AA), Mr.
Thomas Marsh & his wife Margaret.

5:303   Executor: said Mr. Thomas Marsh. Date:
11 July 1672. Witnesses: Robert Burle,
Ralph Williams, John Bicknall.

10 August 1672. Thomas Marsh (g) was
granted administration on said estate.
Appraisers: Francis Stockett, William
Jones, Henry Lewis. Thomas Taylour (g)
to administer oath.

Will of George Strong (AA) was proved by
John Beamon & Mathew Harden on 1 July
1672. Inventory of George Strong.
Date: 1 July 1672.

5:304   List of debts: William Davis, William
Neale, Barnard Eglestone. Amount:
#6976. Appraisers: Richard Mosse,
William Slade.

5:305   Came Hester Nichols, widow of Capt.
Edward Maynard captain of ship William
of Dover which came in August 1670 on
the ship belonging to Sir William
Davidson Knight Baronet & gentleman of
ENG. Before Henry Outgers (notary
public, Amsterdam, Holland). Date: 14
December 1671. Mentions: bills in the
hands of Mr. Henry Phipps, Mr. Conrad
Clenck.

5:306   Acknowledged by Jacob de Wogolaen.
Date: 18 December 1671. [Text in
Dutch.]

5:307   ...

5:308   19 August 1672. Henry Phipps (merchant)
was granted administration on estate of
Edward Maynard (mariner). Signed:
Patrick Forrest, Thomas Hatton.
Appraisers: John Blomfeild, Henry Neale.
John Warren (g) to administer oath.

Mr. William Muffett (CV) was granted
administration on estate of Richard
Millard (DO). Date: 15 July 1672.
Signed: Richard Bayly. Appraisers:
William Jones, Tho. Browne. William
Wroughton (g) to administer oath. Date:
13 August 1672.

5:309   29 August 1672. Francis Sanders who
married Mary widow of Ralph Bassell (AA)
was granted administration on his

Court Session: <no date>

estate. Appraisers: Thomas Dawbone, Walter Carr. Samuell Chew, Esq. to administer oath.

Inventory of William Grant. Date: 10 April 1672. Amount: #7075. Appraisers: George Puddington, Henry Ridgely.

5:310 Inventory of John Payne (CH). Date: 13 March 1671/2. Servant: Thomas Bradshaw. Amount: #9530. Appraisers: Archibald Wahob, Owen Jones.

5:311 Inventory of James Wilson (CV).
5:312 Amount: #8625. Date: 8 June 1672. Appraisers: J. Tilley, William House.

Inventory of Andrew Hendeson.
5:313 Date: 1 August 1672. Appraisers: Francis Hutchins, Edward Coudere.

Will of William Stanley (also William Standly, KE) was proved by Christopher Andrewes & Edward Best on 16 February 1671. Before: James Ringgold. Inventory of William Standly. Appraisers: Robert Parkes, Robert Neave. Date: 10 May 1672.
5:314 Mentions: chattel sold to Christopher Andrewes.

Inventory of Henry Lambe (KE). Date: 6 July 1671. Appraisers: Tobyas Wells, John Winchester.
5:315 List of debts: Thomas Knighton, Robert Turner. Amount: #4120.

Inventory of John Hawkins. Date: 14 May 1672.
5:316 Servants: James Robinson (boy), Francis Collins (boy). List of debts: John Damering, John Gilbert, James Megregory, Daniell Macary, Thomas Wamsley, Humphrey Nichols,
5:317 Mr. Styles, Charles James. Amount: #15467. Appraisers: Henry Ward, Geo. Robotham. Fees posted on 10 September 1672.

Will of Walter Walterling (SM). Date; 30 August 1672.
5:318 Bequests: daughter Mary Walterlyn, 2

Court Session: <no date>

grandchildren Grace Barnes & Elisabeth
Barnes, Mary Walterlin, 2 other
daughters Grace & Patience. Executor:
son John Barnes. Signed: Walter
Walterlyn. Witnesses: William Asbeston,
Henry Smith.

5:319   14 September 1672. Said will proved.
John Barnes was granted administration
on said estate. Bondsmen: William
Asbeston, Henry Smith. Appraisers:
Thomas Peerce, Thomas Spinke. Mr. Tho.
Dent to administer oath.

Will of Richard Upgate (blacksmith, St.
Clement's Mannor, SM). Bequests: son
John Upgate, daughter Mary wife of
Thomas Reeves,
5:320   wife "Bluff Point" on east side of
Wiccacomika River. Executrix: wife Anne
Upgate. Date: 9 November 1671. Signed:
Richard Upgat. Witnesses: Gerrard Slye,
Tho. Gerrard, Tho. Lomax, Mary Snow.
Will proved by Gerrard Slye & Thomas
Gerrard on 3 August 1672.

21 September 1672. Anne Upgate relict
was granted administration on said
estate. Appraisers: John Tennison,
James Greene. Benjamin Sally to
administer oath.

Will of William Boulding (Bohemia River,
BA). Bequests: Mary Thwayte & her 2
children William Thwayte & Thomas
Thwayte (under age, which were born in
my house in Abbington Parish in
Gloucester Co. VA)
5:321   all estate in MD & VA. Date: 26 August
1671. Signed: William Boulden.
Witnesses: John Gardner, George Broccas,
Roger Fretwell, William Brokes.

30 September 1672. Mary Thwayte was
granted administration on said estate.
Appraisers: Hugh Fowck, William Price.
Thomas Howell (g, SO) to administer
oath.

Will of Hugh Cornellison (Bethany).
Date: 15 July 1672. Bequests: Mr.
Edward Cantwell, Mary Cooke, Richard

Court Session: <no date>

5:322
Mackey,
Morene Cornelius, son of John Franklyn,
Daniel Mackary, William Sincler chattel
to pay Peter Alrick & Thomas Woolstone,
Thomas Smith, James Hallwell. Signed:
Hugh Cornellis. Witnesses: William
Sincler, James Howell, Thomas Smith.

1 October 1672. Edward Cantwell (BA)
was granted administration on said
estate. Appraisers: James Magreger,
Augustin Herman. Capt. Thomas Howell
to administer oath.

5:323
Will of Stephen Mountague (CH). Date:
21 June 1672.
Mentions: 300 a. at Cingannuxon to be
sold. Bequests: Mary Emanson (daughter
of Nicholas Emanson & his wife
Elisabeth) 100 a. surveyed by Mr.
Richard Edelen at Matawoman adjoining
"Howland". Executor: George Godfrey.
Witnesses: Nicholas Solby, John Hanson.

5:324
4 October 1672. Will proved by John
Hanson.
George Godfrey was granted
administration on said estate. Benjamin
Rozer (g) to get oath of Nicholas Solby.
Appraisers: Thomas Hussey, Ralph Coates.
Benj. Rozer (g) to administer oath.

9 October 1672. William Stevens (g, SO)
for Luce Weeden was granted continuance
for inventory of James Weeden (SO).
Some of estate is in WO & some in SO.
Appraisers: John Viccerous, George Day.
William Stevens to administer oath.

5:325
Will of George Eaves (SO). Bequests:
Thomas Hilliard (son of John Hilliard)
"Guift" 100 a. &
"Warwick" 200 a. Date: 16 November
1671. Witnesses: William Tomkins, Henry
Harmon, Edward Dickeson.

Will of John Lawrence was proved by
William Royden & Peter Dillaroch on last
day of March 1672. Before: Tobias
Wells.

Court Session: <no date>

Will of John Ringold was proved by William Toulson & Richard Hill on 17 September 1672. Before: Thomas South.

Will of Jacob Neale was proved by Ralph Williams & Robert Burly on 2 September 1672. Before: Thomas Taylor.

Henry Beedle, age 24, deposed on 7 August 1672 that last April, the deponent was riding with Benjamin Wells who said he was co-partnered with his brother. Richard Wells.

5:326 Samuell Chew, Esq., age 41, deposed on 7 August 1672 that the deponent was riding with Benjamin Wells who said he was co-partnered with his brother. Richard Wells.

5:327 Inventory of James Godscrosse.
...
5:328 Amount: #47909. Appraisers: Arthur Ludford, Samuell Goosey. Sworn by Edward Keene. Date: 14 October 1672.

Inventory of Michaell Farmer.
5:329 Amount: #14027. Appraisers: Arthur Ludford, Samuell Goosey. Sworn by Edward Keene. Date: 14 October 1672.

5:330 Inventory of Francis Parrot. List of debts: James Elton (CV),
5:331 Benjamin Cloyster (CV) & Daniell Blade (CV). Amount: #29948. Appraisers: Edw. Roe, Anto. Mayle. Date: 13 September 1672.

Inventory of Lancelott Hallett (merchant, BA). Date: last day of August 1672.
5:332 Amount: #110055. Appraisers: Thomas Howell, Tho. Salmon.

5:333 Inventory of Hance de Ring (BA). Date: 5 July 1672.
5:334 List of debts: Col. Utye, Cornel. Boyce, William Vandenan, John Shackerly. Amount: #25198. Appraisers: Jacob Claus de Young Tho. Salmon.

Inventory of Henry Jones (BA). Date: 22 March 1671/2.

Court Session: <no date>

5:335   Amount: #12667. Appraisers: William
Dunkerton, Richard Leake.

Inventory of Mary Goldhawke executrix of
George Goldhawke (cooper, KE). Date: 26
June 1672.
5:336   List of debts: Thomas Bright, Joshua
Meriton, Peter Harrison, Marthew Woods,
Francis Pyne, Charles de la Roch, George
Yates,
5:337   Cuthbert Witham, William Deale.
Appraisers: John Ingram, John
Winchester.

Inventory of Francis Jenkins (cooper,
CH). Date: 15 June 1672. Appraisers:
James Walker, John Cage.
5:338   List of debts: Mrs. Ellinor Beane, Mr.
John Worland, Mr. John Cage, Henry
Hardy. Amount: #3277. Administrator:
George Credwell (CH).

Inventory of John Godfrey (BA).
5:339   List of debts: Thomas Taldersbe, Thomas
Cole, Edward Horththun. Mentions: 100
a. Amount: #11516. Date: 26 July 1672.
Appraisers: Richard Gwyn, Nicholas
Rickston.

Inventory of Capt. John Collier. Date:
20 July 1672. Appraisers: John Hill,
William Yorke. Sworn by Capt. Thomas
Howell (BA).
5:340   Amount: #12172. List of debts: Lodowick
Williams, Thomas Cooke, Peter Russell,
Mr. Tho. Longe, Giles Stevens.

5:341   Inventory of Mr. Benjamin Wells.
Appraisers: Mr. Richard Ewen, Mr.
Robert Franklin. Date: 18 September
1672.
5:342   Mentions: coat of arms.
5:343   Amount: #41567.

Accounts of Capt. Tho. Stockett.
Executors: Francis & Henry Stockett.
Appraisers: John Welsh, Robert Franklin.

Inventory of Richard Acton (AA).
Appraisers: Capt. Tho. Beeson, Richard
Beard. Date: 26 August 1672.
5:344   ...

5:345   Amount: £100.8.5.

Inventory of papers of John Parker
(merchant) in hands of James Williams,
at whose house said Parker died, in
presence of said Williams & Mordecay
Hunton. Mentions: letters of
administration on estate of (N) Pyne,
bill of George Parker, account of ship
John of Weymouth, account of Mr.
Rousby,

5:346   charter party from Barbados, invoice
from NYC, goods disposed by John
Parkert, account of John Pitt, bond of
Francis Dorrington, account of John
Edmondson, inventory of remaining
rigging of John of Weymouth, (N) Parker
& (N) Drady charter party. In his
pocketbook: bill of William Kirum, bill
of John Edmondson, bill of William
Parrot, bill of Richard Baylie, bill of
William Jones, bill of Robert Turner,
bill from Capt. Maning, note of Mr.
Blomfeild, discharge of Richard Keene,
bill of John Pollard, bill of William
Crump, note of (N) Maning on (N) Ingram,
bill of John Brooke, bill of Thomas
Chandler, discharge of John Edmondson to
Parker, receipt from Mr. Rousby, bill of
William King,

5:347   bill of Thomas Howell, note of William
Stanlye, release of Richard Hooper, bill
of Robert Carvile, agreement between (N)
Royston & (N) Parker, bill of Tho.
Knighton. Inventory of John Parker at
house of William King, in presence of
James Williams & Guy White. List of
debts: Henry Hough, William Crosse,
Thomas Pritchet, Obadiah Evans,

5:348   Francis Pyne, Demetrius Cartwright.
Signed: James Williams, Guy White, John
Baynard. Mentions: servant Charles
Barnwell (boy), widow Pyne.

29 October 1672. Emma wife of William
Roswell (St. Winifred's, St. Clement's
Hundred) deposed that May 20 years ago
she saw Robert son of Robert Cole (St.
Clement's Hundred) baptized by Mr.
Starky & she thought him to be 6-8
months old. Signed: Eme Roswell.

Court Session: <no date>

John Piper (Chaptico Bay, St. Clement's
Hundred) deposed that the deponent has
been free about 20 years & Robert son of
Robert Cole (St. Clement's Hundred) was
born about 1 year earlier.

4 November 1672. Benjamin Rozer (g) was
granted administration on estate of
Lawrence Little (CH). Appraisers:
Edmond Lindsey, George Godfrey. Henry
Addams (g) to administer oath.

5:349   Will of James Trueman (CV). Bequests:
wife Ann Truman 1/3rd, remainder to 3
daughters: Martha, Mary, & Elisabeth.
Overseer: wife Ann then brothers Thomas
& Nathaniell. Date: 29 July 1672.
Signed: James Truman. Witnesses:
Nathaniell Truman, Arthur Storer,
Christopher Pinckney.
5:350   Will proved by Christopher Pinckney &
Arthur Storer on 1 November 1672. Ann
Truman relict was granted administration
on said estate. Bondsman: Thomas
Truman, Esq. Appraisers: William
Groome, Arthur Ludford. Tho. Truman,
Esq. to administer oath.

Inventory of Thomas Booth (d. 1671).
Amount: #7909. Date: 19 October 1672.
Appraisers: Richard Ladd, Michaell
Higgen.

5:351   Inventory of John Elly (d. 1671).
Amount: #17567. Date: 19 October 1672.
Appraisers: Richard Ladd, Michaell
Higgen.

5:352   Inventory of Elisabeth Withers. Date:
16 February 1671. Administratrix of
Samuell Withers. Appraisers: Mr.
Robert Burle, Mr. George Puddington.
Servants mentioned: Josias Lanham (age
19), Edmond Sealer (age 21), Roger
Powell (age 22), Thomas Hebb (age 20),
James Balderston (age 18), Elisabeth
Cooke, Negro Clare (age 13).
5:353   Amount (servants & chattel): £197.10.6.
5:354   ...
5:355   <does not exist>
5:356   ...
5:357   Amount: £42.8.9.

Will of John Parker (Cruckhorne, SO).
Bequests: wife Mary Parker currency put
into Company with Aughter Moody & Co. of
Dorchester in 1668, wife currency from
my father-in-law, wife currency out of
Company belonging to Thomas Hide
(merchant, Weymouth),

5:358   sister Mary Knap, brother-in-law Henry
Knap, William Berry (Patuxent) my
interest in the ship John of Weymouth,
William Harris (mate of said ship),
account of William Twist & Co. Date: 16
September 1671. Witnesses: Thomas
Angell, Nicholas Smart, Henry Smart,
Henry Hemen.

5:359   8 November 1672. Robert Ridgely is to
receive:
* a patent for "Willard's Purchase"
200 a. of Dr. Swanston.
* an assignment from Daniell Willard
to Hugh Stanly.
* a patent for 400 a. granted to Mr.
Thomas Hatton & a transcript of the
assignment.
* a certificate of Patrick Forrest of
receipt from Hugh Stanley for the
use of Margret relict of Thomas
Hatton.

A return for the use of John & Edward
Stanley orphans of John Stanley (dec'd)
& heirs of Hugh Stanley (dec'd), 600 a.
in possession of Francis Swanston (g)
"Willard's Purchase" 200 a. & 400 a.
granted to Mr. Thomas Hatton.

5:359½   9 November 1672. Thomas Wynn attorney
for executor of George Manwaring was
granted continuance.

    Indenture between Charles Calvert, Esq.
on behalf of John Stanley & Edward
Stanley sons of John Stanley (dec'd) and
Francis Swanston (chirurgeon, CV). Land
granted to Thomas Hatton (g) in 1654 on
west side of Patuxent River near
Frodsham Creek [metes & bounds] 400 a.,
assigned to Hugh Stanley (Patuxent)

5:360   and land granted to Daniell Willard heir
of George Willard (dec'd) "Willard's
Purchase" in October 1663 on west side
of Patuxent River adjoining land of

Court Session: <no date>

James Godsgrace (p) [metes & bounds] 200
a. assigned to Hugh Stanley in November
1666. Will of Hugh Stanley was proved
30 July 1667. Said Hugh bequeathed said
land to his wife Dorothy then to his
brother John Stanley then to John
Stanley & Edward Stanley (parties to the
indenture). Said Dorothy & John are
both dec'd, & said John & Edward are
infants of "very tender years".

5:361 On 15 May last, William Groome (g, CV) &
John Bigger (g, CV) evaluated the
orphans' lands on 30 May. Charles
Calvert on behalf of the orphans demised
the lands to Francis Swanston for 7
years.

5:362 Signed: Francis Swanston. Witnesses:
Robert Ridgely, John Faning. Francis
Swanston (chirurgeon, CV) was bound to
Charles Calvert, Esq. Date: 9 November
1672.

5:363 Inventory of Mr. Francis Pope (CH).
Appraisers: Mr. Robert Hinley (CH), Mr.
John Douglas (CH).

5:364 ...
5:365 Amount: #32930. Date: 8 May 1672.

Will of Robert Joyner (SM). Bequests:
wife Mary Joyner plantation "Scotland"
then to son Robert Joyner, son Robert
(under age), daughter Mary Joyner
5:366 (under age), daughter Cathrine Joyner
(under age). Executrix: wife Mary
Joyner. Overseer: Mr. William Rowsell.
Date: 28 January 1669. Witnesses: John
Warreck, Robert Drury, John Dayne. Will
proved by John Warreck & Robert Drury on
12 November 1672.

5:367 Inventory of Mr. John Lewis (Bristoll).
Appraisers: Thomas Peerce, Thomas Spink.
Date: 27 October 1671. List of debts:
John Powill, Clemment, Isack Glover.
Amount: #2872. List of bills: Jaspar
Allen, Demetrius Cartwright,
5:368 Thomas Clark, William King, William
Thompson, William Inness, Joseph Dawkins
& Sam. Sprigg, William Hambleton, John
Peerce, John Clement, Richard West due
to Richard Smith, Demetrius Cartwright,
John How, Mr. Steuart, John Brooke due

to Will. Hambleton, Richard Baylie. Further list of bills: Clement Chiverell, John ThomSon, Richard Chapman, Thomas Clarke, Roger Baker, Guy White, Samuell Sprigg, James Newill, John Powell, Abell James, Vincent Atchinson, Samell Neale, Robert Large, John Barnes, Thomas Locker, Isack Glover. Amount: #9412.

5:369   Valuation of the property of Francis Swanston. Date: 30 May 1672. Signed: William Groome, John Bigger.

Inventory of Mary Peake executrix of George Peake. Appraisers: Thomas Billingsley, John Russell. Date: 7 February 1672.

5:370   ...
5:371   Amount: #29321.

Inventory of Edward Parker. Date: 1 February 1669. Signed: Elisabeth Young. Inventory of Edward Parker (SM). Appraisers: Thomas Stone (p, CH), Will. Gater (p, CH). Sworn by Mr. John Bowles (CH). Date: 14 May 1672.

5:372   Amount: #3550.

25 November 1672. Thomas Taunt who married Ann widow & relict of Christopher Gardner (AA) was granted administration on his estate. Appraisers: Robert Franklyn, Robert Lookwood. Samuell Chew, Esq. to administer oath.

Marriage agreement between William Durand (TA) & Elisabeth Aylee (TA), declared before Richard Wollman & Capt. Phillemon Lloyd.

5:373   Mentions: plantation on Wye River: if no issue by said Elisabeth, then devised to grandchild Samuell Withers (under age 21). Date: 2 August 1672. Witnesses: William Hemsley, William Stevenson, William Power. Affirmed by said William Durand on 6 August 1672. Witnesses: William Stevenson, William Hemsley. Recorded: 7 August 1672. Affirmed by William Hemsley on 9 December 1672.

5:374   19 November 1672. Elisabeth Durand
widow of William Durand was granted
administration on his estate. Bondsmen:
Phillip Stevenson, George Aldredge.
Appraisers: William Hemsley, Edward
Steevens. Mr. Richard Woolman to
administer oath.

10 December 1672. George Robbins
(merchant, TA) who married Margarett
widow of Nicholas Goldbery (merchant,
KE) was granted administration on his
estate. Bondsmen: Edward Wincles, John
Eason. Appraisers: Thomas Osborne,
Michaell Miller. John Wright to
administer oath.

Accounts of John Hatton. Patents:
"Persummon Point" 400 a. (originally
granted to James Rigbie), "Spry Hill"
600 a. (originally granted to Oliver
Spry), "Harmer's Mount" 350 a.
(originally granted to Gothofrid
Harmer), "White Clifts" 300 a. (sold by
Will. Hemsley to said Hatton). List of
bills: Capt. John Weeks, Mr. Bayly,
5:375   Godfrey Bayley, Will. Leeds, John
Jenkens, Abraham Coffens, Godfrey
Harman, Jacob Mighelson, William
Standley, Sam. Skipwith, Geo. Saughier,
Tho. Tolley, Oliver Spry, John Stansby,
Tho. Odonnel, James Rigby, Seth Foster,
Sander Towerson, Nicholas Pickard,
Morgan Williams, John Winchester, John
Spuxdance, Andrew Elinor, John Eason,
Josias Lambert, William Hemsley, Abraham
Bishop, John Morgan, William Bise.
Amount: #15858. Date: 10 September
1672. Witnesses: John Morecroft, Ro.
Carvill.

5:376   Will of John Felton (DO). Bequests:
wife Katherine Felton. Executrix: said
wife. Date: 21 April 1670. Witnesses:
A. Wright, Sarah Barclett, John Edmond,
Tho. Harris, Will. Bridges, Richard
Mansell.

21 December 1672. John Phillips who
married Kathrine relict of John Felton
was granted administration on his
estate. Appraisers: William Wraughton,

William Jones. Mr. Daniell Clerke to administer oath.

5:377 Will of Stephen Mountague was proved by Nicholas Solby on 17 October 1672.

11 December 1672. Thomas Armiger who married Anne widow of Francis Trippus (BA) was granted administration on his estate. Bondsmen: James Phillips, Lodowike Williams. Appraisers: Godfrey Harmer, William Hollis. George Uty to administer oath.

Will of William Boulding (BA) was proved by George Broccas & William Broccas on 12 November 1672. Before: Thomas Howell. Inventory of William Boulding (BA). Date: 13 November 1672. Appraisers: William Price, Hugh Fouch.

5:378 ...
5:379 Amount: #25682.

5:380 Luke Gardner (g, SM), age 50, deposed that on 8 January, he was at the house of Mr. Henry Neale at Newtowne, when said Neale desired the deponent & Mr. Henry Warren to take note of his will. Bequests: ½ to his wife Anne, other ½ to his son Henry, Richard Gardner, John Gardner. Date: 22 January 1672.

William Farding (p, SM), age 27, deposed that he was the overseer to Mr. Henry Neale of Newtowne who was very ill on 8 January last, & Capt. Gardner & Mr. Warren (the "preist") being at his house, made note of his will & the deponent deposed that the above written by
5:381 Luke Gardner is correct. Date: 22 January 1672.

Ann Neale widow of Henry Neale was granted administration on his estate. Bondsman: Capt. Luke Gardner Appraisers: James Pattison, Edward Clerke. Luke Gardner to administer oath.

Will of George Goodwin (carpenter, SM). Bequests: Henry Exon to be paid by Mr.

Court Session: <no date>

Tho. Dent & Tho. Griffin & Maj.
Fitzherbert & Tho. Wyn. Executor: said
Henry Exon. Date: 7 January 1672.
Witnesses: Tho. Cafford, Winefred Horne,
M. Eke (?).

5:382   22 January 1672. Will proved by Thomas
Cafford & Winifred Horne. Henry Exon
was granted administration on said
estate. Appraisers: Thomas Griffin,
Edward Horne.

Inventory of Stephen Mountague (CH).
Appraisers: Thomas Hussey (CH), Ralph
Coates (CH). Date: 19 October 1672.
5:383   Mentions: "Mountague's Mountayne" 200
a., "Mountague's Addition" 100 a.
Amount: #18041.

Inventory of Capt. John Norwood. Date:
20 November 1672.
5:384   Mentions: Mrs. Norwood.
5:385   Servants: Will. Dorman, John Jordeene.
5:386   List of debts: estate of Mr. Pine, Mr.
Devall, Mr. Jobe Walston. Amount:
#38042. Appraisers: Thomas Marsh, John
Beamon.

Inventory of George Peake (g, CV).
5:387   ...
5:388   Date: 19 April 1671. Appraisers: John
Cobreth, Marke Clare.
5:389   Kalom Mackloglin who married Mary
administratrix of James Lindsey (CH) to
pass accounts. Date: 1 October 1672.
Signed: Kallom Mackloglin.

Inventory of Mr. James Lindsey (CH).
Date: 22 April 1671.
5:390   Amount: #14010. Accounts. Payments to:
Dr. Lumer, Mr. Pettaway, Mr. Henry
Warren, John Owing, Mr. Benjamin Rozer,
Denis Oswolivant, Ralph Coates for
Edward Lindsey, Ralph Coates for Mr.
Boner. Amount: #15975. Date: 9 January
1672. Discharge was granted.

5:391   John Stansby (CV) was granted
administration on estate of George Peake
(g, CV). Estate is unadministered by
Mary Peake late wife & executrix. Date:
28 January 1672. Bondsman: John Griggs.

Court Session: \<no date\>

Appraisers: John Cobreth, John Throster.
Edward Keene to administer oath.

5:392   3 February 1672. Charles Carpenter (p,
SM) was granted administration on estate
of Richard Parker (SM). Bondsman:
Walter Hall (g). Appraisers: John
Blomfeild, Richard Burket. John Warren
(g) to administer oath.

Will of Samuell Spicer. Executors:
Richard Owen, John Raven. Bequests:
Mary Raven (daughter of said John Raven)
chattel at plantation of John Edwards at
Fishing Creek, Daniell Robeson. Date: 1
January 1672. Witnesses: Richard
Dawson, Elisabeth Ginnet. Will proved
12 February 1672. Richard Dawson & John
Raven were granted administration on
said estate. Appraisers: John Brooke,
Edward Cooke. Daniell Clerke (g) to
administer oath.

5:393   Inventory of William Lewis. Date: 20
June 1670.
5:394   ...
5:395   List of debts: Jacob Brymington, John
Cocks, Ralph Fishbourne, Christopher
Stoper, Hugh Sherwood, Francis Bellers,
Henry Clay, Ralph Fishbourne, Henry
Clay, Richard Woolman, John Poore,
George Collison, Anthony Mayle, Edmond
Webb, Robert Fuller, Michaell Rogers,
Thomas Taylor, Henry Clay. Servants:
John Browne, John Hoy,
5:396   John Burrows, Elisabeth Bailiffe.
Overseer: Ralph Fishborne. Appraisers:
William Southbee, Thomas Taylor.
Neighbors: William Leeds, Edmond Webb.

Inventory of Mr. James Trueman. Date:
15 January 1672.
5:397-8 ...
5:399   Amount: #64260. Appraisers: William
Groome, Arthur Ludford.

Will of Hugh Cornellison (BA) was proved
by William Sinckler, Thomas Smith, &
James Holloway on 21 December 1672.

24 February 1672. Samuell Crossy was
granted administration on estate of John

Court Session: <no date>

Harrington (CH). Bondsman: Garret
Vanswering. Appraisers: William Hinsey,
John Worland. Mr. Robert Henley to
administer oath.

5:400 Will of John Hatton (salter, London).
[Paragraph in Latin.] Date: 14 December
1654.

5:401 Bequests: sister Sara Hatton, sister
Susann, sister Hanna Hatton, brothers
Henry & Samuell Hatton, brother Thomas
Hatton all lands left me by my father
John Hatton (dec'd), Robert Lewellin
(salter, London). Executors: brother
Thomas Hatton, Robert Lewellin.
Witnesses: Richard Colchester, Hercules
Comander, Sr. [Paragraph in Latin]
Signed: Simon Rolleston. Will of

5:402 John Hatton (VA) from Guilbert
Archbishop of Canterbury, dated 28 July
1669, was recorded by William Mericke
Knight, Doctor of Laws. Robert Lewellin
is dec'd.

5:403 Thomas Hatton was granted administration
on said estate, by his procurator
Samuell Hatton. Date: 9 December 1672.

5:404 Bondsmen: Daniell Clerke (DO), Edward
Roe (TA). Witnesses: Edward Savage,
Tho. Taylor, Henry Turner, Henry Trippe.

5:405 Inventory of John Hatton. Patents
mentioned: "Pursimmon Point" 400 a.
(granted to James Rigbie), "Spry Hill"
600 a. (granted to Olliver Spry),
"Herman's Mount" 350 a. (granted to
Gothofred Herman), "White Clifts" 350 a.
(bought of William Hemsley). List of
bills: Capt. John Weekes, Mr. Bally,
Godfry Bally, Mr. Hatton, William Leeds,
John Jenckins, Abraham Coffin, Godfry
Herman, Jacob Mighellson, William
Stanlye, Samuell Skipwith, George
Saughier, Thomas Tolly, Olliver Spry,
John Stansby, Thomas Oddonell, James
Rigby, Seth Foster, Saunder Towerson,
Nicholas Pickard, Morgan Williams, John
Winchester,

5:406 John Spurdance, Andrew Ellinor, John
Eason, Josias Lambert, William Hemsley,
Abraham Bishop, John Morgan, William
Bisse. Received by Samuell Hatton
attorney of Thomas Hatton of Tewksury,
County Glocester. Witnesses: John

Court Session: <no date>

Morecroft, Robert Carvile. Date: 24 February 1672.

Will of John Deareing. Date: 9 February 1670.

5:407 Mentions: "Deareing Gallyer" 100 a. on Herring Creek Swamp & "Vellmead" 400 a. on the Ridge to be sold. Bequests: son John Deareing pt. "Freeman's Fancy" 200 a. (out of 300 a.) at head of South River & pt. "Abbenton" 600 a. (out of 875 a.) adjoining "Freeman's Fancy", wife Alce Deareing "Deareings Increase" 200 a. on north side of Poptapsco River for her life then to son John Deareing, John Gorsuch. Overseers: Thomas Houcker, Robert Franckling. Witnesses: John Grace, Roger Sedwell. Request by my neighbor Thomas Hocker (also Thomas Hoocker) to be granted administration on estate of a "poore man". Date: 7 March 1672/3.

5:408 Signed: Thomas Taylor, from the Ridge. Robert Ridgely to grant administration to Thomas Hooker (one of the overseers). Date: 12 March 1672/3. Thomas Hooker (AA) was granted administration on estate of John Deareing (AA). Mr. Richard Ball (BA) to prove the will. Appraisers: John Watkins, George Pascall. Thomas Taylor (g) to administer oath.

5:409 Richard Edelen was granted administration on estate of Isack Marshall (CH), as greatest creditor. Appraisers: John Ward, Edward Price. Mr. John Stone to administer oath.

Inventory of Mr. George Manwering (CH). Appraisers: Ignatius Cousens, Thomas Hussey, sworn on 22 May 1671.

5:410 Mentions: boat co-partnered with Mr. Henry Warren. Servants: John Brawsgrove, Ralfe Bartley & his wife, Richard Martine. Mentions: 70 a. leased from Mr. Warren.

5:411 List of debts: Samuell Cressy, Mrs. Young, Witter, Thomas King, Edmond Lindsey & Capt. James Neale, Mr. Hussey for widow Shirtliffe, Thomas Wyn. Amount: #20994. Date: 13 March 1672.

Court Session: <no date>

Accounts. Date: 24 March 1672. Signed:
Henry Addams, Tho. Mathews.
5:412 Payments to: sheriff for Mr. Tho.
Notley, Mr. Henry Warren, Mr. Rozer.
Amount: #21703. Signed: Henry Addams,
Tho. Matthews.

Will of Mathew Harding (inholder, AA).
Bequests: Mrs. Katherne Stockett wife
of Mr. Henry Stockett & her daughter
Francis. Executors: MM Francis
Stockett, Henry Stockett. Date: 22
February 1672. Witnesses: John Oakley,
Judath Marsh.
5:413 Memorandum (to aforegoing will): Robert
Wilson & William Powell & our maid
Margarett witnessed that John Beamon
promised me the whole estate that was
joint should he predeceased me. Signed:
Math. Harding. Witnesses: John Oakley,
Judath Marsh. Francis Stockett & Henry
Stockett were granted administration on
said estate. Mr. Tho. Taylor to prove
will. Appraisers: Thomas Marsh, Robert
Burle.

Will of Thomas Sunderbee (cooper,
Bristoll). Date: 17 February 1672.
Bequests: wife, brother Charles
Sunderbee, cousin John Harris, Thomas
Harris. Witnesses: Peter Perkes, Icell
Perry, Joseph Hiscox. Will proved by
Peter Perkes & Joseph Hiscox on 28 March
1673. John Harris (mariner, Bristoll)
was granted administration on estate of
Thomas Sunderle (Bristoll). Bondsman:
Christopher Birkhead. Appraisers:
Joseph Hitchcox, Peter Perkes.

5:414 Inventory of Hugh Cornellis (Bohemiah
River). Date: 23 February 1672.
Mentions: 150 a. Amount: #15672.
Appraisers: Augustine Herrmen, James
Makriger.

5:415 Inventory of George Peake (CV).
Appraisers: John Cobreth, John Troster.
Date: 27 February 1672.
5:416 List of debts: Joseph Riggs. Amount:
#35701.

Court Session: <no date>

5:417 Will of Mathew Stone (p, CH). Date: 24 December 1672. Bequests: William Marshall, Sr., William Marshall, Jr., John Fernly (son of Francis Fernly), Jonathon Marler, Elisabeth Cormihill, said Elisabeth Cormiell chattel at Thomas Baker. Executors: William Marshall, Sr., Jonathon Marler. Witnesses: William Marshall, Johnathon Marler, William Marshall, Jr.

5:418 2 April 1673. Will proved by William Marshall, Sr. & Jonathon Marler. William Marshall, Sr. & Jonathon Marler renounce executorship of said estate. Before: Robert Ridgely, John Griggs.

Will of Henry Moore. Bequests: son Henry (under age 18) & daughter Elisabeth (under age 16) plantation, son John "Moore's Folly" 50 a. at Port Tobacco, son Thomas "Wheatland" upper half bought of William Boyden, wife Elisabeth other half of said land, Mr. Henry Warren debt from estate of Mr. George Manwaring. Executrix: wife Elisabeth Moore. Guardians for children: Ignatius Courseene, Jesse Wharton. Witnesses: Jesse Wharton, William Guyther, Mathias Obryan.

5:419 8 April 1673. Elisabeth More relict & executrix of Henry More was granted administration on his estate. Appraisers: Fran. Thornton, Fran. Addams. Benjamin Rozer (g) to administer oath.

Will of John Dearing (AA) proved by Roger Sedwell & John Grace on 23 March 1672/3. Signed: Richard Ball at his house on Potapsco River (BA).

Will of George Eaves was proved by William Tomkins & Edward Dickenson on 3 December 1672. Signed: Will. Stevens.

Roger Brooke brother of Henry Brooke (CV, dec'd) was granted administration on his estate. Bondsman: Charles Boteler. Appraisers: Phillip Harwood,

Page 64

Court Session: <no date>

Richard Hacksby. Baker Brooke, Esq. to administer oath. Date: 21 March 1672.

5:420 Inventory of Jacob Neale. Appraisers: Francis Stockett, Henry Lewis. Date: 3 September 1672. Amount: #25431.

Inventory of Richard Millard (also Richard Miller, DO). Date: 8 February 1672/3. Appraisers: Tho. Browne, William Jones.

5:421 List of debts: Thomas Cobham, Stephen Zealous, John Crawly, William Burton, William Jones,

5:422 Thomas Cobham, William Harper, Thomas Purnill, Daniell Chapman, Thomas Purnill, Thomas Browne, Henry Turner, Thomas How, estate of John Taylor for Tho. Cobham, John Felton, Daniell Chapman, Thomas Howton, Thomas Purill to Mr. Pickering, Thomas Purnill. Amount: #21368.

5:423 Accounts of Robert Coberthwayt. Administrator: John Anderson from March 1671 to March 1673. Payments to: Dr. Hough, Mr. Christopher Rousby, John Bigger, Francis Hutchins, Mordecay Hunton, Richard Keene, James Guthery, Dormand Magrowgh. Payments since account given to Mr. Tho. Trueman: Mr. William Groome, Dr. John Pearce. Amount: #4370. Amount of inventory: 6570. Received from: James Preston, Moses Oling.

Will of Clement Herbert (p, TA). Date: 21 August 1671. Bequests: wife Elisabeth Herbert. Witnesses: William Garge, William Tollard.

5:424 Mr. Richard Woolman (TA) to prove said will.

Will of Moses Harris (AA). Bequests: Elisabeth Champe 100 a. at head of Roade River adjoining Andrew Roberts & Richard Cydings & John Larkins. Executrix: said Elisabeth. Date: 21 February 1672/3. Witnesses: Edward Allely, Thomas Taylor.

11 April 1673. Said will proved by Thomas Taylor, Esq. Mr. Richard Ball

to obtain oath of other witness.

5:425   Charles Delaroch (inholder, CV) to be
         recompensed for taking accounts of
         estate of John Taylor (also John
         Taylour, p, CV). Date: 22 April 1673.

         Philip Calvert, Esq. (Chancellor) was
         commissioned as Judge or Commissary
         General for Probate. Date: 23 April.
5:426-427 ...

5:428   26 April 1673. Petition of Edward
         Winckles attorney for Jonathon Hopkinson
         (inholder, TA), who is departing on
         voyage to ENG, for administration on
         estate of William Power (TA), as
         principle creditor. "No wife nor any
         son of his kindred within this
         province."

         Petition of said Edward as attorney for
         said Jonathon for administration on
         estate of Evan Thomas (TA), as principle
         creditor. Deceased "left neither widow
         nor kindred within this province."
5:429   Edward Wincles attorney for Jonathon
         Hopkinson was granted administration on
         estate of William Power.
5:430   Appraisers: Edward Stevenson, Thomas
         Emerson. Philip Stevenson (g) to
         administer oath.

         Edward Wincles attorney for Jonathon
         Hopkinson was granted administration on
         estate of Evan Thomas.
5:431   Appraisers: Edward Stevenson, Thomas
         Emerson. Philip Stevenson (g) to
         administer oath.

5:432   <does not exist>

5:433   Thomas Hawkins (Popleys Island) was
         granted administration on estate of
         Alexander Dhynoyossa.

         Capt. Wheatly attorney for William
         Barrett was granted administration on
         estate of Humphry Warren (CH).

         John Morecroft was granted
         administration on estate of John Parker.

Inventory of John Taylor. Date: 24 April 1673. Appraisers: John Halfhead, Jr., William Burges. List of debts: Mr. Rousby Amount: #1585.

5:434   3 May 1673. Daniell Clarke (DO) exhibited the bond of John Phillips & Ramond Staplefort on the estate of John Felton (DO).

Daniell Clarke (DO) exhibited oath to appraisers of Samuell Spice.

William Thomas (p, DO) deposed that Jacob Wymake (DO, now dec'd) was intending to take a voyage to ENG for recovery of his health, & made his will on 22 March 1670 & the following May departed on the Vinchorne of Bristoll, Thomas Cooper (commander), & in the company of Edward Perrin (merchant, Bristoll). Said Jacob is since dec'd at the house of Edward Perrin in Bristoll; said Edward is ready to testify. Witnesses to the will live very remote from Office for Probate of Wills. Commission to Daniell Clarke to take oaths of William Thompson & William Willoughby said witnesses. Said William Thomas was granted administration on said estate.

5:435   Appraisers: William Worgan, Thomas Skinner.

5:436   Daniel Clark to administer oath.

5 May 1673. Will of Henry Hawkins (TA), dated 24 April 1672, was exhibited. Witnesses: Nathaniel Read, Griffeth Steevens.

5:437   Jonathon Sybery (g, TA) to examine the witnesses. Said Jonathon to take oath of Phillemon Lloyd regarding said will.

5:438   Philemon Lloyd is cited as brother to Henry Hawkins.

5:439   9 May 1673. Thomas Howell who married Ellinor relict of Humphry Warren (Hatton's Point, CH) petitioned for administration on his estate. Cites suit by Capt. William Wheatly attorney for William Barret (merchant, London). John Morecroft is attorney for Wheatly

Court Session: <no date>

who is attorney for Barret.

5:440   Inventory of Walter Walterling. List of
               debts: Mathias Diacosta, Edward Hard,
               Rich. Moy, Thomas Doxey,
5:441   Elisabeth Greene, John Barnes, Elisabeth
               Young. Signed: John Barnes.
               Appraisers: Thomas Pearce, Thomas
               Spinck. Further list of debts: Will.
               Osbeston, Daniell Clocker, Georg
               Marshall, James Lewis, Tho. James,
               William Turbillvill, Constant Daniell,
               Georg Charlseworth, Edward Jollee,
               Joseph Hackney, Tho. Pearce, Tho.
               Pritchet, John Thompson, John Griffin,
               Curtis Fletcher, Georg Haynes, Robert
               Large, John Reynolds, Henry Ryder,
               Daniel Deanie, Hugh Mannin. Amount:
               #2985. Further list of debts: Mr.
               Thomas Mathews,
5:442   Dr. Morecroft, Mr. Kenhelm Cheseldine,
               Mr. Walter Ball, Mr. Rich. Moy, Hannah
               Price, the Governor, accountant, the
               Secretary, Francis, Capt. Gardner, James
               Pevis, Hannah Rigell, Thomas Pearce,
               Robert Lardge, Henry Rider, the Cooper,
               Samuel Brockhouse, Mr. Will.
               Turbillvill, the Carpenter, Maj.
               Fitzherbert, John Hayles, Mr.
               Vansweringen, Sanders, Henry, John
               Barnes. Amount: #19638. Signed: John
               Barnes.

5:443   Thomas Howell (p, CH) who married
               Ellinor relict of Humphry Warren, Sr.
               (Hatton's Point, CH) was granted
               administration on his estate. Sureties:
               James Walter, Giles Tompkinson. Date: 9
               May 1673.
5:444   Appraisers: Robert Henly, John Douglas.
               John Boules (g, CH) to administer oath.

5:445   Petition of Thomas Vaughan who married
               Sara relict of Richard Russell (St.
               Michaell's Hundred, SM) for
               administration on said estate. Witness
               to said will: Roger Shehee. Sheriff
               (SM) to prove will. Sheriff (CV) to
               Humphry Limbrey.

               13 May 1673. Thomas Trueman, Esq.
               exhibited depositions of John Smith &

Court Session: \<no date\>

David Cuningham regarding the will of
John Bigger, Sr. John Bigger, Jr. "had
laboured to conceal" estate of John
Bigger, Sr. & betrayed the trust
"reposed in him by his deceased
kinsman."

5:446 Said John Bigger, Jr. has forfeited the
administration. Administration was
granted to Robert Lashly, for use &
benefit of wife of said Bigger, Sr.

- John Smith, age 24, deposed that
  John Bigger, Sr. had certain chattel
  when he came to the house of his
  kinsman John Bigger, Jr.
- Daniel Cuninham, age 24, deposed the
  same. Date: 17 March 1672.

Accounts of John Bigger, Sr.
Administrator: John Bigger, Jr. Date: 2
October 1669. Mentions: dec'd's "wyfe"
& children. Payments to: William
Grosse, John Auldwheele, John Sinckler &
his man Tom & William Sempler, Lt.
William Bell, Alexander Magruder, Thomas
Blanford,

5:447 James Kanedy, Tho. Barbour, Henry
Trulock, John Wright, Patricke Mackeand,
for beef in Barbadoes that his brother
had, John Nicholls, accountant.

Robert Lashly (p, CV) was granted
administration on estate of John Bigger,
Sr. (CV).

5:448 Allexander Dynoyossa son of Allexander
Dynoyossa (Popleys Island, KE) was
granted administration on his father's
estate. Mentions: debt to Thomas
Hawkins (overseer),

5:449 administrator's brothers & sisters newly
arrived in the Province. Surety:
Garrett Vansweringen, Appraisers: John
Wright, Robert Dunn. Arthur Wright (g)
to administer oath.

5:450 16 May 1673. Summons to John Bigger,
Jr. to render accounts of John Bigger,
Sr.

23 May 1673. Thomas Vaughan who married
Sara relict of Richard Russell (St.
Michael's Hundred, SM) exhibited his
will.

Will of Richard Russell. Overseer: John Thompson.

5:451 Bequests: eldest daughter Elisabeth Russell "Russell's Plantation", daughter Mary Russell, Roger Shehee, wife. Date: 18 September 1672. Witnesses: Humphry Limbrey, Roger Shehee. Codicil: bequests: Sara Coleman, Humphry Limbrey. Date: 18 September 1672. Codicil:

5:452 Wife has estate until children are of age. Date: 18 September 1672.

Jane Paine widow of Thomas Paine (St. Jerome's, St. Michael's Hundred, SM) exhibited his will & petitioned that Nathaniell Garrett, John Smalpeice, & John Reynolds be named executors. All three

5:453 separately renounced executorship. Said Jane was granted administration. Will of Thomas Paine (p, St. Jerome's, SM).

5:454 Bequests: eldest son Isaack (under age 18) "Paine's Lott" (BA), son Joseph (under age 18) "Holt" (BA), wife Jane plantation & land in SM, 5 daughters (under age 17) Mary & Sara & Elisabeth & Hannah & Rachell.

5:545 Executors: Nathaniell Garrett, John Smallpeice, John Reynolds. Date: 12 March 1672. Witnesses: Will. Calvert, Robert Ridgely, Joseph Hackney. Appraisers: Joseph Brough, Georg Marshall. Col. Will. Calvert to administer oath.

5:456 29 May 1673. John Hedge (taylor, TA) was granted administration on estate of Thomas Taylor, (KE) who died single, with "no person of blood in the Province", as principle creditor. Appraisers: Nathaniell Evatt, John Hinson. Signed: Richard Fullinggam. James Ringold (g) to administer oath.

Notice to sheriff of TA for accounting of intestate estates.

5:457 Same to sheriffs of: KE, AA, BA, SM, CH, SO, CV, DO.

30 May 1673. Charles de la Roch (inholder, CV) was granted administration on estate of John Taylor

(CV). Appraisers: John Halfhead, Jr.,
William Burgess. Signed: John Bigger.

5:458 John Bigger, Jr. was granted continuance
on estate of John Bigger, Sr.

Inventory of Daniell Johnson.
Administratrix: Elisabeth Kilborne
(relict). Amount: #51778.

5:459 Accounts. Payments to: Richard Dod &
James Hayse, Mr. Morecroft, Mr. Jenifer,
Joseph Pearce, Mr. Roswell per (N)
Lindsey, Mr. Rozer, Mr. Humphry Warren,
John Burras, Edward Abbott (taylor),
John Cox, Geo. Godfrey, Jeremiah
Cannady,

5:450 Mr. Notley, Mr. Cosden, Mr. Hill,
Francis Wyne, John Farrell, Robert
Henly, Mr. Bonner. Amount: #23478.
Further payments to: Fran. Taylor, James
Smallwood, Thomas Mathewes, Samuell
Cressey, Owen Jones, William James
(runaway),

5:461 George Knight (runaway), Thomas Cosman
(since dead, insolvent), Nicholas Turner
(runaway), Ambroze Farlo (gone to VA),
Mr. Morecroft, Edward Pearce, Robert
Ware. Distribution: administratrix, her
son Daniell Johnson. Amount: #51778.

5:462 Signed: Fran. Kilborn & his wife
Elisabeth Kilborn.

5:463 Inventory of William Durand.
Administratrix: Elisabeth Durand.
Appraisers: William Hemsley, Edward
Steevens. Richard Woolman administered
oath. Date: 24 April 1673.

5:464 List of debts: Mr. Edward Steevens,
Edmund Webb, Tho. Broomdoun, John Pooly,
Francis Smith. Amount: #21849.

5:465 3 June 1673. Sheriff (SM) to summon
Abell James to give account of estate of
Edward Duberg.

Citation vs. estate of John Parker.

4 June 1673. Inventory of John Bigger.
Executor: John Bigger. Witnesses to
will: Daniel Cuningham, John Smith.
List of debts: William Cross, John
Adwell, John Sinckler & his 2 freemen,

Court Session: <no date>

5:466　Ninian Beale, Alexander Magruder, Tho.
Blanford, Thomas Barber, Henry Trulocke,
John Wright. Date: 4 June 1667.

Will of Jacob Waymacke. Date: 22 March
1670. Bequests: William Thomas (Fishing
Creek, Little Choptank, DO) "Spring
Garden". Witnesses: William Thompson,
William Willoby.

5:467　Will proved 26 May 1673. Witness:
Daniell Clarke (DO).

3 June 1673. Inventory of Jacob
Waymacke. Appraisers: William Worgan,
Thom. Skinner. Date: 31 May 1673.
Mentions: 50 a. Amount: #5500.

5:468　Will of Luke Barber (Micham Hall, SM).
Bequests: wife Elisabeth Barber use of
"Micham Hall" then to eldest son Luke
Barber then to his eldest son if none
then to his brother Edward Barber then
to his eldest son if none then to his
brother Thomas Barber then to his eldest
son if none then to female heirs of Luke
etc.,

5:469　Edward "Luke Land" 500 a. at Choptico
then to his eldest son if none then to
his brother Luke then to his eldest son
if none then to his brother Thomas then
to his eldest son if none then to female
heirs of Edward etc., youngest son
Thomas "Micham Hills" at Choptico then
to his eldest son if none then to his
brother Luke then to his eldest son if
none then to his brother Edward then to
his eldest son if none then to female
heirs of Thomas etc., eldest daughter
Elisabeth, youngest daughter Mary, Capt.
Richard Bankes (Poplar Hill) & Mr.
Randall Hinson (Poplar Hill).

5:470　Signed: Luke Barbier. Date: 30 July
1664.

4 June 1673. Walter Hall (Cross Mannor)
exhibited said will. Elisabeth widow
made her will just after the death of
her husband, constituting Col. Lewis
Stockett as executor.

5:471　George Beckwith to prove the will.

Court Session: <no date>

Inventory of John Felton. Appraisers: William Wraughton, William Jones. Date: 1 May 1673. Amount: #10470.

5:472 Marke Cordea attorney for Capt. Robert Crossman vs. estate of Georg Manwering. Caveat.

Ignatius Warren (Newtowne, SM) who married Mary daughter of Robert Cole (dec'd) vs. Capt. Luke Gardner executor of said Cole (St. Clement's Bay, SM). Re: his wife's legacy.

10 June 1673. John Halfhead & William Burges (appraisers of estate of John Taylor) took their oath.

5:473 Inventory of John Rigold (KE). Appraisers: John Hinson, Nathaniel Evett. Date: 19 September 1672.
5:474 List of debts: William Savage, Thomas Boone. Amount: #25653.

5:475 Inventory of Mr. Henry Neale. Appraisers: James Pattison, Edward Clarke. Date: 4 February 1672.
5:476 ...
5:477 List of debts: John Jers, James Greenwell, Henry Taylor, Edward Louder, William Mickin, Richard Gary, Garrett Vanswering, Pope Allen, John Allen, Charles Carpenter. Amount: #15788. Further list of debts: Richard Slater (runaway), Peter Carward (runaway), John Place. Signed: Ann Neale.

5:478 Will of Edward Dubery (SM). Bequests: Diana James, Mr. Abell James. Executor: Mr. Abell James. Date: 26 November 1672. Witnesses: Leonard Greene, Thomas Moseley. Will proved by Leonard Greene & Thomas Mosely on 13 June 1673. Abell James was granted administration on said estate.
5:479 Appraisers: Patricke Forrest, William Watts. Thomas Dent (g) to administer oath.

5:480 Inventory of William Poore (TA). Appraisers: Edward Steevenson, Thomas Emerson. Mentions: items at house of

Court Session: <no date>

Mr. Hemsley. List of debts: William
Abrahams, Leonard Damells, Thomas
Vaughan, Nicholas Hackett, Edward
Ellgate, John Glover.

Inventory of Evan Thomas. Appraisers:
Edward Steevenson, Thomas Emerson (same
as previous entry). Mentions: chattel
sold by Mr. Steven Tully to Simon
Harris. List of debts: Jonas Davis,
Nathaniell Reade, Francis Bellowes &
Simon Harris. Before: Phillip
Steevenson.

5:481 Mr. Thomas Thatcher (clarke, Boston,
MA, NE) who married Margaret Sheafe
(widow, Boston) sole daughter & one of
executrices of Henry Webb (merchant,
Boston) & Elisabeth Gibbs wife of Robert
Gibbs (merchant, Boston) another of
executrices of said Henry & daughter of
said Margarett by her first husband
Jacob Sheafe (merchant, Boston). Said
Thomas & Margarett on behalf of
Mehittable Sheafe (under age, daughter
of said Jacob & Margarett) made PoA to
Robert Gibbs aforesaid on 21 September
1669 to recover all debts due the estate
of said Henry from William Batten
(formerly of Boston, since of MD). Said
Robert Gibbs appeared on 24 October 1672
before Robert Howard (notary, Boston)
5:482 & made PoA to Samuell Winslow (merchant,
MD) to recover for estate of said Henry.
5:483 Witnesses: John Jackson, George Coysh,
Richard Price, John Grey. Affirmed by
Charles Calvert. Date: 23 November
1672.
5:484 Administration on estate of Henry Webb
(merchant, Boston, NE) was granted on 28
December 1663 by John Endecott. He made
his will on 5 April 1660, & died not
long after that. Executrices: his
daughter Margarett Sheafe, his
granddaughters Elisabeth & Mehittabell
Sheafe. Mr. Robert Gibbs (merchant,
Boston) married said Elisabeth. Will of
said Henry Webb.
5:485 Bequests: my only daughter Margarett
late wife of Jacob Sheaffe,
5:486 her daughter Elisabeth,
5:487 my grandchild Elisabeth Sheaffe (under

Page 74

age 21) my mansion & land adjoining
Capt. Leveritt & mill at Yorke Falls
5:488 & if no male heir then to my grandchild
Mehittabell Sheaffe & if no issue then
to Hartford College,
5:489 grandchild Mehittabell
5:490 (under age 21), my sister Jane late wife
of my brother John Webb (Eitherly,
Hampshire), cousin Elisabeth Blackleeth
wife of John Blackleeth then to her
daughter Elisabeth Blackleeth,
5:491 cousin Francis Orum & her 2 children
Elisabeth & John Orum, John & Samuel
Sanford who are sons of my late sister
Elisabeth Sanford, wife's sister Barbary
Sewell wife of Reynold Sewell (joyner,
Salsbury), David Sewell & Elisabeth
5:492 my wife's cousins, eldest son of Capt.
Edward Hutchinson, Mr. Edward Rawson,
the poor of Boston,
5:493 Mr. Richard Bellingham or his wife,
Hervard Colledge land bought of Henry
Philips & Samuel Oliver,
5:494 Mr. John Wilson (pastor), Mr. John
Norton (teacher), Mr. Thomas Thatcher
(pastor of the Church of Christ), Mr.
May & Mr. Powell (elders of the new
church), Mr. Miller (teacher of
Barnstable). Executrices: daughter
Margarett Sheaffe & 2 grandchildren
Elisabeth & Mehittabell Sheaffe.
5:495 Overseers: Mr. Edward Rawson, elder
James Penn, Mr. Anthony Stoddard, Capt.
Edward Hutchinson. Date: 5 April 1660.
5:496 Witnesses: Thomas Buttolph, Thomas
Scottow, Samuell Robinson. Will proved
by Thomas Buttow & Thomas Scottow on 13
September 1660. Samuell Winslow
attorney for Robert Gibbs who married
Elisabeth Sheaffe (one of the
executrices) was granted administration
on said estate.
5:497 Date: 17 June 1673.

Will of John Collett. Executor: Henry
Haselwood. Bequests: Henry Haselwood
plantation &
5:498 "Turkyhill" 100 a., Peter Ellis. Said
Henry is to sell to Martin Muginbrug
"Colleton" 250 a. on Saxafrax River.
Further bequests: cousin Mary Gouldsmith
chattel with coat of arms, cousin Mathew

Gouldsmith "Elck Neck" 600 a. on
Gunpowder River & "Smallhope" 50 a.,
sister Elisabeth Gouldsmith "Collett's
Point" 400 a. on Bush River,

5:499 2 cousins Mathew Gouldsmith (under age
14) & his sister Elisabeth if both die
without issue then to my cousin
Elisabeth Collet (daughter of uncle
Nicholas Collet (London)). Date: 26
March 1673. Witnesses: Peter Ellis,
Edward Goffe. Will proved 21 June 1673.

5:500 Henry Hasellwood was granted
administration on said estate.
Appraisers: James Inch, Thomas Salmon.
George Wells (g) to administer oath.

Estate of Isaacke Marshall appraised by
John Ward & Edward Price. John Stone
(g, CH) administered oath. Date: 2 May
1673.

William Berry (p, Patuxent River)
renounced administration on estate of
John Parker (merchant). Date: 3 June
1673. Witness: Edward Sauvage.

5:501 Thomas Kemp, age 52, deposed that (N)
Bigger, Sr. was at the deponent's house
about 3 months before his death &
complained about his cousin John Bigger,
Jr. Mentioned: John Smith, Daniel Payd.
Date: 14 June 1673. Before: Thomas
Trueman.

28 June 1673. The widow of James White
(AA) was granted administration on his
estate. Appraisers: John Welch, Robert
Franklin. Samuel Chew, Esq. to
administer oath.

Will of Henry More (CH) was proved by
Mathias Obryand on 9 May 1673

5:502 & Jesse Wharton, Esq. on 14 May 1673.
Signed: Benjamin Rozer. Elisabeth More
was granted administration on said
estate on 25 May 1673. Appraisers:
Francis Adams, Francis Thornton. Date:
8 April 1673. Said appraisers took oath
on 10 May 1673.

5:503 Inventory of Henry More (CH). Date: 14
May 1673.

5:504 Appraisers: Francis Thornton, Francis

Court Session: <no date>

Adams.

1 July 1673. Samuel Hatton attorney for
Thomas Hatton executor of John Hatton
was granted continuance. Nathaniell
Heathcoate is to render accounts of
items in his possession.

5:505   Inventory of Edward Maynard.
Administrator: Henry Phipps. List of
debts (CV): John Pollard, Demetrius
Cartwright, Christopher Rousby, John
Holland, William Berry, Jesper Allen,
Capt. Perry, Rich. Bayley, William King,
Capt. Carleton. Amount: #14012.
Further list of debts (CV): Charles
Calvert (Governor), Henry Cox,
Allexander Magruder, John Pearce,
Francis Swimfeild, Robert Tyler, William
Jones, William White. Amount: #3922.
Accounts. Payments to: (N), Pollard,
Demetrius Cartwright,
5:506   Henry Phipps.

4 July 1673. Luke Gardner (g, St.
Clement's Hundred) surviving executor of
Robert Cole (St. Clement's Hundred) was
granted continuance.

John Bigger, Jr. & Dan. Cuningham
(witness) appeared to prove will of John
Bigger, Sr. (CV). Said Cuningham could
not attest to validity of said will.

Edward Keene (g, Hunsing Creek (?), CV)
presented the PoA from Henry Resfne from
time of his departure from the Province.
Mentions: said Henry's children in ENG:
Newill, Thomas, Ann, Mary. Said Henry
is since dead.
5:507   Edward Keene was granted administration
on said estate. Appraisers: William
How, John Tittmarsh. Tobias Norton or
William Groome to administer oath.

Inventory of John Deareing (AA).
Appraisers: John Wattkins, George
Paschall. Date: 21 June 1673.
Mentions: "Velmeade" 900 a. on south
side of South River (patented 21 January
1667), "Deareing's Gallier" 100 a. on
Herring Creek swamp on south side of

Court Session: <no date>

South Creek (patented 20 June 1668).
List of debts: Francis Poteete, John
Woodfine, John Karkhick, James Foote,
Henry Perpoint, Thomas Plumer, William
Cole, William Chandler, Thomas Danborne.
Amount: #12915.

5:508   John Smallpeece renounced administration
on estate of Thomas Paine (St. Jerome's,
SM). John Reynolds renounced
administration on estate of Thomas Paine
(St. Jerome's, SM). Witness: Peter
Eure.

5:509   Jane Paine was granted administration on
estate of said Thomas.

5:510   Sureties: Col. William Calvert, John
Smallpeece. Appraisers: William Claw,
Thomas Wright. Col. William Calvert to
administer oath. Inventory of Thomas
Paine. Date: 29 May 1673.

5:511   ...

5:512   Servants: Robert Cofile, Morgin Pramch,
Oliver Criss, old Negro woman.

5:513-514 ...

5:515   Mentions: 19 books (by title).

5:516-520 ...

5:521   List of debts: William Baker, John
Burridge, Geo. Mitchell (SO), Joseph
Leduke, Joseph Hackney, George Walker,
Henry Smith, Thomas Locer, Thomas
Knight, Mr. Vansweringen, the
Chancellor. Amount: #44155.

5:522   Accounts of Edward Burton.
Administratrix: relict Mary Ringold wife
of James Ringold. Amount of inventory:
#22187. Payments to: Daniel Jenifer,
Mr. Jenifer, Cornelius Howard, Charles
Delaroch, Richard Moore, Mr. Harris,
Mathias Smith, David Poole,

5:523   James Godfrey, Mathias Smith, Philip
Shapleigh, Tobias Wells, Disburough
Bennit, the Secretary, Abra. Heaman
(Biddiford), Robert Dunn. Amount:
#20569. Mentions: bill of Thomas
Hutton. Date: 24 July 1673.

5:524   Mentions: an orphan. Discharge was
granted.

Accounts of Thomas Hinson.
Administrators (sons): Thomas Hinson,
John Hinson. Amount of inventory:

Court Session: <no date>

#92451. Mentions: brothers & sisters of
administrators. Payments to: James
Ringold & his father, Capt. Robert
Morris, Mr. Collett, Dr. Tilghman,
Joseph Weekes, Robert Denny, Christop
Barnes, Simon Carpenter,
5:525 Mr. William Coursey, Capt. Crosscomb,
Mary Steevenson, John Smith (merchant,
London), Thomas Ellis, Capt. Lloyd, the
Secretary, Mr. Smith, Marke Cordea, Mr.
Collett,
5:526 schooling for Charles Hinson (orphan),
5:527 Joseph Weekes for his wife (a child's
part), Thomas South for his wife (a
child's part), Charles Hinson (brother,
under age, his part). Amount: #93500.
5:528 Date: 24 July 1673.

Inventory of Richard Parkes (chirurgeon,
SM). Date: 19 February 1673. Amount:
#2535. Appraisers: John Blomfeild,
Richard Birckett.
5:529 Administrator: Charles Carpenter.
Accounts. Payments to: brother, John
Noble (Parkers). Amount: #3673. Date:
26 July 1673.

5:530 Inventory of Samuell Spicer. Date: 22
May 1673. List of debts: Anthony
Dawson, Mr. Henry Trippe, Mr. Thomas
Taylor. Amount: #5413. Appraisers:
John Brooke, Edward Cooke.

Will of James White (cooper, AA).
Bequests: daughter Margarett White
"Eglington" 300 a. on Patuxent River,
5:530½ daughter Elisabeth White, son James
White 200 a. Executrix: wife Susanna.
Date: 29 December 1672. Witnesses: John
Stanseby, Samuell Lane, Robert Lockwood.

21 July 1673. Will proved by Mr.
Samuell Lane & Robert Lockwood. Signed:
Sam. Chew. Date: 28 June 1673.
Appraisers: John Welch, Robert Franklin.
Samuell Chew, Esq. to administer oath.
5:531 Susanna White relict was granted
administration on said estate. Date: 8
August 1673.

Richard Keene vs. estate of William
Jackson (brickmaker, CV). Caveat.

Court Session: <no date>

12 August 1673. Thomas Vaughan (g, TA) assignee of John Clemons (TA) was granted administration on estate of John Leaven (TA), as greatest creditor, in lieu of John Morecroft. Appraisers: John Standley, John Ingram. Jonathon Sybery (g) to administer oath.

5:532 18 August 1673. William Chandborne (BA) who married Susanna relict of Richard Foxon (BA) was granted administration on said estate. Appraisers: William Toulson, Issack Harniss. Capt. Thomas Howell to administer oath.

20 August 1673. John Allen for John Fanning vs. estate of William Jackson (CV). Caveat.

John Allen vs. estate of William Jackson (CV). Caveat.

5:533 Inventory of John Collett (BA). Date: 8 August 1673.

5:534-535 ...

5:536 List of debts: John Depee, John Mascard, William Picks, Richard James, Robert Hawkins, John Ryely, Richard Leake, Francis Child, Richard Farrendell, Thomas South, Charles James. Amount: #58637. Appraisers: Thomas Salmon, James Inch.

5:537 Thomas Hussy (CH) & Ralph Coates (CH), sworn by Mr. Benjamin Rozer, appraised the estate of Stephen Mountague (CH) on 25 October 1672. On 18 August 1673, the administrator petitioned for an appraisal of "Howland" 200 a. on Mattawoman. Amount: #3600. Date: 18 August 1673.

5:538 Accounts of Steephen Mountague (CH). Executor: George Godfrey. Amount of inventory: #18041. Amount of additional inventory: #3600.

5:539 Payments to: accountant, Mr. Rozer, the Secretary,

5:540 Jarvis Crumpp, John Wright, Francis Wyne, Stephen Mirtye, Mr. Morecroft, John Grunby, Joseph Wharton, John Wood, John Allen, Robert Doyne, Richard Moy. Amount: #22413. Date: 28 August 1673.

5:541   Inventory of Francis Tripper. Date: 7
        May 1673. List of debts: Henry
        Mitchell, Richard Faredall. Amount:
        #7863. Appraisers: William Holis,
        Godfrey Harmer.
5:542   29 August 1673. Luke Gardner (g,
        Cannone Neck, SM) surviving executor of
        Robert Cole (St. Clement's Hundred, SM)
        exhibited accounts on his estate.
        Mentions: daughter Mary Cole who married
        Ignatius Warren, son Robert Cole (who
        will be of age by 17 October 1673).

        Michaell Higgen executor of William
        Dweare (Barbadoes). Will proved by
        George Sealeing & George Adams
        (witnesses).
5:543   Will of William Dweare (Barbadoes).
        Date: 19 September 1672 as per Catholic
        Church of Rome. Bequests: Michael
        Higgen, Joane Clark, Catholique Priest,
5:544   youngest son of William McDowell,
        Michaell Higgen the younger. Witnesses:
        George Sealeing, George Adams.

        30 August 1673. Michael Higgen
        executor of said will was granted
        administration. Appraisers: John
        Clarke, John Diar. Thomas Sprigg (g) to
        administer oath.

        Accounts of Thomas Taylor (KE).
        Administrator: John Wedge. Amount of
        inventory: #2286.
5:545   Amount of accounts: #2286. Date: 2
        September 1673. Inventory of Thomas
        Taylor. Date: 5 August 1673. List of
        debts: Richard Huttchins, Thomas Boone.
        Appraisers: Nathaniell Evett, John
        Lunford.

6:1   Oath of an Inventor. Oath of an
        Administrator. Oath of an Appraiser.

        2 September 1673. Samuell Cressy who
        married Susannah relict & executrix of
        William Robbesson (CH) exhibited
        accounts. Mentions: son (under age) of
        said Robesson.
6:2   Appraisers: Francis Pope, Thomas Baker.
        Amount of inventory: #18940. Payments
        to: Daniel Johnson, Capt. William

Boreman, Rich. Randall, Walter Story,
John Long (merchant, London), Thomas
Standbridge, Francis Pope & Thomas
Baker, Secretary. Mentions: Susanna
relict of testator & wife of
administrator.

6:3 Amount: #15864. Signed: Sa. Cressey.
Date: 2 September 1673. Administrator:
Samuell Cressey (g). Distribution to:
George (son), Susanna (relict & mother
of said George). Mentions: Charles
(brother of said George, since dec'd).

2 September 1673. Samuel Cressey
administrator of John Harrington (CH).
The widow of dec'd conveyed away the
estate. Mentions: Robert Henly, John
Worland, Henry Adams (g, justice). New
appraisers: John Boules (g), William
Henley.

6:4 Will of Thomas Wright (p, SM). Date: 22
August 1673. Bequests: Joseph Edloe,
Joseph Hackney his 2 sons John & Thomas,
William Lucas, Jr., wife. Executrix:
said wife. Witnesses: Joseph Hackney,
William Newport. Will proved 3
September 1673. Jane Wright widow &
relict of Thomas Wright (p, St.
Jerome's, SM) was granted administration
on his estate. Appraisers: Joseph
Hackney, William Claw. Col. Calvert to
administer oath.

6:5 Will of Mr. George Foxwell (merchant,
Boston NE & VA) from Sir William Berkely
(Knight, Governor of VA) with date 30
October 1672. Executor: Mr. Robert
Edmond (merchant, late of same place,
now resident of Nansemon).

6:6 12 September 1673. Marke Cordea (g,
Cross Mannor, SM) was granted
administration on estate of John Brookes
(p, SM), as greatest creditor.
Appraisers: Samuell Brockhouse, John
Askin. Col. Calvert to administer oath.

John Thompson overseer of Richard
Russell (p, SM, dec'd) renounced
administration on his estate. Witness:
Peter Eure.

Court Session: <no date>

19 September 1673. Joseph Brough &
Richard Attwood to appraise estate of
Richard Russell. Col. William Calvert
to administer oath.

6:7   Will of Henry Hawkins. Bequests: son of
William Saucall, Mary eldest daughter of
Richard Woolman time of my servant
Edward Bone, her brother Richard
Woolman, her sister Rebecca Woolman, her
next sister Alice Woolman, Elisabeth
Woolman, Henry Costin, John Turley,
Thomas Henfry, Edward Bone & Steven Sone
& William Curre, Sarah Smith, William
Smith, Henry Pratt, old Beasely, Negro
old Paule, Robert Noble, William
Hewbery, Alis wife of Richard Woolman &
Alis & Elisabeth her 2 youngest
daughters, Richard Woollman, Sr.,
brother Phillemon Lloyd & his wife,
their son Edward my plantation, Dennis
Moccono.
6:8   Residue: Edw. Lloyd, Susanna Maria
Bennett. Executor: Phillemon Lloyd.
Date: 24 April 1662. Witnesses: Nath.
Reade, Griffeth Steevens.
  • Nath. Read deposed on 15 August 1673
     that he knew the testator for some 6
     years prior to the date of the will,
     & that the will was written in April
     1672. Mr. Woolman wrote the will &
     put in the wrong date--the children
     were not born nor was Capt. Lloyd
     married. The other witness is
     runaway. Signed: Jona. Sybery.
     Date: 8 September 1673 at Wye.
6:9   Philemon Lloyd was granted
administration on said estate.
Appraisers: Rich. Woolman, William
Hemsley. Said Sybery to administer
oath.

22 September 1673. Phillemon Lloyd to
prove will of Charles Masters (TA).
Appraisers: William Hemsly, Jonathon
Sybery.

6:10   Robert Burle (AA) & Thomas Marsh (AA) to
prove will of Nathaniell Stinchcombe &
will of Tomassine Stinchcombe (widow &
executrix of said Nathaniell). Thomas
Turner (AA) is executor of said

Court Session: <no date>

Tomassine. Date: 24 September 1673.
Appraisers: Thomas Buckingham, Ralph
Halkins.

Will of Clement Herbert (TA) was proved
by witnesses: William Gary, William
Tollard. Date: 21 June. Signed:
Richard Wollman.

6:11   Inventory of Henry Brooke (g, CV).
Date: 7 July 1673. Appraisers: Philip
Harwood, Richard Axby.

26 September 1673. Thomas Roper (p, AA)
was granted administration on estate of
Okey Rowland (AA).
6:12   Surety: Henry Peirepoint. Appraisers:
George Puddington, Henry Ridgley.
William Burges (g, AA) to administer
oath.

2 October 1673. Arthur Wright (KE) was
granted administration on estate of
Joshua Meriton (chirurgeon, KE), as
greatest creditor. Sureties: Rich. Moy,
Francis Ashbury. Appraisers: Michaell
Miller, Francis Ashbury. William Head
(KE) to administer oath.

Inventory of Christopher Gardiner.
Date: 7 May 1673.
6:13   Amount: #13245. Appraisers: Robert
Francklin, Robert Lockwood.

Will of John Reynolds (carpenter, St.
Jerome's). Date: 24 August 1673.
6:14   Bequests: Isaacke Paine & Joseph Paine &
Rachaell Paine, Nicholas Guither,
youngest daughter of Edward Jolly, John
Smallpeece, William Claw, Thomas James,
Thomas Locker. Executors: William Claw,
John Smallpeece. Witnesses: Richard
Chapman, Nicholas Guither. Will proved
3 October 1673.

6:15   3 October 1673. William Claw (St.
Clare's, SM) & John Smallpeece were
granted administration on said estate.
Appraisers: Walter Hall, William Lucas.
William Calvert, Esq. to administer
oath.

Court Session: <no date>

15 October 1673. Georg Beckwith & James Williams to appraise estate of Henry Keene (CV). Thomas Sprigg (g) to administer oath.

6:16   Dr. John Morecroft is empowered to take PoA from John Clemons (TA) to Thomas Vaughan (TA) concerning estate of John Leanin. Date: 14 August 1673. Witnesses: John Standley, Philip Herbert, John Davis.

6:17   17 October 1673. Luke Gardner (g) surviving executor of Robert Cole (St. Clement's Mannor) & Robert Cole (son of said dec'd) & Ignatius Warren who married Mary (daughter of said dec'd) approved accounts of the dec'd.

24 October 1673. Thomas Wakefeild one of executors of Jonathon Marler exhibited his will, witnessed by Christop Hitchcock, Roger Wray, & Mathew Wood, & petitioned for administration. Other executor is John Worland. Witnesses would not attest to content of will.

6:18   Will of Jonathon Marler (CH). Bequests: Thomas Wakefeild "Manchester" 180 a., brother John Marler (Manchester) 100 a. leased to John Gimbo, said John Marler & Samuell all land in ENG, John Worland 100 a. bought of John Douglas. Executors: Thomas Wakefeild, John Worland. Date: 29 July 1673. Witnesses: Christopher Hitchcock, Roger Wray, Mathew Wood. Codicil: bequest: Col. Maleny (?). Date: 29 July.

6:19   Said will was proved by Christopher Hitchcock & Roger Wray on 24 October 1673. Thomas Wakefeild & John Worland were granted administration on said estate. Appraisers: Thomas Hussey, Ralph Coates. Robert Henley (g) to administer oath.

Jemima Hardy, wife of Henry Hardy, executrix of Thomas Pearcy (CH) exhibited accounts on his estate. John Bowles (g) to administer oath.

Will of Anthony Lecompt (DO).
6:20   Bequests: eldest son John Lecompt land

on other side of creek from my house &
50 a. bought of William Willoughby, 3
sons Moses Lecompt & Philip Lecompt &
Anthony Lecompt all rest of lands,
eldest daughter Hester Lecompt, daughter
Katherine Lecompt, Nicholas Trip.
Executrix: wife Hester Lecompt. Date: 9
September 1673. Witnesses: Jacob Seth,
John Snookes, Margarett Bryant. Will
proved by Jacob Seth & John Snookes on
25 October 1673. Hester Lecompt (widow
& relict) was granted administration.
Appraisers: William Ford, John Webb.
Thomas Skinner (g) to administer oath.

6:21 25 October 1673. John Wright (g, KE)
was granted administration on estate of
John Boulton (tanner, KE), who died with
"no wife nor children nor relations in
this country", as greatest creditor.
Security: Arthur Wright. Appraisers:
Isaacke Winchester, Francis Chissell.
William Head (g) to administer oath.

last October 1673. Dorothy Dorington
relict of Henry Robinson (Clifts)
exhibited his will, proved by John More.
Edward Keene (g) to take oath of other
witness. Said Dorothy was granted
administration. Appraisers: John
Cobreth, James Humber. Said Edward to
administer oath.

James Humber executor of Cornelius Regan
(CV) exhibited his will. Edward Keene
(g) to take oath of witnesses: John
Lech, Marke Clare.

6:22 Samuell Hatton administrator of John
Hatton vs. Nathaniell Heathcoate.
Caveat. Mentions: (N) Brewer. Signed:
(N) Morecroft.

6:23 1 November 1673. Mary Hooper widow &
relict of Richard Hooper (CV) was
granted administration on his estate.
Surety: Richard Smith. Appraisers:
Nathaniell Ashcomb, Samuell Borne.
Thomas Sprigg (g) to administer oath.

Mary Hooper was granted administration
on estate of William Hopkins (CV).

Surety: Richard Smith. Appraisers: Nathaniell Ashcomb, Samuell Borne. Thomas Sprigg (g) to administer oath.

John Gerrard (g) son of Thomas Gerrard exhibited his will. Witnesses are in VA. Said John was granted administration. Appraisers: Nehemiah Blackstone, Gerrard Sly (g). Benjamin Solley (g) to administer oath.

6:24   5 November 1673. John Stone (g) to prove will of Joseph Harison (CH). Appraisers: John Ward, Jeremiah Dickison. John Stone to administer oath.

11 November 1673. Henry Adams (g) to prove will of William Marshall (CH). Appraisers: John Coates, Hew Thomas. Henry Adams to administer oath.

John Allen (g) was granted administration on estate of William Jackson (brickmaker, CV), as greatest creditor. Appraisers: William Barton, Jr., John Coates. Henry Adams (g) to administer oath.

12 November 1673. Thomas Taylor, Esq. to prove will of Ralph Williams (AA). Executors: Robert Burle, Thomas Marsh. Appraisers: Richard Moss, William Hopkins. Tho. Taylor to administer oath.

William Baker to prove will of Henry Jubbar (mariner, Poole, ENG).

6:25   15 November 1673. Benjamin Rozer to prove will of Mathew Stone, Sr. (CV). Executor: Mathew Stone, Jr.

William Chandborne (p, BA) who married the relict of Richard Foxon (BA) was granted administration on his estate.

John Bowles (CH) who married Margary (now dec'd) widow & executrix of Capt. William Battin (CH) was granted administration on his estate.

6:26   John Bowles (CH) was granted
administration on estate of his late
wife Margary late wife & executrix of
Capt. William Battin (CH).

18 November 1673. Vincent Attcheson was
granted administration on estate of
Thomas Snow (TA), as principle creditor.
Surety: Robert Dunn. Appraisers: John
Bowles, Thomas Parker. Henry Hosier to
administer oath.

6:27   Will of Daniell Holland (Northumberland
Co. VA). Bequests: wife Joyce Holland
20 a. in Newman's Neck leased to John
Freeman, daughter Elisabeth (under age
15). Date: 31 March 1672. Witnesses:
Edward Elliott, Jeremy Robins, Francis
Cussam, Paule Willbery, Mary Cussam.
Will proved by Edward Elliott, Jer.
Robins, Francis Cussam, & Paule Wimbery
on 17 April 1672 in Northumberland Co.
Court. Per Mr. Thomas Hobson (clerk),
John Askwith was granted administration
in Northumberland Co.

6:28   Joyce Shapleigh relict & executrix of
Daniell Holland was granted
administration in MD.

John Worland one of the executors of
Jonathon Marler renounced the
administration on his estate. Date: 8
November 1673 at Pukawaxon. Signed:
Robert Henley.

6:29   Thomas Wakefeild the other executor of
Jonathon Marler was granted
administration on his estate. Date: 11
November 1673.

Inventory of Lawrence Little (CH).
Date: 20 December 1672. Administrator:
Benjamin Rozer. List of debts: Thomas
Craxon, Henry Adams. Amount: #1528.

6:30   Accounts of said Little. Amount: #1785.
Date: 11 November 1673.

Accounts of Samuell Burford (CH).
Administrator: Benjamin Rozer. Amount
of inventory: #7300. Payments to: John
Allen, Ann Fowke, Dominicke Bodkin paid
to Robert Doyne, accountant. Amount:
#8129.

6:31   Date: 11 November 1673.

Inventory of John Steevens (KE).
Appraisers: Tobias Wells, John Ingram.
Date: 9 August 1672. List of debts:
Thomas Wright, John Tassell. Amount:
#2780. Administrator: Michaell Miller.
Mentions: items in hands of William
Head.

6:32   Accounts of Alexander Towerson.
Payments to: Tobias Wells, Capt.
Phillimon Lloyd, Nicholas Wyatt, Francis
Pyne, William Hambleton, Samuell
Winslow. Amount: #4629.
Administratrix: Sarah Harrison. Date:
13 November 1673.

Accounts of Thomas Pearcy. Executrix:
Jemima Hardy. Amount of inventory:
#22848. Payments: Benjamin Rozer,
6:33   Robert Sly, John Newton, John Worland.
Amount: #13929. Signed: Henry Hardy,
Jemima Hardy. Discharge was granted on
24 October 1673.

Inventory of Henry Keene. Date: 25
October 1673. Appraisers: George
Beckwith, James Williams.
6:34   Amount: #4558.

Inventory of William Dweare.
Appraisers: John Clarke, John Dyer.
Date: 10 October 1673. Amount: #5283.

6:35   Inventory of Edward Dubery (SM).
Appraisers: Patricke Forrest, William
Watts. Date: 30 August 1673. List of
debts: Chancellor, John Booth, William
Baker, Robert Jones, John Dugins.
Amount: #91714.

Inventory of Richard Foxon.
6:36   Amount: #11383. Date: 1 November 1673.
Appraisers: William Towlson, Isaacke
Winchester.

Inventory of Daniell Holland
(Northumberland Co. VA). Date: 25
November 1673. List of debts: Thomas
Taylor, William Georgoe, John Brookes,
William Jones, Daniel Puddiford, William

Court Session: <no date>

Rotton, Richard Pattey. Amount: #10504.
Administrator: Philip Shapleigh.

6:37   Inventory of James White (AA). Date: 30
        July 1673.
6:38   ...
6:39   List of debts: William Horne, William
        Andrewes, William Peerie, Robert Costin,
        John Wattkins, John Eason, Richard Ewen,
        William Smicke, William Magrah, Francis
        Johnson. Mentions: widow. Appraisers:
        Ro. Franklin, John Welsh. Amount:
        #59787.

6:40   Inventory of John Leanen. Date: 20
        August. List of debts: William Ladd,
        Mr. Philip Steevenson, William Phinney,
        Francis Bellocs, Richard Steevens,
        William Mountagne, John Ingram, James
        Clayland,
6:41   Vincent Loe, William Hemsly, Richard
        Jackson, Edward Winckles, William
        Mountagne. Amount: #24570. Appraisers:
        John Standley, John Ingram.

        27 November 1673. John Allen (g) was
        granted administration on estate of
        Nicholas Solby (CH), as principle
        creditor. Surety: Gerrard Sly.
        Appraisers: John Coates, William Barton,
        Jr. Thomas Hussy (g) to administer
        oath.

        Benjamin Rozer (CH) administrator of
        Lawrence Little (CH)
6:42   was granted discharge.

        Said Benjamin Rozer administrator of
        Samuell Burford (CH) was granted
        discharge.

        George Godfrey (CH) administrator of
        Steephen Mountagne (CH) was granted
        discharge.

        28 November 1673. Mary Thomas widow of
        John Thomas (CH) was granted
        administration on his estate.
        Appraisers: Nathaniell Eaton, John
        Lemar. Benjamin Rozer (g) to administer
        oath.

Court Session: <no date>

Tho. Taylor, Esq. to prove will of James Stringer.

6:43 James Thompson (CV) administrator of William Greene (CV) was granted discharge. Date: 3 December 1673.

3 December 1673. William Dare, William Twiss, John West, Philip Standsley, Thomas Price, & Thomas Hide creditors vs. estate of John Parlet (CV). Caveat.

6:44 6 December 1673. John Warder (Pukaiwaxon, CH) exhibited the nuncupative will of Richard Wattson (Pukaiwaxon). Marke Richardson (Pukaiwaxon) deposed that said Richard desired wife & child of John Warder to receive all & then died on 13 November last. Mentions: Mathew Hill (clarke). Martin Descura deposed the same. John Warder, his wife Margery, & his son William were granted administration on said estate. Appraisers: Thomas Pope, John Worland. Robert Henly (CH) to administer oath.

10 December 1673. John Brookes, John Pollard, & Henry Tripp to appraise estate of Anthony Lecompte (DO). Thomas Skinner to administer oath.

6:45 12 December 1673. Jonathon Squire cousin & heir of the whole blood of John Morecroft (g, SM) was granted administration. Said John died childless & unmarried. Sureties: Walter Hall, Richard Bayley. Appraisers: Patricke Forrest, Georg Mackall. Garrett Vansweringen (g) to administer oath.

Richard Smith (St. Leonard's, CV) administrator of Thomas Manning (Clifts, CV) exhibited accounts. Mentions: John Manning (son of said Thomas, under age 21). Discharge granted.

6:46 Accounts of Capt. Thomas Manning (g, CV). Administrator: Richard Smith. Date of administration: 8 March 1670. Amount of inventory: #62889. Payments to: John Price, Charles James, William

Court Session: <no date>

Worgan, William Powre, John Nevill,
Henry Sterling, Steephen Beason, Joseph
Horsey, John Parker, Andrew Cooke, James
Elton & his wife, wife of Georg Selog,
Thomas Place, Henry Mitchell,

6:47 Marke Hill, William Cossins, accountant
& his security & John Manning, Richard
Smith, John Elly, Dr. Joules, William
Cossins & John Burges, Roger Baker,
Richard Lad, Johns Hollins, Dr. Jones,
William Willson, Edw. Keene, Mr. Notley
attorney for (N) Corseliss, John
Grammer, Mr. Christop Rousby, Nehemiah
Covington, Peter Sharpe,

6:48 schooling for young boys, Benjamin
Cloyster. Mentions: Mrs. Manning buried
at same time. Amount: #16542.

15 December 1673. John Gerrard son &
one of executors of Thomas Gerrard (g,
Macholik VA, formerly of St. Clement's
Mannor SM) exhibited his will, witnessed
by John Waugh, Isaake Allerton, John
Lee, & John Coouper. Will proved by
Maj. Isaack Allerton & Capt. John Lee.
Will of Thomas Gerard, Esq. (Macholick,
Westmoreland CO. VA). Date: 5 February
1672.

6:49 Mentions: wife Susanna (dec'd).
Executors: son John Gerrard, wife Rose.

6:50 Bequests: daughter Mary (under age 21)
land in Mistress White Neck leading from
Mattapony Bridge to my son-in-law (N)
Blackstone or John Shanks & "St.
Katherine's Island" in occupation of
John Dennis & 300 a. in Broad Neck
between Mr. Cole & Mr. Dobson & 100 a.
"Westwood Lodge" in occupation of
Samuell, son Justinian ½ of

6:51 "St. Clement's Mannor" & other ½ to wife
Rose then to male heirs by said Rose,
youngest son John ½ "Bastfoord Mannor" &
other ½ to wife,

6:52 youngest son John "Gerrard's Reserve"
(Lower Macholicks, Westmoreland Co. VA)
& other ½ to wife, grandchild Gerard
Paton, 3 sons & 5 daughters, sons-in-law
& daughters-in-law & grandchildren,
chattel for Gerrard Tucker (under age
18),

6:53 Negro Thomas (boy), Mr. John Wauge,
eldest son Justinian land in ENG,

Court Session: <no date>

6:54 ...

6:55 Witnesses: John Waugh, Isaacke Allerton, John Lee, John Coouper. Said John Gerrard was granted administration.

6:56 17 December 1673. Joseph Chew (AA) who married Margarett relict & administratrix of Thomas Miles (inholder, AA) exhibited accounts. Mentions: orphans.

6:57 Amount of inventory: #87896. Payments to (10 November 1669): Capt. Thomas Stockett, William Roper, John Browne, Joseph Taylor, Thomas Marsh, Henry Robinson, Capt. William Burges, Richard Bayley, Robert Peaka, Tho. Cole, Edward Parrish, William Richardson, Samuell Chew, Henry Allison, Abraham Burkitt, Robert Hopper, Philip Shapleigh, William Cole, Capt. Thomas Stockett, Thomas Ford, John Hillen,

6:58 Samuell Lane & Francis Stockett, Thomas Francis, James White, Thomas Hookes, John Welsh, David Fry, Abraham Clark, Thomas Jordaine, William Juell, William Sringall, John Larkin, Thomas Herne, Henry Hall, Robert Franklin, Henry Stockett, James Chilcott, John Welsh, Thomas Ellis, Nan. Heathcoate, Philip Thomas, William Tranes, Edward Lake,

6:59 John Nevill, William Kemp, John Bennitt, Dennis Mackunna, Robert Bennett, Timothy Owen, John Gray, Heugh Hitchcock, Henry Robinson, Steephen Beason, Rich. Nevill, William Hopkins, Paule Bussy, John Body, John Read, Edward Mason, William Ellis, Auth. Stockley, Nathaniell Smith, Humphry Emerton, Robert Lesby, William Spanbridge (?), John Hawkins, John Gray, David Jones, Ambroze Farlo,

6:60 John Hobson, Georg Pascall, William Gunnill, Richard Arnold, Thomas Wattkins, William Andrule, accountant. Amount: #89719. Date: 17 December 1673.

6:61 Joseph Chew was granted administration on estate of Thomas Miles. Appraisers: John Wattkins, Fardinando Battee. Mr. John Welch to administer oath.

30 December 1673. Thomas Taylor (AA) to prove will of Nicholas Wyatt (p, AA).

Court Session: <no date>

Appraisers: Cornelius Haward, Mathew
Haward. Thomas Taylor, Esq. to
administer oath.

Robert Burle (g, AA) to prove will of
John Browne. Appraisers: William
Hopkins, Mathew Haward. Robert Burle
(g) to administer oath.

6:62   8 January 1673/4. William Coursey (g) &
Peter Sayer (g) on behalf of Frances one
of the daughters & co-heirs of Henry
Morgan (KE, d. 1663) petitioned. No
estate was probated. Not long after
said Henry's decease, Frances (mother of
said Frances) married Jonathon Sybery.
Said Frances the mother is now dead for
2 years. Administration granted for her
father & her mother for herself & her
sister Barbara Morgan (now in ENG).

6:63   10 January 1673. William Coursey (g) on
behalf of orphan of William Shirt (TA)
petitioned. Said William left a widow &
one child. Said widow married Bonham
Turner. Said widow drowned. Said
William Coursey & Philip Steevenson to
swear Bonham Turner. Appraisers:
William Finney, Trustram Thomas.
William Coursey (g) to administer oath.

        Prenuptial Agreement between Marke
        Cordea (g, Cross Mannor, SM) & Hester
        Lecompte (widow & executrix of Anthony
        Lecompte (DO)). Said Anthony bequeathed
        to: daughters Hester & Katherine
        Lecompte,
6:64   sons John & Moses & Philip & Anthony,
        when the children reach age 20.
6:65   Date: 10 January 1673. Witnesses: Gar.
        Vansweringen, Peter Eure, Matheus
        Garardi Van Alren Walrave. Bondsmen:
        Walter Hall (g, SM), Garet Vansweringen
        (g, SM).
6:66   Witnesses: Henry Carew, Peter Eure.

6:67   13 January 1673. Roger Baker (St.
        Leonard's Creek, CV) was granted
        administration on estate of Henry Jubbar
        (Poole, Dorset, ENG), as greatest
        creditor. Appraisers: George Beckwith,
        Richard Bayley. Thomas Spigge (g) to

administer oath.

Randall Hanson (also Randall Hinson)
only surviving executor of Luke Barbier
(Micham Hall, SM) renounced
administration on said estate.
Witnesses: Peter Eure, Tho. Wynne.

6:68 Joachim Guibert who married Elisabeth
eldest daughter of Luke Barbier was
granted administration on said estate,
for the children: Luke, Elisabeth,
Edward, Thomas, Mary, Ann Barbier.
Appraisers: James Pattison, Henry
Spinke. John Jourdaine (g) to
administer oath.

Elisabeth Preston widow & executrix of
James Preston (Preston's Neck, CV)
exhibited his will. Said will to be
proved by witnesses: John Clifford,
Edward Bentall. Will of James Preston
(Patuxent). Date: 20 December 1673.

6:69 Bequests: wife Elisabeth Preston &
daughter Rebecca Preston, sister Rebecca
Preston, sister Sarah wife of William
Ford.

6:70 Overseers: William Ford, William
Steevens, Jr., Thomas Preston.
Executrix: wife Elisabeth Preston.
Witnesses: John Clifford, Edward
Bentall, Edward Day, Thomas Browne.

6:71 Will proved by John Clifford & Edward
Bentall on 13 January 1673. Elisabeth
Preston widow was granted
administration.

23 January 1673. John Welsh (g, AA)
exhibited oath of John Wattkins &
Fardinando Battee, appraisers of estate
of Thomas Miles, unadministered by
Margrett the relict. Administrator is
Joseph Chew (AA).

6:72 Said Margrett was late wife of Joseph
Chew. Date: 22 December 1673.

Richard Smith (g, St. Leonard's, CV) is
administrator of Thomas Manning (Clifts,
CV) during the minority of John Manning
(son & heir of said Thomas).

6:73 Said Richard was granted discharge.

27 January 1673. George Parker for Cornelius Howard (AA) was granted administration on estate of Georg Good, who died with neither wife, child, nor kinsman in the Province. Thomas Taylor, Esq. to administer oath to said Cornelius as administrator of said Richard Good [sic].

6:74 Jane Hough widow & executrix of Henry Hough (chirurgeon, Patuxent River, CV) exhibited his will, proved by Mordecai Hunton, Gervas Shaw, & Edward Cowdrey. Will of Henry Hough. Date: 16 December 1673.

6:75 Executrix: wife Jane Hough. Bequests: wife, son Henry Hough. Witnesses: M. Hunton, Gervas Shawe, Edward Cowdrey. Will proved 27 January 1673. Jane Hough was granted administration. Appraisers: William Groome, Frances Hutchins. Ed. Keene (g) to administer oath.

6:76 Inventory of Mr. Jonathon Marler (CH). Appraisers: Mr. Tho. Hussy (g, CH), Ralph Coates (CH). Robert Henly swore appraisers. Date: 19 November 1673. Amount: #12990.

6:77 Inventory of Richard Wattson (g, CH). Appraisers: Thomas Pope, John Worland. Robert Henly swore appraisers. Date: 10 December 1673 at Pukewaxon.

6:78 List of debts: Georg Newman, Gerratt Rowles, Mr. Young, Thomas Frankes. Amount: #17770.

6:79 30 January 1673. Thomas Gibson (CH) was granted administration on estate of William Cotton (CH), who died unmarried and childless, as greatest creditor. Surety: Charles De la Roch (inholder, St. John's, SMC). Appraisers: John Douglas, Peeter Carr. Robert Henly to administer oath.

4 February 1673. Thomas Dent (g, SM) & William Hatton (SM) are executors of William Wilkinson (clarke), who bequeathed to Elisabeth Budden chattel in hands of

6:80 said executors until her death. The

executors have maintained her for 10 years & said Elisabeth is recently dec'd. Thomas Dent & William Hatton were granted administration on estate of Elisabeth Budden, as greatest creditors.

6 February 1673. Elisabeth Norwood (CV) widow of John Nordwood (CV) exhibited his nuncupative will, proved by William Singleton & Michaell Higgen. Bequests: his wife. Surety: William Singleton. Appraisers: Mic. Higgen, William Singleton. Edward Keene (g) to administer oath.

6:81 Francis Chissell (KE) was granted administration on estate of Richard Morris (KE), who died leaving no widow but an orphan age 3, as greatest creditor. Surety: Charles De la Roch. Appraisers: Miles Miller, Vallentine Southerne. Tho. Osberne (g) to administer oath.

11 February 1673. William Steevens (Pocomoke, SO) exhibited the will of James Weeden (SO). Appraisers: Edward Wale, Jeffry Minshall. William Steevens (g) to administer oath.

12 February 1673. Philemon Lloyd (g) & Richard Woolman (g) to appraise the estate of Frances Sybery relict of Henry Morgan (TA). William Coursey (g) to administer oath.

6:82 14 February 1673. Caveat vs. estate of Robert Cole (St. Clement's Mannor). Signed: Capt. Luke Gardner.

Caveat to widow & creditors of Jacob Neale, regarding acceptance of accounts of Thomas Marsh executor of said Jacob.

Caveat to Kenelm M<page torn> regarding the estate of Nicholas Solsby.

Henry Hosier (KE) on behalf of his daughter Mary Hosier (under age 17) exhibited the will of Lewis Steevens & was granted administration on said estate. James Ringold to administer

oath.

16 February 1673. Mathew Stone (Pomton Mannor, CH) exhibited the nuncupative will of his uncle Mathew Stone. Benjamin Rozer (CH) to prove will.

6:83 Henry Ward attorney for Elisabeth Steevens widow of Richard Steevens (TA) was granted administration on his estate. Appraisers: William Bishop, John Chaffe. Thomas Hinson (g) to administer oath.

John Dowlin (KE) exhibited the will of John Carraway (BA), as principle legatee. Henry Hosier (g, KE) to prove will. Appraisers: Lewis Bryan, Nicholas Rugsten. Richard Ball (g, BA) to administer oath.

6:84 Thomas Parker who married Elisabeth relict of Henry Gott (KE) was granted administration on his estate. Bondsmen: Vincent Attcheson, John Wright. Appraisers: John Bowles, Lawrence Simons. Henry Hosier (g) to administer oath.

Will of James Weedon (g, Pocomoke). Bequests: son William Weedon (under age 18) "Nonesuch House" occupied by Edward Pitt (draper) on London Bridge in Parish of St. Magnus the Martir
6:85 then to daughter Ann Weedon (under age 18) then to wife Lucee Weedone then to brother William Weedon (London), daughter Ann Weedon, [testator plans to move to Rehoboth Bay near Whorekill Creek], son William & daughter Ann 1000 a.,
6:86 brother William Weedon & William Steevens (Pocomoke) chattel due from my house on London Bridge, wife Luce. Executrix: wife. Overseers: brother William Weedon (g, London), Mr. William Steevens (Pocomoke). Date: 12 January 1670. Witnesses: John Rhoads, Pier Piera.
6:87 Will proved 10 April 1672. Luce Weedon widow was granted administration on 11 April 1672.

6:88

Will of Cornelius Regann (Hunting Creek, CV). Executor: James Hughmes. Bequests: John son of John Leach, John Leatch, Sarah daughter of said James Hughmes, Joseph Tilly. Date: 6 October 1673. Signed: Cornelius Regan. Witnesses: John Rogars, James Clerke. Will proved 27 November 1673.

Will of Henry Robbinson (p, Clifts, CV). Date: 17 October 1672.

6:89

Bequests: only son Henry Robinson (under age 21), son Henry Robinson & his mother Dorothy Robinson my wife,

6:90

Francis Dorington (Clifts) 200 a., Thomas Morris 200 a., wife Dorothy 200 a. Executrix: wife. Signed: Henry Robinson. Witnesses: John More, John Taylor. Will proved by John More on 31 October 1673.

6:91

Will proved by John Taylor on 27 November 1673.

Will of Nathaniell Stinchcomb (AA). Bequests: brother John Stinchcomb, 3 children of brother Nicholas & children of sister Rebecca Handcock, John Merriken (servant), wife Tomasine Stinchcomb.

6:92

Overseers: Richard Moss, Edward Pomffrett. Date: 11 June 1670. Signed: Nath. Stinshcomb. Witnesses: Edward Allety, William Coboren. Will proved 24 November 1673.

Will of Tomasin Stinshcomb (late executrix of Nathaniel Stinshcomb (AA)).

6:93

Bequests: sons Nathaniell (under age) & John Stinshcomb (under age) lands, Blansh Burkley & Susanna Neale, John Stinshcomb (brother of said Nathaniell (dec'd)) & sister Rebecca Hancock (sister of said Nathaniell (dec'd)) & my mother Joane Mastey.

6:94

Executor: Thomas Turner (AA). Overseers: Richard Moss (AA), Thomas Homward (AA). Date: 13 August 1673. Witnesses: John Persley, Miles Gibson. Will proved by Miles Gibson on 26 November 1673.

6:95

Will proved by John Persley on 5 December 1673. Bondsmen: Corn. Howard,

Court Session: <no date>

Math. Howard.

Will of Joseph Harrison (CH). Date: 28
August 1673. Bequests: sons Francis &
Joseph Harrison land on Maine Creek, son
Francis Harrison chattel bought of Mr.
Thomas Dent,

6:96   son Richard Harrison, daughter Mary
Harrison, wife Elisabeth Harrison, Luke
Greene, children (under age): Elisabeth,
Katherine, Joseph, Benjamin Harrison.
Executrix: wife Elisabeth Harrison.
Overseers: Mr. Zachary Wade (g, CH),
Mr. Randall Hinson (g, SM). Witnesses:
Jeremiah Dickison, Thomas Shuttleworth.

6:97   Will proved 26 December 1673.

Inventory of Okey Rowland. Appraisers:
George Puddington, Henry Ridgley. Date:
6 October 1673.

6:98   List of debts: John Keele. Amount:
#7439.

Inventory of Henry Robinson (CV). Date:
27 November 1673.

6:99-100 ...
6:101 List of debts: Jeffry Menley, John
Dobson, John Eason, William Read,
Spencer Hales, John Gary, William Kent.
Amount: #46724. Appraisers: John
Cobreth, James Humbes.

Inventory of Cornelius Ragan (CV).
Date: 29 November 1673.

6:102 Amount: #6793. Appraisers: John Leache,
Marke Clare.

Inventory of Tomasin Stinchcomb (widow &
executrix of Nathaniell Stinchcomb).
Date: 3 December 1673. Servants
mentions: Martin Morgan, Benjamin
Dogget, David Stradling, Frances
Stradling.

6:103-108 ...
6:109 List of debts: Thomas Cleverly, William
Sarall, Edward Lunn, Nathaniell Stiles,
John Richardson (KE), Joseph Chew, John
Winchester (KE), Capt. Tho. Todd (BA),
Humphry Kileley, Henry Woolchurch, John
Browne, Jr. (NE), Richard Hittson (TA),
Truston Thomas (TA), Augustine Harman
(BA), William Coursey (TA) & Trusram

Court Session: <no date>

Thomas (TA). Amount: #84690.
Appraisers: Tho. Buckingham, Ralph
Halkins.

6:110   24 February 1673. Thomas Trueman, Esq.
executor of John Wright (CV) exhibited
his will. Will of John Wright.
Bequests: William Eyles, Philip
Cookesey, John Atwell, Mr. Thomas
Trueman. Executor: said Thomas. Date:
9 February 1673. Witnesses: Robert
Philips, Eliza. Price. Will proved 24
February 1673. Thomas Trueman, Esq. was
granted administration. Appraisers:
Robert Lastly, John Atwell. William
Groome (g) to administer oath.

6:111   25 February 1673. Henry Adams (g, CH)
exhibited will of William Marshall (CH).
Administrator: Francis Wyne. Robert
Henley & Thomas Notely (g) renounced
administration on said estate. Will of
William Marshall (CH). Date: 22 April
1673.

6:112   Bequests: son William Marshall (under
age 21) 100 a. on west side of
Wiccocomocoe River adjoining
"Pickquascoe" & 150 a. & 100 a.
adjoining Edward Phillpott & bought of
Capt. Hugh Oneale & Thomas Gervis & 200
a. at head of Pickquascoe, son Joshua
Marshall & daughter Elisabeth Marshall
(under age 21) 525 a. "Two Friends"
(SM) on Piles Fresh.

6:113   Executors: Mr. Thomas Notley, Mr.
Robert Henley, Mr. Francis Wyne.

6:114   Brother Mr. Francis Wyne is to have
charge over son Joshua (under age 21).
Witnesses: Zachary Wade, Ed. Price,
Jonathon Marler. Will proved by
Zacharia Wade & Edward Price in December
1673.

6:115   Robert Henley renounced administration
on said estate. Date: 23 December 1673.
Witnesses: John Stone, James Lewellin.
Thomas Notley renounced administration
on said estate. Date: 23 February 1673.
Witnesses: Benjamin Solley, John
Llewellin. Francis Wyne granted
administration. Date: 11 November 1673.

6:116   Will of Nicholas Wyatt (p, AA).
        Executrix: wife Dammaras Wyatt.
        Bequests: son Samuel Wyatt (under age
        18) plantation "The Quarter", daughter
        Sarah plantation near the widow Gibbens.
        Date: 10 December 1671. Witnesses: Cor.
        Howard, Robert Gugen. Will proved by
        Robert Goodgin on 22 January 1673. Will
        proved by Cornelius Howard at house of
        Damarus Wyatt on 24 January 1673.
6:117   Damarus Wyatt was granted administration
        on said estate. Date: 22 January 1673.

        3 March 1673. Mathew Erickson for Eliz.
        Ereckson (KI) widow of John Erickson was
        granted administration on his estate.
        Appraisers: Issaace Winchester, Thomas
        Bright. John Wright (KI) to administer
        oath.

6:118   Mathew Read petitioned for
        administration on estate of Richard
        Morris, as creditor, in lieu of Francis
        Chissell. Denied.

        Luke Gardner sole surviving executor of
        Robert Cole (St. Clement's Bay, SM), at
        the request of Robert Cole (son & heir)
        & Ignatious Warren who married Mary
        daughter of said dec'd, reviewed the
        accounts of said estate.
6:119   ...
6:120   Said Robert Cole departed for ENG on 9
        March 1661. Mentions: chattel given his
        son Robert by John Thimbleby,
6:121   servant of Mr. Slye. Inventory of said
        estate. Servants mentioned: John Elton,
        Robert Gates, John Johnson, Isbell
        Jones.
6:122-123 ...
6:124   Mentions: Mary Sheppey. Signed: Robert
        Cole. Date: 25 April 1662.
6:125   List of debts: Richard Sheppy, Richard
        Bennitt, Col. Evans, Joseph Alliny,
        Mathew Rowse, Dr. Lumbrozio, John
        Shankes, Mr. Rouse, Peter Mills, Mr.
        Brittaine, Mr. Foxhould,
6:126   Mr. Salley, John Prentice. Amount:
        #95800.
6:127   Accounts of said estate. Payments to:
        Ignatius Warren who married Mary
        (daughter), Robert Cole (child's

portion), Francis Knott (his 1/8th part), Mr. Slye, Mr. Francis Fitzherbert (legacy), executor for William Cole (son) & Edward Cole (son).

6:128 Servants mentioned: Samuell Hewson, Daniel Pritchard, Timothy Mahaun.

6:129-131 ...

6:132 Further payments to: Mr. Fitzherbert, Mr. Barton, Capt. Cooke for passage for Mary Cole, Capt. Martin,

6:133 Joseph Alluy, Richard Sheppy, Walter Beane, John Ellton & Robert Gates (servants), Fran. Cole & Francis Knott, William Cole, (N) Johnson (servant), Mary Cole, John Elton & John Rey (servants), Robert Cole & Francis Knott, Eliz. Cole, John Elton, John Rey, Mary Cole,

6:134 Robert Gates, Robert Cole & Francis Knott, William Cole, Edward Cole, Mary Cole, Eliz. Cole, John Elton, Robert Gates, John Johnson, John Rey, Robert Gates, Robert Cole, Mary Cole, William Cole, John Rey,

6:135 Eliz. Cole, Robert Cole & Frances Cole, Negro Cloise (of Mr. Slye) for caring for Ann Knott, Ann Thornton, John Johnson, Francis Knott, Robert Cole, William Felsteed, Robert Cole & Francis Knott, William Felsteed, John Rey, William Cole, Mr. Sterling,

6:136 Mr. Piles, John Rey, John Hilton, Robert Cole & Francis Knott, Eliz. Cole, John Hillton, the church, Mrs. Cole (in ENG),

6:137 William Felsteed, William & Edward Cole, Eliz. Cole, the church, Vincent Mansfeild, John Rey, Richard Foster,

6:137! John Johnson, John Hillton, Ann Thorneton, John Johnson, John Rey, William Felsteed, Betty Cole, (N) Johnson, the Frenchman, Betty Cole, William,

6:138 William & Edward Cole, Isbell, Ann Thorneton, Thomas Bennett, Betty, the church, William Cole, Edward & Bettee Cole,

6:139 Betty Cole, Mr. Foxwell, (N) Johnson, Francis Knott, William & Noel, William Cole, Robert Cole, (N) Johnson, Betty,

6:140 the carpenter, Betty, Dorithy Sittwell,

6:141-142 ...

6:143 (N) Gerrard,

6:144   for bringing John Prentice from VA,
Fran. Knott, Edward Cole, Betty (now
dec'd), Mr. Gerrard, Edward Cole,
6:145   Capt. Mathew Paine for passage of
Edward Cole to ENG, John Standley for
bringing a runaway servant from VA,
Edward Cole, William Cole,
6:146   William Cole, expenses for William Cole
when he was bound out as an apprentice,
Mr. Sly for Francis Knott. Amount:
#96983. Luke Gardner one of the
executors of Robert Cole delivered
chattel to Ignatius Warren & to Robert
Cole (when he was 18), Francis Knott,
Mr. Fitzherbert for Edward & William
Cole.
6:147   Date: 14 February 1673.

4 March 1673. Samuell Brockas sworn as
appraiser for estate of John Brookes.

7 March 1673. Robert Carvile attorney
for Robert Lasley administrator of John
Bigger, Sr. (CV) exhibited an account
dated 4 June last by John Bigger, Jr. &
petitioned for delivery of said items.

6:148   10 March 1673. Lodowicke Williams (BA)
who married Mary daughter & heir of
James Stringer (AA) exhibited his estate
by William Fuller. Ann (the widow &
mother of said Mary) married John
Collier (since dec'd) & then married
William York. Said widow is dec'd
intestate, leaving children by said
Collier (infants, brothers & sisters of
half blood to Mary). Said Lodowick was
granted administration on estate of
James Stringer, as well as estate of
John Collier for John, Philip, William,
Sarah, Eliza., & Jane Collier (infants),
said Mary Williams being next of blood.
Appraisers: Edward Swanson,
6:149   James Collier. George Utie (g) to
administer oath.

Sarah Harris widow & executrix of George
Harris (KE) exhibited his will. John
Wright (KE) to prove will.

6:150   13 March 1673. Katherine Whittle
(Poplar Hill, SM) widow of William

Court Session: <no date>

Whittle (SM, d. 5 March) was granted administration on his estate. Peter Carwardine had insisted said William to make provisions for his wife & children. Sureties: Peter Carwardine, Philip Jones. Appraisers: Will. Kenedy, John Cooke. John Warren (g) to administer oath.

Inventory of John Boulton (tanner, KE). Appraisers: Francis Chissell, Issaacke Winchester. Date: 22 December 1673.
6:151 List of debts: Tobias Wells, John Ereckson, Thomas Bright, Edward Jones, William Head. Amount: #9468.

6:152 Appraisers for estate of Joshua Merriton (chirurgeon, KE) were sworn. Date: 11 October 1673. Signed: William Head.

Inventory of Richard Uppdate. Amount: #9505. Appraisers: John Teneson, James Greene. Date: 9 January 1673.

6:153 Inventory of Ralph Williams (AA). Appraisers: Richard Moss, William Hopkins. Date: 21 January 1673.
6:154-157 ...
6:158 List of debts: Dr. Jourdin, Steephen Burle, William Granger, Samuell Allcocke, Humphry Little, Joseph Chew, Ralphs Hawkins, Cornelius Howard, Mathew Howard, Thomas Turner, Henry Jowles, John Beaman, Francis Smith,
6:159 Tho. Taylor (KE), John Larkins, Tho. Long, Richard Pether, George Yates, Robert Proctor, William Head, Henry Sewall, John Keeley, Robert Burle, Mr. Richard Ball, Thomas Hinson, Vincent Low, Esq., George Yates, Mr. John Welsh, Edward Dorsey,
6:160 William Neale, Richard Keene, James Kyley, James Rigbey, Tho. Philips & Richard Wlate (?), George Strong, Capt. John Norwood, Dr. Jacob Neale, Richard Bennet, chattel sent to ENG via Capt. James Connaway, Robert Burle, Edward Lunn, James Rigbey,
6:161 Mr. Richard Ball, Edward Pomfrett, Capt. Tho. Stockett, William Jones, Olliver Hollaway, William Powstney, John Curvell, Ralph Hawkins, Francis Petitt,

6:162
Richard Ruckstone, William Hawkins, George Strong, Hanna Strong, John Birknell, Nathaniell Stinshcomb, Henry Constable, William Long, Thomas Turner, George Holland, Richard Bayley, Quinton Parker, Mr. George Parker, Ann Norwood, Richard Bayley, Tho. Turner for Josias Hall. Amount: #96089. Mentions: James Rigbey who lived at house of Mr. Ralph Hawkins,

6:163
250 a. in town neck, 215 a. "Alltogeather" bought of Richard Deaner, 20/30 a. in town neck.

6:164
Inventory of Thomas Gerard, Esq. at Mattapony. Appraisers: Gerard Slye, Nehemiah Blakistone (g). Date: 8 November 1673. List of debts: Henry Asbery, Robert Sampson, John Grace, Mr. Garett Vansweringen. Signed: John Gerard.

6:165
Inventory of Dr. Luke Barbier. Appraisers: Henry Spincke, James Pattison. Date: 19 February 1673. Items at Micham Hall.

6:166
...

6:167
Items at Chaptico.

6:168
Amount: #27096. Administrator: Joachim Guibert.

6:169
Inventory of John Brookes (SM). Date: 5 March 1673. List of debts: George Wright. Amount: #2100. Appraisers: Sam. Brockhouse, John Ascat.
Will of Thomas Billingsley (CV). Bequests: brother Francis Billingsley, John Troster, Jr., daughters Elisabeth & Sarah Billingsley "Billingsley Chance" 300 a. on Chicconocomocoe River adjoining Henry Hooper, daughter Mary Billingsley "Billingsley's Folly" 100 a. on same river, wife Elisabeth Billingsley & son Thomas Billingsley (under age 18) "Jeamoth".

6:170
Executrix: wife Elisabeth Billingsley. Overseers: brother Francis Billingsley, Richard Hooper, Dr. John Stansby, John Troster. Date: 26 March 1673. Witnesses: David Morgan, Walter Wattkins, Ann Morgan. Will proved by Walter Wattkins (CV) & David Morgan (CV)

Court Session: <no date>

6:171 on 12 March 1673/4. Appraisers: John
Standsby (CV), John Troster (CV).
Inventory of Thomas Billingsley. Date:
16 March 1673/4. Mr. Edward Keene
administered oath.
6:172 Amount: #25696.

Inventory of William Whittle (Poplar
Hill).
6:173 Date: 19 March 1673. Appraisers: John
Cooke, William Canadee. Amount: #12139.
List of debts: Samuell Cressey, John
Wade, Abell James, Robert Thomas,
William Harris, Mr. Moy,
6:174 Robert Thomas, Peter Carwardine, John
Booth, Mr. Sanders, Thomas Reynolds.
Amount: #4272. Additional list of
debts: Richard Hatton.

Will of Ralph Williams (merchant,
Bristoll, now AA). Bequests: youngest
daughter Rebecca Williams (now in
Bristoll) chattel held by my cousin
Thomas Day (merchant, Bristoll),
6:175 married daughter Elisabeth Millen
(living in London), daughter Rebecca
Williams then to cousin John Willcocks
(Bristoll), wife Margrett King
(Chepstow), cousin Thomas Day.
Executors: cousin Thomas Day (merchant,
Bristoll), Robert Burle, Thomas Marsh
(g, AA). Date: 13 August 1672.
Witnesses: Robert Burle, John Birknall.
6:176 Codicil: bequests: servant William
Mansfeild, Mr. Thomas Marsh, servant
Mary Evans & her daughter. Date: 18
September 1673. Witnesses: Abraham
Chille, William Mansfeild. Will proved
by William Mansfeild on 9 December 1673.
Will proved by Abraham Chille on 14
January 1673.

Court Session: 1674

6:177 27 March 1674. Bonham Turner
relinquished his administration on
estate of William Shirt (TA), on behalf
of Katherine daughter of said William.
William Finney was granted
administration on said estate.
Appraisers: Trustram Thomas, Jonas
Davis. Richard Wolman to administer

oath.

28 March 1674. Anthony Dauson (DO)
exhibited the will of Henry Osborne
(CV), citing as executrix his wife
Katherine Osborne. Said widow gave
chattel to her son Henry Osborne. Then
she married Richard Steevens. Henry the
son is since dec'd. Chattel passes to
Rebecca wife of said Dauson & to Sara
Osborne (sisters of the whole blood of
said Henry Osborne the younger).

6:178 Said Anthony was granted administration
on estate of Henry Osborne the younger,
on behalf of his wife Rebecca & Sarah
Osborne (her sister, under age).
Appraisers: William Steevens (g), Morris
Mathewes. Daniell Clarke (g) to
administer oath.

James Collier (BA) married the widow of
Edward Ayres (Bush River, BA), who died
leaving a widow (now dec'd) and 1
daughter Elisabeth. Said Collier was
granted administration on his estate.
Appraisers: Edward Swanson, Lodowicke
Williams.

6:179 George Utie (g) to administer oath.

William Yorke (BA) who married Ann
relict of John Collier (BA) & formerly
wife of James Stringer (AA) rendered
accounts of said estates found amongst
papers. Mentions: 150 a.

6:180 Mary Williams daughter of said James
Stringer is to be paid from the estate
of John Collier. Inventory of James
Stringer & John Collier, by Lodowicke
Williams.

6:181 Appraisers: Edward Swanson, James
Collier.

6:182 Inventory of James Stringer.
Appraisers: Thomas Howell, Robert
Clarkson. Date: 16 September 1656.

6:183 Mentions: 150 a. on South River. List
of debts: Richard Attlon, Robert
Cumfrey. Amount: #15753. Accounts of
James Stringer. Payments to: carpenter
of Mr. Leech, boatswain of Mr. Cutts,
boatswain of Capt. Varnell,

6:184 Mr. Hatton, Mr. Morris, Mr. Thomas,

Steeven Gary. Payments (per John Collier): Mr. Sronge, Mr. Browne, Mr. Marsh, Mr. Beard, Mr. Utie, Mr. Fuller, Mr. Hatton, Mr. Koyd, Mr. Cutts, Mr. Thomas, Heaster Goshum. Amount: #6080. Amount of inventory: #15753. Payments: by widow Stringer, by John Collier, 150 a. due to Mary the heir, Ann Collier relict of said Stringer, Mary Williams sole heir of Stringer. Amount of accounts: #15753.

6:185 Accounts of John Collier (d. April 1672). Administrators: wife Ann, 6 small children. Amount of inventory: #12721. Payments to: Richard Metcalfe, Thomas Salman, Walter Tucker & Company, John Scott, Francis Lovelace, William Salsbury, Thomas Cooke, Jeremy Eaton by William Yorke, William Palmer, Steeven White, (N) Thurston for John Boone, Lodowick Williams (legacy). Amount: #4143.

6:186 31 March 1674. William Yorke who married Ann relict & administratrix of John Collier (BA) exhibited an account of the estate of James Stringer (1st husband of said Ann). The Judge refused said accounts. Said Yorke also exhibited accounts of estate of John Collier by Ann Yorke relict & administratrix of said John & late wife of said Yorke. The Judge considered that said Yorke was one of the appraisers of the estate of said Collier and after marrying said Ann, managed the entire administration.

6:187 Accounts were read over to Lodowicke Williams administrator of said John Collier. Payment to Mary wife of said Lodowicke as child's part of James Stringer & Ann Yorke.

6:188 Inventory of Samuell Burford (CH). Date: 4 November 1671. Administrator: Benjamin Rozer. List of debts: Clement Theobalds, John Allen, Nathaniell Ashford, Henry More, Ann Fowke, Jeremias Dickison, Nicho. Solby, John Payne, Bryant Common, Francis Wyne, Philip Browne, Philip Gibbon, Thomas Witter.

Amount: #7300.

6:189 Thobyas Wells (KE) executor of Mary Pine widow of Francis Pine executor of Thomas Bradnox (KE) petitioned that the will be proved by Thomas Osborne (g, KE). Appraisers: John Ingram, Arthur Wright (g).

Said Tobias Wells was granted administration on estate of William Leppen, as greatest creditor. Appraisers: John Ingram, Arthur Wright.

1 April 1674. John Walton executor of John Burger (KE) petitioned for William Head to prove the will. Said Walton was granted administration. Appraisers: Issacke Winchester, William Laurence.

3 April 1674. Justinian Gerrard (g, Bramley, SM) was granted administration on estate of Robert Huchison (SM), as greatest creditor.
6:190 Said Huchison/Hutchison has neither wife, child, nor relation in the Province. Appraisers: John Gouldsmith, Robertt Cole. William Roswell (g) to administer oath.

6 April 1674. Catherine Whittle widow & administratrix of William Whittle (Poplar Hill, SM) exhibited the inventory by William Kennedy & John Coock & distribution in thirds: 2 parts to children of said William by former wife: John Whittle, Peter Carwardine for Thomas Whittle.
6:191 Said John & Thomas are under 21.

8 April 1674. Stephen Tully (sheriff, TA) to cause Edward Winkels to exhibit accounts on estate of William Power (TA) & on estate of Evan Thomas (TA).

Richard Moore (KE) was granted administration on estate of John Browne (KE), who died leaving neither wife nor children nor person of his own blood in the Province. Dec'd had judgements against Richard Peerie (KE), Edward Hull et. al. Mentions: Rebecca wife of said

6:192 Moore.
Appraisers: Robert Turner, Peeter Evans.
John Wright (g) to administer oath.
Mentions: Edward Hall.

9 April 1674. Edward Hall (KE) &
Richard More both exhibited claims
against the estate of John Browne.
Arthur Wright (g, KE) administrator of
Josuah Meriton (KE) exhibited claims
against said Browne. Said More was
granted administration.

6:193 Joane Tyler widow of Robert Tyler
(Ressurection Mannor, CV) exhibited his
will, proved by Mr. Thomas Sprigg &
John Hales. Will of Robert Tyler.
Executrix: wife Joane Tyler. Bequests:
wife Joane "Brough" 750 a. on west side
of north fork of Patuxent River (CV),
son Robertt (under age 16) 60 a.
adjoining Edward Isaacks & land bought
of Thomas Boudell,
6:194 son Robertt 375 a. land bought of Thomas
Boudell, son Robertt Negro Anthony (boy)
& Negro Sue (girl), daughter Elisabeth
(under age 16) Negro William (boy).
Overseers: Mr. Thomas Sprigg, Samuell
Taylor, Robertt Taylor. Date: 11
September 1673. Witnesses: Thomas
Sprigge, John Hales, William Thompton.
6:195 Will of Robertt Taylor proved by John
Hales & Thomas Sprigg (g, CV) on 9 April
1674. Joane Tylor was granted
administration.

10 April 1674. Thomas Vaughan (St.
Michael's Hundred) who married Sara
relict of Richard Russel showed that
Humphry Limbrey would not appear to
prove said will. Sara was granted
administration. Security: William Lucas
(St. Jerom's, SM). [Will was proved by
Roger Shehee on 23 May.]

6:196 15 April 1674. John Gouldsmith & Thomas
Carvill executors of John Piper
(Basford, SM) were granted
administration on said estate. Will was
proved by Samuell Maddox & John Grace.
Will of John Piper. Date: 22 October
1673. Executors: John Gouldsmith,

Thomas Carvill. Bequests: wife Marguerit Piper then to Robert Browne (½) &

6:197 son (under age 19, ¼) of my cousin John Piper (Mattox Creek, VA) & other ¼ to my godchildren: John Corthes the younger, James Luan, John Carvill, Clement Roberths, Jeane Grenlaw. Mentions: John Portwood, children of John Gouldsmith. Witnesses: Samuell Mattox, Samuell Cooksey, Roderick Lloyd, John Grace. Will proved by Samuel Mattox & John Grace on 15 April 1674. Thomas Notley (g) to administer oath to said Gouldsmith & Carvill. Appraisers: Thomas Gerrard (g), Samuell Dobson. Capt. William Boreman to administer oath.

16 April 1674. William Hambleton (g) to prove will of Henry Frith (TA). Witnesses are aged & unable to travel. Elisabeth Frith relict was granted administration. Said Elisabeth has since remarried.

6:198 Appraisers: Seth, Foster, Edm. Webbe. William Hambleton (g) to administer oath.

Philip Linn (CH) was granted administration on estate of James Lluellin (chirurgeon, CH), as greatest creditor. Appraisers: William Boyden, Thomas Baker. Benjamin Rozer (g, CH) to administer oath.

23 April. Jane Paine administratrix of Thomas Paine to exhibit accounts.

24 April. William Melton (Patuxent, CV) was granted administration on estate of John Foster (Cliffes, CV), who died leaving neither wife nor children nor any person of the blood in this Province, as greatest creditor. Appraisers: Richard Stallings, Mark Clare. Edward Keene (g, CV) to administer oath.

6:199 27 April. Nathaniell Lamplugh (mate on ship St. Nicholas whose master is John Johnson & is riding at anchor in St. Michael's River TA) was granted administration on estate of James Woode (chirurgeon, Wapping, ENG). Appraisers: Andrew Skinner, John Kennimont. William Hambleton (g, TA) to administer oath.

8 May. Hester Cordea relict of Antoine le Comte (DO) was granted continuance.

12 May. Mary Stacey wife of William Stacey (Patuxent Mannor, CV) was granted administration on estate of Richard Stacey (Patuxent Mannor, CV). Witnesses to will: James Garret, George Rowell.
6:200 Will of Richard Stacey. Bequests: William Stacey, Mary Stacey wife of said William. Date: 14 April 1674. Witnesses: James Garett, George Rowell. Appraisers: Robertt Lesley, John Bigger. William Groome (g) to administer oath.

John Rawlins (Tresquakin, DO) on behalf of Henry Bradley executor of his brother Samuel Bradley exhibited the will.
6:201 John Patricke proved the will; the other witness is gone out of the Province. Will of Samuel Bradley. Date: 7 December 1673. Bequests: brother Henery Bradley, landlady Philadelphia Rawlings (Transquakin). Executor: said brother. Witnesses: John Patricke, Daniell Clarcke. Said Henry was granted administration. Appraisers: John Rawlins, Thomas Harpin. Richard Winsmore (g, DO) to administer oath.

14 May. William Parcker took oath. Date: 1 May 1674. Signed: Edw. Keene (g).
6:202 John & George Parker took oath. Date: 1 May 1674. Signed: Edw. Keene (g, CV).

Inventory of Mr. William Jackson. Date: 1 August 1673.

Inventory of John Noorwood (d. 1673).
6:203 List of debts: Edward Wells, Edward Goods, Edward Turner, Thomas Bancks, William Brougham, Cornelius Jones, Andrew Higgs, Thomas Williams, Benjamin Cloister, William McDaniell, John Green, William Turner, Thomas Pagett, John Dyer. Amount: #20355. Date: 11 April

1674. Appraisers: Michael Higguen, William Singleton.

6:204 Inventory of Henry Jubbar (marriner, TA) in the hands of Thomas Gant (CV). Appraiser: Richard Bayley. Date: 6 June 1673. Amount: #9506. Administrator: Roger Baker.

Inventory of Thomas Snow (carpenter, KE). Amount: #1560. Date: 9 April 1674. Appraisers: John Boules, Thomas Parcker. Sworn by: Henry Hosier.

6:205 15 May. Inventory of John Reannalls (St. Jerome). Date: 21 March 1673. Appraisers: William Lucas, Walter Hall. Sworn by: William Calvert, Esq. Amount: #1255. Mentions: land "Fresh Ponneck".

Inventory of Richard Morris (KE). Appraisers: Michael Miller, Vallentine Southern. Date: 16 March 1673.
6:206 List of debts: Mary Pyne. Amount: #4917.

Inventory of John Wright (CV). Appraisers: Robert Lasley, John Aldwell. Date: 23 March 1673. Signed: Robert Lasbey, John Alwell.

6:207 Will of Isack Burger (p, KE). Bequests: Mary Walton daughter of John & Jone Walton "Shipppoint" 50 a. of 100 a. bought by myself & John Walton, Ruth Jones, Richard Jones, Jr., Margueritt Hill, Nathaniell Hull, Elisabeth Walton, Matthias Smith. Executor: John Walton.
6:208 Date: 18 October 1673. Witnesses: M. Miller, Edward Jones. Will proved 2 May 1674. Inventory of Isack Burger (KE). Appraisers: Isack Winchester, William Lawrence. Date: 8 May 1674. Amount: #6387.

6:209 Will of George Harris (KE). Bequests: Heaster Jenkins, wife Sarah then to my sister's son John Smith (ENG). Executrix: wife. Witnesses: Disboro Bennett, Nathaniel Fuller. Will proved by Disboro Bennett on 10 April 1674.

6:210   Inventory of John Browne (KI). Date: 30
        April 1674.
6:211   Amount: #10892. Appraisers: Robert
        Turner, Pet. Evans.

        Inventory of Falck Brinnell. Date: 29
        April 1674.
6:212   Inventory of Nicholas Uajat (also
        Nicholas Wyat, AA). Date: 13 April
        1674. Appraisers: Cornelius Howard,
        Mathew Howard (gentlemen).
6:213-214 ...
6:215   16 May. Continuation...
6:216   ...
6:217   Servants: Edward Morgan, Ellin, Negro
        John. Amount: #65788. Executrix:
        Damorus Wyat.

6:218   Inventory of John Eurickson (KE).
        Appraisers: Isack Winchester, Thomas
        Bright.
6:219   List of debts: Laurence Arnold,
        Valentine Southern, Thomas Bright,
        Richard Griffin, Thomas Currie, Joshua
        Meriton, Mary Pine, Isack Winchester,
        Xopo Haper, William Head, Jeremie Eaton,
        Richard Pecker, Charles Banckes, John
        Wright, Mathew Read. Amount: #36595.
        Date: 8 May 1675.

        Inventory of William Marshall (p,
        Pegasco, CH) in the hands of Francis
        Wyne (cooper, CH). Date: 6 April 1674.
        Appraisers: John Court, Hugh Thomas
        (gentlemen).
6:220   Servants: Christopher Johnson, Robert
        Gibson, John Auborn, Thomas Noocke,
        Negro Tongoe (boy), Negro Moggiste
        (woman).
6:221   List of debts: Nathaniell Button, John
        Roberts. Amount: #49340. Further list
        of debts: John Roberts, Nicholas Solby,
        Achiball Wanhap, Hugh Thomas, Nicholas
        Clements, Francis Wyne, John Gould, John
        Dent, John Guin, John Sprigg, Henery
        Bonner. Amount: #13526.

6:222   Inventory of Henry Gott (KE) in the
        hands of Thomas Parcker (Chester River,
        KE). Date: 12 May 1674. Amount:
        #13418. Appraisers: John Boules,

Laurence Symons. Sworn by: Henry Hosier.

6:223
6:224
Inventory of Richard Hooper. Amount: #28439. Date: 20 February 1673/4. Appraisers: Nathaniell Ashcom, Samuell Boume.

Inventory of William Hopkins. Amount: #6620. Date: 20 February 1673/4. Appraisers: Nathaniell Ashcom, Samuell Boume.

Inventory of Joshua Meriton (KE). Appraisers: Michael Miller, Francis Asbury. Date: 30 October 1673/4 [sic].
6:225 Amount: #8533.

Accounts of James Trueman (CV). Date: 10 March 1672. Administratrix: Anne Trueman (widow). Payments to: John Price, Mr. John Cox, Dr. Swanston, George Rouell, Mr. William Bury, John Sinkler, Philip Coony, Feago, Mr. Borter, Thomas Sheradon, the coopers, George Hawes, the sawyers, Brother Horer, Mr. Clerck (ENG), brother Thomas Trueman. Amount: #11717.

Mary Thomas widow of John Thomas (Stafford Co. VA) was granted administration on his estate. Date: 26 January 1673. Signed: Benjamin Rozer.

6:226
Robert Henly & John Duglass are appraisers of estate of Humphry Warren, Sr. Date: 24 March 1673/4. Signed: John Bowles (CH).

Thomas & Samuell Dobson are appraisers of estate of John Piper. Date: 27 April 1674. Signed: William Boarman.

Richard Baley is appraiser of estate of Henry Jubbar (Poole, ENG). Date: 11 April 1674. Signed: Tho. Sprigg.

16 May. William Parker (Cliffes, CV) by his attorney George Parker exhibited his oath as administrator of estate of his father William Parker. Appraisers: John Hance, George Parker.

6:227 20 May. Anne Bineham (BA) widow of James Bineham (BA) was granted administration on his estate. Her husband was murdered by Indians last year; she was wounded & left with 1 child. Signed: Hanna Binehames. Appraisers: James Philips, Thomas Jones.

6:228 Mary Harmer (BA) widow of Godfry Harmer came to court. John Waterton (one of the witnesses to will of Godfry Harmer (BA)) petitioned for administration. Appraisers: MM John Scott, Thomas Morley (both of Gunpowder River). Will of Godfry Harmer (Gunpowder River, BA). Bequests: daughter Sarah, daughter Elisabeth, daughter Mary. Executrix: wife Mary.

6:229 Date: 12 February 1673. Witnesses: John Waterton, Charles Jones. George Utie (g) to administer oath.

6:230 Lewis Brien & Nicholas Ruxton are appraisers of estate of John Carraway (d. 16 February 1673). Appraisal dated: 22 April 1674. Returned by Henry Hosier (Chester River) on 9 May 1674. Warrant issued to Richard Ball (BA) on 22 April 1674. Will of John Carraway (north side of Tatonco River, BA). Bequests: Francis Peteet, Elisabeth Boulin, Elisabeth Doulan, son of John Boulin, John Boulin to pay Capt. Tod, John Boulin. Date: 30 June 1673. Witness: William Emett. Will proved on 22 March 1673/4 before Henry Hosier. Inventory of John Carroway (BA). Appraisers: Lewis Brien, Nicholas Ruxston.

6:231 Amount: #4665. Date: 8 May 1674.

Inventory of Edward Ayrs. Appraisers: Edward Swanston, Lodowick Williams. Date: 27 April 1674. Administrator: James Collier. Amount: #2374.

6:231½ 21 May. John Doulin was granted administration on estate of John Carraway.

Thomas Carvill was sworn as one of
executors of John Pyper by Thomas
Notley. Date: 17 April 1674.

22 May. Thomas Taylor, Esq. (AA)
attorney for John Keynes (Marlebrough,
Wiltshire, ENG) executor of Joseph
Burger (AA) exhibited will. Will of
Joseph Burger (merchant, Marleborough,
Wiltshire, ENG). Bequests: brothers
William & Samuell & Jeremiah & sisters
Ann & Mary

6:232 land bought of Richard Evens, mother
(wife of John Keynes), brothers Mr.
Isack & Daniell Burger & sister
Elisabeth Parker. Executor:
father-in-law John Keynes (g,
Marleborough). Date: 22 October 1672.
Witnesses: Robert Gough, William Elles.

6:233 <Paragraph in Latin.>

Sir Robert Hanson (Knight, Lord Mayor of
London) at the request of John Keynes
(g, Marleborough, Wiltshire) is executor
of Joseph Burger (merchant, Marleborough
& AA) & was granted administration by
Prerogative Court of Archbishop of
Canterbury. Thomas Taylor was granted
administration on behalf of John Keynes.

6:234 Thomas Carleton (sheriff, BA) exhibited
that Roger Robertt (taylor, BA) is
dec'd, left neither wife, child, nor
other person of blood in the Province.
Mentions: bill of John Gilbert
(merchant).

Jane Paine administratrix of Thomas
Paine (St. Jerom's, SM) was granted
continuance.

Benjamin Rozer (g, CH) exhibited that
Robert Prouse (CH) died in VA, and that
there is no person with rights. Said
Benjamin was granted administration, as
greatest creditor. Appraisers: John
Mans, Henry Aspinall.

6:235 23 May. Jonas Davis who married
Elisabeth relict of William Durand (TA)
exhibited his inventory.

Richard Wollman (g, TA) exhibited oath of Tristram Thomas & Joannas Davis. Securities: William Finny, Philip Stephenson, David Johnson for the estate of William Shirt (TA).

25 May. Elisabeth widow of James Warner (AA) exhibited his will. Thomas Marsh (AA) to prove will. Appraisers: Cornelius Howard, Richard Hill. Will of James Warner. Bequests: wife Elisabeth Warner then to daughter Johanna Sewell plantation. Date: 13 February 1673. Witnesses: Abraham Child, John Jacobe.

6:236 Codicil: Bequests: son Samuell Howard, (N) Philips, son Henry Sewell, Abraham Child. Witnesses: Abraham Child, John Jacobe.

26 May. Philemon Lloid (g, TA) exhibited will of Charles Masters (TA). Will of Charles Masters. Date: 3 May 1672. Bequests: Elisabeth youngest daughter of Richard Wollman "The Vineyard", Rebecca Wollman, Mary Wollman, Richard Wollman, Jr. chattel at Mr. Thomas. Witnesses: Edward Winckles, Even Griffett. Will proved by Edward Winckles on 9 May 1674. Mr. Richard Wollman was granted administration. Appraisers: MM Jonathon Sybrey, William Hemsley. Phi. Lloid to administer oath. Date: 13 May 1674.

6:237 Philemon Lloid was granted administration on estate of Henry Hawkins. Appraisers: Richard Wollman, William Hemsley. Jonathon Sibrey (g, TA) to administer oath. Date: 6 April 1674. Appraisers took oath to appraise estate of Mr. Richard Hawkins.

Francis Knott (p, SM) discharged Capt. William Boreman of the estate of Ellinor White. Date: 23 February 1673. Witness: Thomas Mathews, Jr.

Discharge was granted on estate of James Whittle.

27 May. William Hambleton (g) exhibited oath of Andrew Skinner & William

Hemsley, appraisers of estate of James
Wood (chirurgeon, Wapping, ENG). Date:
15 May 1674. (N) Kennimont is ignorant
of the price of medicines. William
Hemsley replaced him. Nathaniell
Lamphugh was granted administration.

Additional inventory of Dr. Luke
Barber. Appraisers: Henry Spinck, James
Padison.

6:238 29 May. Francis Hopewell (CV) who
married Anne daughter of William Whittle
(SM) exhibited that Catherin widow &
administratrix of said William
distributed the estate as follows: 1/3rd
to herself, 1/3rd to John Whittle
(eldest son, near age 21), remaining
1/3rd to Peeter Carwardin (SM) for the
use of Thomas Whittle (youngest son).
Petitioner never received anything.

6:239 30 May. Thomas Nottley (merchant) was
granted administration on estate of
Morgan Taylor (CH), as greatest
creditor. Appraisers: John Lluellin,
Humphry Warren. Robert Roelants to
administer oath.

Robertt Burle is one of the executors of
Ralph Williams (AA). The other executor
is Thomas Marsh who resides out of the
jurisdiction of the court.
6:240 Will was proved by William Mansfeild on
9 December 1673, and by Abraham Child on
14 January 1673.

1 June. Richard Wollman was granted
administration on estate of Charles
Masters.

Edward Winckles administrator of William
Power & administrator of Evan Thomas
exhibited accounts. Discharge was
granted for both.

Nathaniel Lamphugh administrator of
James Wood (chirurgeon, Wapping)
exhibited inventory.
6:241 Mentions: payments to: James Clayland,
William Hemsley. Signed: Michael
Rochford.

2 June. Charles de la Roche administrator of John Taylor exhibited accounts. Discharge was granted.

4 June. Joseph Wickes executor of Mary Goldhawke (KE) exhibited accounts. Continuance was granted to produce legible accounts.

6:242 5 June. Joseph Wickes administrator of Mary Goldhawke (KE) exhibited accounts. Discharge was granted.

Brine Odaly one of executors of Roger Sheehee (SM) exhibited the will. Witnesses: Daniell Divine, Hugh Manning. Suit entered by Constantyne Daniell. Said Daniell to appear with Bryen Odaly & Constantine Okeef.

Anne Neale executrix of Henry Neale (Britton's Bay) exhibited accounts. Continuance was granted to produce legible accounts.

6:243 6 June. Sheriff (CV) to cause Edward Leiley (CV) to give accounts on the estate of John Bigger (CV).

Sheriff (BA) to cause Thomas Booker (AA) to give accounts on estate of John Dearing (AA).

9 June. Emmamuel Ratcliff (St. George's Hundred, SM) exhibited the will of Daniell Gover. Will of Daniell Gover. Date: 23 May 1674. Bequests: brother Emanuel Ratcliff, Elisabeth Exons, Henry Exons. Witnesses: George Fenix, Edward leCroft. Will proved 9 June 1674. Judge pronounced the will void. Emmanuell Ratcliff was granted administration on estate of his brother-in-law Daniell Gover. Appraisers: William Harper, John Macky.
6:244 Mr. Thomas Dent to administer oath.

Marck Cordea who married relict of Antoine le Compte (DO) exhibited the inventory.

11 June. Kenelme Cheslidyne & Robertt Ridgely attorneys for Margarett Penry vs. Thomas Howell & George Wells & Johanna Goldsmith. Robertt Carvile attorney for Thomas Howell administrator of Francis Wright exhibited accounts.

6:245 Mentions: Thomas Howell & Maior Goldsmith as overseers of the estate of Francis Wright & inventory of October 1667. Appraisers: James Frisby, John Vanhake. Deposition of John Cleaver. Payments to: Henry Haslewood. Dec'd's brother Raphaell is sole executor.

6:246 Judge pronounced said inventory & accounts void.

12 June. Anne Neale widow & administratrix of Henry Neale (g, New Town, SM) & relict & executrix of William Tetershall (g, SM) exhibited accounts. Distribution: executrix, Lawrence Tetershall (her son, under age), Mary Tetershall (her daughter, under age). Discharge was granted.

Said Anne Neale exhibited inventory of Henry Neale, which contained items which belonged to her children Lawrence & Mary Tetershall.

6:247 Accounts cited distribution to the children of said Henry after the widow's 1/3rd.

Bryen Odaly & Constantine Keef executors of Roger Shehee appeared. Testimony by Constantyne Daniell & his witnesses, Daniell Divine (witness), Hugh Manning (witness). Appraisers: William Marshall, Thomas Docksie. Col. William Calvert to administer oath. Will of Roger Shehee. Date: 25 April 1674. Executors: my countrymen Bryen Odally & Constantyne Okieffe. Bequests: son Edmond Shehee (now in VA).

6:248 Witnesses: Daniell Divine, Hugh Manning. Codicil: Bequests: church, Mr. Foster, Bettie Manning, Teigue Wany (?), Constantyne Okeef, Mr. Hall, Bryen Odaly, Constantine O'Daniell, Love O'Daniell. Will proved 12 June 1674.

Court Session: 1674

Abell James (SM) executor of Edward
Dubrey (SM) exhibited accounts.
Discharge was granted.

16 June. William Harper (St. George
Hundred) attorney for Joseph Tucker
(master of Francis & Mary of Bristoll)
attorney for William Donning & Thomas
Smart (merchants, Bristoll) creditors to
the estate of William Hatoft (St. Inigos
Hundred, SM) presented PoA.

6:249   Mentions: William Hattoft (of Bristoll,
died in VA or MD), Maior Edward
Fitzherbert, Caleb Baker.

6:250   Date: 14 October 1673. Witnesses: Symon
Pukmer, William Cottell. Will proved by
Symon Pukmer on 15 April 1673. Will
proved by William Cottell on 29 April
1674. Joseph Tucker PoA to William
Harper.

6:251   ...
6:252   Date: 12 May 1674. Witnesses: P.
Boteler, Robert Ridgely, Tho. Dent.

Robertt Ridgely attorney for William
Harper vs. Edward Fitzherbert, Esq. &
Caleb Baker executors of said Hattoft &
Garrett Vanswearingen one of securities
of said Edward & Caleb & John Barns (St.
Inigoes Hundred) executor of Walter
Walterlyn (St. Inigoes Hundred) the
other security.

6:253   7 June. Stephen Tully (TA) son & heir
of John Tully (master of the good ship
Releife of London) was granted
administration on his estate. Mathew
Ward (TA) to administer oath.

William Lawrence who married relict of
William Elliott (KI) exhibited accounts.
Mentions: payment due to William (orphan
of dec'd).

19 June. Anne Neale administratrix of
Henry Neale (New Towne, SM) exhibited
accounts. Discharge was granted.

6:254   20 June. Henry Dauson (DO)
administrator of Henry Orsborne (CV)
exhibited inventory. Appraisers:
William Steephens, Morrish Mathews.

Page 123

24 June. Justinian Gerrard (Bramely,
SM) administrator of Robertt Hutchison
(SM) exhibited inventory.

26 June. Jonathon Squire administrator
of John Morecroft by his attorney
Kenelme Cheslidyne was granted
continuance.

27 June. Jane Paine relict &
administratrix of Thomas Paine exhibited
accounts.

Mark Cordea (g) administrator of John
Broock exhibited accounts.

Thomas Gibson administrator of William
Cotton (CH) exhibited inventory &
accounts.

29 June. George Robins (Peache Blossom,
TA) was granted administration on estate
of Thomas Willmer (merchant, London),
who died single, unmarried, childless, &
left no person in the Province with the
right of claim, as greatest creditor.
6:255 The goods & chattel (of said Willmer)
are to be of use to the mother & brother
of the dec'd. Appraisers: Thomas
Vaughan, Richard Bayly, John Glover,
James Morufee (?). Richard Wollman to
administer oath.

30 June. Jonathon Squire exhibited the
inventory of John Morecroft.

1 July. Henry Adams (CH) to swear
Thomas Howell administrator of Humphry
Warren (CH).

3 July. Edward Keen (g, CV)
administrator of Henry Refue (CV)
exhibited inventory. Mentions: debtor
John Larkins. Richard Lad (g) to
administer oath.

Robertt Ridgely attorney for William
Harper attorney for Joseph Tucker
attorney for William Donning & Thomas
Smart (merchants, Bristoll) 2 of
creditors of William Hattoft (dec'd) vs.
Edward Fitzherbert & Caleb Baker

executors of William Hattoft & Kenelm
Chesledyn attorney for Garret
Vansweringen & John Barnes. Continuance
was granted.

6:256   10 July. Thomas Hooker one of the
executors of John Dearing (AA) exhibited
inventory.

Robertt Lesly administrator of John
Bigger (CV) exhibited his accounts.
Mentions: John Bigger (Patuxent River)
where dec'd lived, wife of dec'd in
Scotland.

Bryen O'Daniell & Constantyn O'Keel
executors of Roger Shehee (SM) exhibited
his inventory. Appraisers: William
Marshall, Thomas Doxsy.

15 July. William Thomas (DO) executor
of Jacob Waymack (DO) exhibited
accounts. Discharge was granted.

17 July. George Wells (BA) one of
executors of Samuell Goldsmith to render
accounts.

6:257   20 July. John Guilbert (CE) chief
creditor to Roger Robertts (CE, dec'd)
exhibited that there was an inventory by
Capt. Thomas Carleton (BA) & there is
additional chattel. Said John Gilbert
granted administration on his estate.
Signed: Richard Keene. Appraisers:
James Frisby, Richard Edmunds. Abraham
Wild (g) to administer oath.

24 July. Thomas Spinck (St. Inigoes
Hundred, SM) exhibited the accounts of
Samuell Neale. Continuance was granted.

Joane Tyler relict & administratrix of
George Reade (CV) exhibited accounts.
Mentions: chattel in hands of Robertt
Taylor (Patuxent River, dec'd, said
George was his executor). Robertt Tyler
was the second husband of the
administratrix. Continuance was
granted.

Philip Lloyd & Joseph Wickes appraised the estate of Symon Carpenter. Inventory made on 2 January 1670. Certified at the request of Mr. Henry Coursey. Date: 5 July 1674.

6:258 James Ringgold exhibited will of Lewis Steephens (Chester River, KE). Will of Lewis Steephens (Chester River, KE). Date: 13 January 1673. Executrix: Mary Hosyer daughter of Mr. Henry Hosier (Longfoord Bay, KE). Signed: Lewis Stephens. Witnesses: Joseph Masones, Morgan Jones. Will proved 2 March 1673.

Benjamin Rozer exhibited bond of Phil. Lynes administrator of James Lewellin (CH).

6:259 Philip Lines & Philip Gibbon bond of 4 May 1674.

Thomas Sprigg exhibited the inventory of Robertt Tyler (CV). Appraisers: William King, John Winfield. Date: 6 July 1674.

George Uty exhibited inventory of Godfry Harmer (BA).

George Uty exhibited oath of Jane Dixon relict & administratrix of John Dixon (BA), sworn on 12 November 1670.

George Uty exhibited will of William Robisson (BA) & inventory. Will of William Robisson

6:260 (p, Bush River, BA). Bequests: wife Henerica Robisson. Date: 24 April 1671. Witnesses: Thomas Heath, Mary Elinge. Will proved April 1672. Edward Swanstone who married Henerica administratrix was granted administration. Date: 26 May 1672. Appraisers: William York, William Osborne. George Uty (g) to administer oath.

28 July. Joane Tyler relict & administratrix of George Reade exhibited accounts. Discharge was granted.

4 August. George Parker (g, CV) one of the witnesses of the will of Henry

Beedle (Hering Creek, AA) exhibited his will, proved by said Parker & John Hance (CV). Sophia Beedle widow & administratrix was granted administration on his estate. Appraisers: Capt. William Burgess, Mr. Richard Evens. Samuell Chew, Esq. to administer oath.

6:261 Will of Henry Beedle (g, Herring Creek, AA). Date: 29 May 1674. Bequests: daughter Sophia Beedle (under age 21, unmarried) 500 a. being 2 tracts of land I had of my father-in-law Mr. William Coursey in TA, wife Sophia "Beedles Outlett", brother William Coursey. Executrix: wife Sophia. Witnesses: John Hance, Geo. Parker. Will proved 4 August 1674. Signed: Michael Rockford (clerk).

6:262 5 August. Thomas Smethwick witness to will of George Nettlefould (AA) exhibited his will. Will of George Nettlefould (p, Rode River, AA). Bequests: wife Maudling Nettlefould plantation but if she marries then ½ to her & other ½ to Mary Dunkin wife of Patrick Dunkin & Phebe Thomas wife of John Thomas, George Burgess son of Capt. William Burgess (AA) plantation after decease of wife. Executrix: wife. Date: 3 July 1674. Witnesses: Thomas Smethwick, George Smith, Humphry Jones. Will proved 5 August 1675. Appraisers: William Burges, John Cumber. Mr. Nathaniell Heathcoate (g) to administer oath. Magdalene Nettlefould widow was granted administration.

6:263 Jonas Davis who married Elisabeth widow of William Durand (TA) was granted continuance.

William Melton administrator of John Troster (Cliffs, CV) exhibited inventory. Appraisers: Richard Stallings, Marck Clare.

6 August. John Wright (KE) on behalf of Sara Shaw widow of John Shaw (AA) was granted administration on his estate. Appraisers: Nicholas Gaseway, Richard

Tyding. Capt. William Burgesse to administer oath.

John Southy (DO) one of the executors of Alexander Roche exhibited his will. Will of Alexander Roche (DO). Bequests: Dennis Cremmin (Barbadoes), Mr. John Southy & John Mackell & Edmund Brannock & John Butten, Mr. John Southy,

6:264 Jane Brannack wife of Edmund Brannack, Owen Murphey. Executors: Mr. John Southy, John Mackell, Edmund Brannock. Date: 15 July 1674. Witnesses: John Butten, Owen Murphey, William Seaell, John Miles. Will proved by John Butten & John Miles on 6 August 1674. John Southy, John Mackell, & Edmund Brannock were granted administration. Appraisers: Thomas Skinner, Thomas Mattie. Dr. Robertt Winsmer to administer oath.

6:265 12 August. Richard Gardner son & heir of Capt. Luke Gardner (SM) exhibited his will. Witnesses: Robertt Carvile, Clement Hill (gentlemen). Will of Luke Gardner (SM). To be buried as Roman Chatholick. Bequests: pastor of church at Newtowne, pastor of church at Portobaccoe, pastor at Gouds (?) Mr. Massey, Mr. Carcu (at Chancellors), wife Elisabeth Gardner plantation at Connoe Neck & St. Clement's Island, eldest son Richard Gardner "Barberton Mannor" on north side of Piscadeway Creek (CH), next eldest son John Gardner "St. John's" (SM) except for 300 a. to son Luke Gardner

6:266 on west side of Amaine Branch, son John Gardner (under age 18) "St. John's Landing" at head of St. Clement Bay, son Luke Gardner (under age 18) "Hillilce" near head of Chaptico Bay & "Gardner's Landing" by Chaptico Bay, son Luke "Grimsditch" (CH) near Mattawoman, youngest son Thomas Gardner (under age 18) 800 a. on branch of Piscadeway Creek & half tract betwixt my brother-in-law Zachary Wade & myself. Children at age 18 & can not sell any land until they are age 25.

6:267 Wife & eldest son guardians of other

sons. Overseers: brother-in-law Maior
Thomas Brooke guardian of youngest son
Thomas then his eldest son Thomas Brooke
guardian. Codicil: bequests:
6:268 the poor, brother-in-law Maior Thomas
Brookes & his children, goddaughter Mary
Brooke, pastor of Newtown Church, pastor
of St. Mary's Church. Date: 4 December
1673. Witnesses: Robertt Carvile,
Clement Hill, Elisabeth Ryder, Richard
Lankfores. Elisabeth widow of said Luke
was granted administration. Appraisers:
Thomas Brooke, Zachary Wade, William
Hatton, Randall Hanson. Benjamin Solley
or John Stone (gentlemen) to administer
oath. Robertt Carvile, g, age 38, of
St. Mary's City, deposed regarding said
will that he saw the dec'd sign said
will.
6:269 Witnesses: Mr. Clement Hill, et. al. &
deposed regarding the contents. Date:
12 August 1674.

6:270 Mary Stacey executrix of Richard Stacey
(CV) exhibited inventory.

14 August. William Hambleton exhibited
the will of Henry Frith. Will of Henry
Frith. Executrix: wife Elisabeth Frith.
Bequests: son Henry Frith (under age 16)
150 a., 3 daughters (under age 14) land.
Overseers: Mr. William Hambleton, Hugh
Sherwood. Witnesses: Humphry Davonport,
William Gaslings, Richard Sherrington.
Will proved by Humphry Davonport &
Richard Sherrington on 23 July 1674.
Elisabeth Frith relict of Henry Frith
now wife of Edward Elliott was granted
administration on his estate.
Appraisers: Mr. Seth Foster, Edmund
Webb. William Hambleton to administer
oath.

6:271 20 August. Since Thomas Marsh has moved
out of AA, Robertt Burle is to take the
probate of the estate of James Warner.

22 August. John Llewellin & Humphry
Warren to appraise estate of Morgan
Taylor (CH). Robertt Roelandts (CH) to
administer oath. Date: 30 May 1674.

Mr. William Barton & Mr. John Coarles to appraise estate of William Jackson (CV). Thomas Mathews (CH) to administer oath. Date: 19 November 1673.

John Coates & William Barton to appraise estate of Nicholas Solsby (CH). Thomas Hussey (CH) to administer oath. Date: 3 February 1673.

Robertt Carvile attorney for Henry Adams & Thomas Mathews executors of George Manwaring vs. Kenelm Chesledyn attorney for Mark Cordea. Continuance was granted.

6:272 25 August. Tobyas Norton administrator of John Francklin (CV) was granted administration on his estate. Appraisers: William Watson, Edward Cook. Date: 15 February 1671. Said Watson & Cook moved to the Eastern Shore. Estate is in partnership with Henry Cox.

John Meeres (CV) son & heir of Thomas Meeres (AA) was granted administration on his estate. Appraisers: Robertt Burle, Richard Hill. Samuell Chew, Esq. to administer oath.

6:273 Jane Paine administratrix of Thomas Paine (St. Jerom's) to pay to her 5 daughters on their day of marriage or age 17, to his 2 sons Isack & Joseph when age 21. Date: 25 August 1674.

27 August. Robertt Burle (AA) one of the executors of Ralph Williams (merchant, AA, formerly of Bristoll) was granted continuance. Other executor is Thomas Marsh, who is removed out of AA to KE.

6:274 Thomas Turner executor of Thomasin Stinchecombe (AA) was granted continuance. Said Thomas has been sick for 7 months.

2 September. Benjamin Solley (g, SM) brother to Edward Solley (CH) was granted administration on his estate. Appraisers: Francis Wyn, Robertt Foat.

John Allen (g) to administer oath.

6 September. Kenelm Chesledyn on behalf
of Margueritt Bushby executrix of Dr.
Robertt Bushby (AA)
6:275   was granted administration on his
estate. Appraisers: Mr. Robertt Burle,
Mr. Richard Hill. Samuell Chew, Esq.
to administer oath.

Thomas Notley (merchant, SM)
administrator of Morgan Taylor (CH)
exhibited accounts. Discharge was
granted.

8 September. Tobias Wells (KE) executor
of Mary Pine was granted continuance.
Will of Mary Pine (KE).
6:276   Bequests: Mr. John Halfhead payment for
700 a. at Langford's Bay sold to John
Readway, wife of said John Halfhead,
Isack Winchester, John Essex, Tobias
Wells. Executor: said Tobias Wells.
Date: 28 December 1673. Witnesses: John
Rodway, Mathias Stevenson, William
Currer, Louis Blangy. Will proved by
William Curre & Louis Blangy on 3 June
1674. Signed: Thomas Osborne.

6:277   Said Tobias Wells administrator of
William Leppen (KE) exhibited inventory
& accounts.

Thomas Dent (g, SM) exhibited oath of
William Harper & John Macky, appraisers
of estate of Daniell Gover (SM), sworn
on 31 August 1674. Also exhibited was
inventory.

14 September. Samuell Chew, Esq. (AA)
exhibited will of Thomas Meers (AA),
with probate & oath Robertt Burle &
Richard Hill,
6:278   appraisers & inventory. Will of Thomas
Meers (Severn, AA). Date: 16 May 1674.
Bequests: cousin Christopher Rowles,
Wenlock Christison (Miles River, TA),
Elisabeth Hawkins wife of William
Hawkins (Broad Creek), Elisabeth
Underwood (orphan servant), Quakers,
6:279   John Gather, 2 orphans, wife Elisabeth
Meers 100 a., wife John Sangoe (Negro

boy), daughter Sarah Homewood wife of
John Homewood, son John Meers.

6:280 Executor: son John. Advisors: Quakers.
Signed: Thomas Meeres. Witnesses: James
Smith, Thomas Eyres, Edward Norris.
Will proved 9 September 1674.

Samuell Chew, Esq. (AA) exhibited oath
of Capt. William Burgess & Richard
Even, appraisers of estate of James
Burgesse (Marlebrough, Wiltshire, ENG),
6:281 sworn on 19 August 1674. Inventory was
exhibited.

15 September. George Marshall (g, SM)
was granted administration on estate of
Joseph Bruff (SM). Appraisers: Brien
Odaly, Thomas Doxsy. William Calvert,
Esq. (SM) to administer oath. Sworn on:
19 September 1674.

6:282 William Chadborne (AA) who married
relict of Richard Foxon (AA) was granted
continuance.

21 September. Ellnor Farguson wife of
William Farguson and relict of Thomas
Phelps (AA) was granted administration
on his estate. Security: said Farguson,
John Howard, Thomas Roper. Appraisers:
Henry Ridgely, Cornelius Howard.
Richard Hill to administer oath.

John Howard attorney for William Roper
(AA) was granted administration on
estate of William Hapwale (AA), who died
unmarried and hath anyone of his blood
in the Province, as greatest creditor.
6:283 Appraisers: Martin duVall, John Gray.
William Burgesse (g) to administer oath.

THomas Roper (AA) administrator of Okey
Rowland (AA) was granted discharge.

24 September. William Burgesse (g, AA)
exhibited the will of George Puddington
(AA), proved by said Burgesse & John
Browne (witnesses). Will of George
Puddington (South River, AA). Date: 15
August 1674.
6:284 Bequests: 2 of my near relations (my
brother or sisters children) passage to

Court Session: 1674

the Province, son-in-law Robertt
Franklin, George Burgesse & William
Burgesse

6:285 Susanna Burgesse (children of Capt.
William Burgesse), kinsman James
Chilsott, kinsman Augustin Skinner,
children of my son Richard Beard,
children of grandson Neale Clerk, wife
Jane Puddington (payment in London),
Edward Burgesse (son of Capt. William
Burgesse). Executor: said Edward.
Witnesses: Nath. Heathcoate, William
Laus, Charity Stone, John Broome,
William Burgesse.

6:286 Will proved by William Burgesse & John
Broome on 24 September 1674. Edward
Burgesse (executor, son of William
(witness)) is out of the country. Said
William was granted administration on
behalf of said Edward. Appraisers:
Nathaniell Heathcoate, Robertt Franclin,
Thomas Francis. Thomas Tailler to
administer oath.

John Gittings (g, CV) exhibited
inventory of John Winfeild (CV) under
the hand of Tho. Sprigg. Said Winfeild
had neither wife, child, nor relation
alive.

6:287 Said Gittings granted administration on
his estate.

George Robins (Peache Blossom, TA)
exhibited the inventory of Thomas
Willmer (merchant, London).

25 September. William Greengoe (smith,
SM) exhibited the will of Miles Edwyn.
Kenelm Chesledyn (g) to prove the will.
Witnesses are remote from the Office.

Nathaniell Heathcoate (g, AA) exhibited
the will of George Nettleford (AA).
Magdalene Nettleford executrix of said
George was sworn on 8 August 1674.

6:288 Appraisers: Capt. William Burgesse, Mr.
John Cumber. Said Heathcote to
administer oath.

Thomas Tailler, Esq. (AA) exhibited oath
of Cornelius Howard, sworn on 11 August
1674. Warrant date: 3 February 1673/4.

Page 133

William Burgess (g, AA) exhibited oath of Sarah Shaw widow & administratrix of John Shaw (AA), sworn on 19 August 1674. Also oath of appraisers Nicholas Gascoway & Richard Tydings, sworn same day.

1 October. Arthur Wright (KE) administrator of Joshua Meriton exhibited accounts. Discharge was granted.

2 October. William Claw & John Smallspeece executors of John Reynolds exhibited accounts. Continuance was granted.

Mary Clagett (CV) relict & administratrix of Richard Hooper (CV) exhibited accounts. Discharge was granted.

Mary Clagett (CV) relict of Richard Hooper (CV) & administratrix of William Hopkins (CV) exhibited accounts. Discharge was granted.

5 October. Alice Tenahill relict of William Tenahill (CV) exhibited his will.

6:290 Will of William Tennahill. Date: 10 June 1666. Bequests: confirmation of gift by David Duncan to my 3 children William & John & Mary Tennahill, sons William & John plantation & 100 a. at head of Poplar Creek bought of Thomas Bennett, wife Alice Tennahill (pregnant). Overseers: John Carnell, Stannop Roberts. Signed: William Tenahills. Witnesses: John Lawson, Richard Ridor. Will proved by John Lawson on 7 May 1667.

6:291 8 October. Dorothy Dorington relict & executrix of Henry Robinson (CV) exhibited accounts.

James Humber (CV) executor of Cornelius Regan (CV) exhibited accounts.

9 October 1674. Distribution of estate of Henry Robinson: Dorothy Dorington

(relict, ½), Henry Robinson (only son, ½).

6:292 Francis Wyn (CH) executor of William Marshall (CH) was granted continuance.

10 October. Elisabeth Davis relict & administratrix of William Durand (TA) exhibited accounts. Discharge was granted.

Richard Wolman (TA) administrator of Charles Masters (TA) was granted continuance, due to his long sickness.

Robertt Winsmore (g, DO) exhibited oath of Owen Murphy witness to will of Alexander Roche (merchant, late of Barbadoes, DO),

6:293 sworn on 17 August last. William Seale was then & now is a prisoner. Appraisers Thomas Skinner & Morris Mathews, were sworn 28 August 1674. Signed: Robertt Winsemore. Inventory was exhibited.

6:294 12 October. James Frisby (CE) son & heir & one of executors of James Frisby (BA) exhibited his will. Will of James Frisby, Sr. (Sassafras River, BA). Bequests: wife (1/3), 3 sons James Frisby, Jr. & William Frisby & Thomas Frisby "Swan Point" & plantation & 150 a on north side of Sassafras River between Hendrick Matson & Marcus Eurrson (?) & plantation on Elisabeth River (VA) 600 a., daughter Mary Frisby (under age 18) Negro Margueritt (girl).

6:295 Executors: wife, son James Frisby, Jr. Date: 22 December 1673. Witnesses: Abraham Stran, Nicholas Dorell. Will proved by Nicholas Dorrell on 12 October 1674. Abraham Stran could not swear. Mary Frisby (widow) & James Frisby (son) were granted administration.

6:296 Appraisers: John Guilbertt, John Coxe. Thomas Howell (g) to administer oath.

13 October. Thomas Hussey (g, CH) exhibited the will of Joseph Pearce (merchant, Darthmouth, Devonshire, ENG), who died at the house of said Thomas.

Witnesses were: Benjamin Rozer, John Jones. Anne Pearce (widow) is cited as executrix. Will of Joseph Pearce (merchant, Darthmouth, Devonshire, now of CH).

6:297 Bequests: wife Anne Pearce. Mentions: children. Executrix: said wife. Date: 22 September 1674. Witnesses: Benjamin Rozer, John Jones.

6:298 Thomas Mathews (g, CH) to prove said will. Benjamin Rozer on behalf of the executrix was granted administration. Appraisers (CH): Thomas Hussey, Ignatius Causin.

14 October. Will of John Nevill (g, CV). Date: 5 October 1673.

6:299 Bequests: Mr. Richard Tillman (TA), Patriack Sullivant (p, TA). Witnesses: Ralph Blackhall, James Barkhurst. One of witnesses lives in TA; the other, in KE. Patrick Sullivant (TA) was granted administration. Mathew Ward (TA) to administer oath. Appraisers (Clifts, CV): John Mannings, William Evans. Richard Lad (g, CV) to administer oath.

6:300 John Walters married Susanna White relict & executrix of James White (AA). Said Susanna is pregnant; continuance was granted.

15 October. Miles Gibson (BA) executor of John Newton (BA) exhibited his will. Said Miles is forced to remain at home because of incursions of the Cinegoe Indians. Appraisers: William Hollis, James Philips. George Utie (g, BA) to administer oath.

John Currer (KE) on behalf of Elisabeth Head widow of William Head

6:301 was granted administration on his estate. Appraisers: Mr. Thomas Osborne, Mathew Riede. William Lawrence (g, KE) to prove will & administer oaths. Said Elisabeth cannot travel because she is pregnant & recently ill. Mentions: Michaell Miller (creditor to dec'd).

6:302   Sarah Harris widow of George Harris (KE) renounced executorship on his estate. John Ingram (KE) was granted administration. Appraisers: Tobias Wells, Isack Winchester. William Lawrence to administer oath.

17 October 1674. John Wright (KE) administrator of John Boulton (KE) exhibited accounts. Discharge was granted.

6:303   Samuell Cressey (CH) administrator of John Harrington (CH) petitioned for new appraisers: John Douglas, William Hemsley. Robertt Henley (g) to administer oath.

Thomas Arminger (BA) administrator of Francis Frippos (BA)

6:304   was granted continuance.

Abraham Wild (g, KE) exhibited oath of Richard Edmunds & James Frisby, appraisers of estate of Roger Robertts (CE). Richard sworn 29 July; James, 6 August. Signed: Abraham Wilde. Inventory dated: 4 August 1674.

6:305   Capt. William Burgesse (g, AA) exhibited oath of Marin DuVall & John Gray, appraisers of estate of William Hapwate (AA), sworn 8 October 1674.

Inventory of George Puddington was exhibited, by appraisers Nathaniell Heathcoate, Robertt Francklin, & Thomas Francis.

Mens Stekelcopp (BA) on behalf of Henry Haslewood executor of John Collett (BA) exhibited accounts. Col. Nathaniell Utie, Esq. to swear said Haslewood to put accounts in order.

19 October. Mathew Ward (g, TA) petitioned for Henry Hosier & John Wells to appraise estate of John Nevill (CV), that part of the estate in TA.

6:306   William Claw & John Smallpeese executors of John Reynolds (SM) were granted continuance.

William Jones (TA), at the request of
Nathaniell Lamphigh administrator of
James Wood (chirurgeon, late of Wapping,
ENG) was granted continuance.

20 October. Will of John Westlock (p,
Wickcocomaw, SO). Executrix: wife
Magdalena Westlock.

6:307   Date: 29 January 1673/4. Witnesses:
William Elgett, Thomas Giles. David
Browne (g) to prove will; said Magdalene
is of great age & witnesses live
remotely. Appraisers: James Weatherly,
Henry Hayman. Said Browne to administer
oath.

William Thomas (St. Jerome's, SM)
exhibited that Joseph leDuc died at his
house. Appraisers (SM): Bryen O'Daly,
Morgan Jones. Coroner William Calvert
to administer oath.

John Gittings (CV) administrator of John
Winfeild (CV) exhibited inventory.

6:308   21 October. Robertt Burle (g, AA)
exhibited the will of James Warner (AA),
proved by witnesses Abraham Childe &
John Jacob on 10 September 1674.
Elisabeth Warner widow & executrix was
granted administration. Appraisers: MM
Cornelius Howard, Richard Hill. Per
order to self & Mr. Thomas Taillor.

6:309   Sarah Harris relict of George Harris
(KE) renounced administration &
petitioned for John Ingram to be granted
administration. Date: 31 January
1673/4. Witnesses: Morgan Williams, R.
Bennett.

22 October. George Wells (g, BA)
administrator of Samuell Goldsmith (BA)
is unable to travel, having been lately
molested by Cineha Indians.
Continuance was granted.

23 October. Will of John Hall (BA) was
exhibited. The witnesses are remote &
unable to travel because of incursion of
Indians. Nathaniell Utie, Esq. (BA) to
prove the will.

6:310   Executor: Bernard Utie. Appraisers:
Samuell Boston, George Wells. Said Utie
to administer oath.

William Thomas (St. Jerom's, SM)
exhibited the inventory of Joseph leDuc.
Appraisers: Morgan Jones, Brien Odaly.

Thomas Waikfield (CH) executor of
Jonathon Marler (CH) exhibited accounts.

6:311   26 October. Richard Tilghman
(chirurgeon, TA) & Joane Colleck
(spinster, TA) executors of Thomas South
(KE) exhibited will. Richard Ellwood is
the sole surviving witness. The other
witness, Joshua Barnes, drowned in the
company of the dec'd. Will of Thomas
South (g, KE). Bequests: maidservant
Joane Colleck, John Keely (of Severne),
Richard Tilghman (TA).

6:312   Executors: Richard Tilghman, Joane
Colleck. Overseers: Mr. Henry Hosier,
James Ringall. Additional bequests:
sister Sarah land then to heirs of my
sister Anne. Renunciation of my wife
Grace Smith. Date: 13 October 1673.
Witnesses: Joshua Barnes, Richard
Ellwood. Mentions: said wife Grace
eloped some years ago. Appraisers:
Ralph Blackhall, Richard Jones.

6:313   James Ringold (g, KE) to administer
oath.

28 October. John Brooks (p, SM) was
granted administration on estate of his
brother Mathew Brooks, who died with
neither wife nor children. Security:
William Boreman (g, SM). Appraisers:
Mr. Robertt Rowlant, Walter Davis.
John Douglasse (g, CH) to administer
oath.

Lydia Solley, widow of Benjamin Solley
(g, SM), was granted administration on
his estate. Said Lydia is weak &
sickly. Security: Dr. John Peerce.

6:314   Appraisers: John Bullock, William
Felsted. William Rosewell (g) to
administer oath. Thomas Oataway
replaced John Bull as an appraiser on 17
February 1674.

29 October. James Boyd who married relict of John Norwood (AA) was granted administration on his estate. Mentions: orphans of the dec'd. Estate is unadministered by Anne Boyd late wife of said James & lately Anne Norwood. Thomas Tailler to administer oath to said James. Appraisers: Dr. William Jones, John Bemont. Robertt Burle to administer oath.

6:315   3 November. Francis Brooke (TA) exhibited the will of Joseph Dellawood, proved by Mary Sanders (witness). The other witness, William Relisford, drowned with the dec'd. Will of Joseph Dellawood (p, TA). Bequests: brother John Dellawood (VA) 100 a. on Chester River (TA), Francis Brooke. Date: 6 October 1674. Witnesses: William Retisford, Mary Sanders. Said Francis was granted administration. Appraisers: Andrew Skinner, Jonas Davis. Philemon Lloyd (g) to administer oath.

6:316   Francis Brooke (TA) exhibited the will of William Retisford, proved by Thomas Maycoke & Dennis Sullivant. Will of William Retchford (TA, also Plymouth, Devonshire). Bequests: wife Mary Retchford (Plymouth). Overseer: Joseph Dellawood then Francis Brookes. List of debts: Jeffryas Crouch, Thomas Hemfreys, Joshua Crouche, Thomas Allen. Date: 6 October 1674. Witnesses: Thomas Maycock, Dennis Sullivant.

6:317   Said Francis was granted administration. Appraisers: Andrew Skinner, Jonas Davis. Philemon Lloyd (g) to administer oath.

6 November. Benjamin Rozer (g, CH) was granted administration on estate of Philip Gibbon (CH), who died with no relations or blood to administer the estate. Appraisers (gentlemen, CH): Ignatius Caussin, John Hartwell. Thomas Mathews (g) to administer oath.

6:318   Hester Cordea relict & executrix of Anthony LeCompte (DO) was granted continuance. Her husband Mark Cordea is absent.

Francis Wyne (CH) executor of William
Marshall (CH) was granted continuance.

7 November 1674.   Court at St.
Mary's.   James Thompson administrator of
William Greene (SM) exhibited accounts.
Residue

6:319 to be secured for the orphan of said
Greene.

11 November.   Richard Gardner (SM) son &
heir of Capt.   Luke Gardner (SM)
exhibited the inventory, on behalf of
Elisabeth Gardner (his mother,
administratrix).   There is an additional
plantation.   Continuance granted.

14 November.   Thomas Notley (g, SM)
exhibited bond of Elisabeth Gardner
widow & administratrix of Capt.   Luke
Gardner.

6:320 Commission was sent to Mr.   Benjamin
Solley & myself to commit administration
to Mrs.   Elisabeth Gardner of the estate
of Capt.   Luke Gardner & on 29 September
last, administered the oath.   Bond by
Mr.   Clement Hill.   Mr. Solley fell sick
& died before he & I could jointly
certify the deed.   Appraisers: Maier
Thomas Brooke, Mr.   William Hatton, Mr.
Randall Hanson.   Date: 9 November.
Signed: Thomas Notley.

John Douglasse (g, CH) exhibited the
oaths of Robertt Rowlants & Walter
Davis, appraisers of estate of Mathew
Brooke (CH), sworn

6:321 29 October 1674.

Jane Ryder (SM) relict & executrix of
Thomas Wright (SM) was granted
continuance.

17 November.   Robertt Burle (g, AA) one
of executors of Ralph Williams
(merchant, AA, late of Bristoll, ENG)

6:322 was granted continuance.   The other
executor is Thomas Marsh (KE).

20 November.   Jane Ryder (SM) relict &
executrix of Thomas Wright (SM)
exhibited accounts.   Discharge was

granted.

Thomas Mathews (CH) exhibited oath of Benjamin Rozer (g) administrator of Philip Gibbon (CH), sworn 12 November 1674.

6:323 Thomas Mathews (g, CH) exhibited will of Joseph Pearce (Dartmouth, Devonshire, ENG), with probate.
- Mr. Benjamin Rozer & John Jones (Portobacco, CH) deposed that they saw Joseph Pearce sign his will. Date: 20 October 1674.
- Mr. Benjamin Rozer sworn as administrator. Date: 19 October 1674.
- Mr. Thomas Hussy & Mr. Ignatius Causine sworn as appraisers. Date: 22 October 1674.

20 November. Henry Hyde (g, St. George's Hundred, SM), one of the overseers of will of Robertt Cager (p, Herring Creek, SM), exhibited that Robertt Cager, son & heir of said dec'd, is now near age 21 & married
6:324 & desires to account to said heir his administration. Accounts were provided to said heir, his wife, her father & brothers. Discharge was granted.

21 November. John Barnes (SM) executor of Walter Walterlin (SM) exhibited accounts. Discharge was granted.

6:325 Jane Ryder (SM) relict & executrix of Thomas Wright (SM) exhibited his inventory. Appraisers: Joseph Haisiney, William Claw.

24 November. Kenelm Chesledyn attorney for Joane Cowell widow of Benjamin Cowell (chirurgeon, London, ENG) exhibited bill due from Richard Tilghman. Said Kenelm was granted administration on the estate.

6:326 26 November. Samuell Chew (g, AA) exhibited the oaths of Robertt Burle & Richard Hill, appraisers of estate of Dr. Robertt Bushby, sworn 9 October

1674. Will of Robertt Bushby (indweller on Severn River, AA). Date: 13 June 1674. Bequests: Francis Jones (daughter of John Jones & Francis), daughter-in-law Francis Degdby,

6:327 brother Thomas Bushby, wife Margueritt Bushby (pregnant). Executrix: wife. Signed: Richard Bushby. Witnesses: James Boyd, Catherin Exton, Mary Polinger. Will proved by James Boyd & Mary Polinger on 10 November 1674.

6:328 last November. William Hopkins for Jane Heliard widow of Daniell Heliard (AA) was granted administration on his estate. Said Jane can't travel to the Office. Appraisers: William Cockey, Bernard Egelstone. Nathaniell Heathcoate (g, AA) to administer oath.

Mary Lile relict & administratrix of Michael Farmer (CV) exhibited accounts. She retained her 1/3rds & gave security to pay residue to her children: Michael, Mary, Elisabeth Farmer.

6:329 Alice Goulson relict & administratrix of James Godscrosse (CV) exhibited accounts. Distribution: her 1/3rds. She gave security to pay residue to her children (now living).

Henry Sewell (AA) exhibited summons to Elisabeth Warner, Johanna Sewall, and the witnesses to the will of James Warner (dec'd). Said Henry petitioned to have will proved. Said Elisabeth Warner did not appear. Said Henry was granted continuance.

4 December. Thomas Marsh (KE) executor of Jacob Neale (chirurgeon, AA) exhibited accounts.

6:330 No widow or creditors. Discharge was granted.

Richard Hill (g, AA) for Dorothy Lusby (widow of Robertt Lusby (AA)) & Jacob Lusby (son & heir of said dec'd) executors, was granted administration on his estate. Widow is unable to travel. Nathaniell Heathcote (g) to prove will

by sole surviving witness; other witness
is dec'd. Appraisers: William Harris,
Sr., William Farguson. Said Heathcote
to administer oath.

John Vanhak (CE) was granted
administration on estate of John Allen
(CE). Said John is unable to travel to
the Office.

6:331   Appraisers: John James, Abraham Wild
(g). Thomas Howell to administer oath.

John Allen (CH) administrator of
Nicholas Solsby (CH) exhibited an
additional inventory.

Sara Vaughan relict & administratrix of
Richard Russell (SM) was granted
continuance.

John Allen (CH) administrator of William
Jackson (CV) petitioned for

6:332   John Rowsby & Spencer Hailes to appraise
additional estate. Christopher Rowsby
(g) to administer oath.

Richard Hill (g, AA) exhibited oath of
Ellenor Fargison administratrix & relict
of Thomas Phelps (AA), sworn 10 November
1674. Also oath of appraisers
(gentlemen, AA) Cornelius Howard & Henry
Ridgely, sworn same day.

Inventory of William Hapwate (AA) was
exhibited, by appraisers Marin duVall &
John Gray.

6:333   12 December. Philip Lynes (CH) for Jane
Lee widow of James Lee (CH) was granted
administration on his estate.
Administratrix cannot travel to the
Office. Appraisers: Alexander White,
Robertt Downs. Zachary Wade (g, CH) to
administer oath.

Philip Lynes (CH) was granted
administration on estate of John Place
(SM), as greatest creditor. Security:
Mr. Benjamin Rozer. Thomas Mathews (g,
CH) to take bond. Appraisers: Justinian
Funnis, Richard Edlin. Capt. William
Boreman (SM) to administer oath.

6:334 13 December. John Beamon (AA) was granted administration on estate of Arthur Briscoe (AA), who died with none of blood to administer estate. Said John is unable to travel to the Office. Capt. William Burgesse (AA) to take the bond. Appraisers: Henry Stockett, Richard Tydings (g).

15 December. William Chadborne (CE) for Elisabeth Pyke relict of William Pyke (AA) was granted administration on his estate.

6:335 Said Elisabeth is unable to travel to the Office. Richard Hill (g, AA) to administer oath. Appraisers: Thomas Watkins, John Edwards.

William Lawrence (g, KE) exhibited the oath of Tobias Wells & Isaack Winchester, appraisers of estate of George Harris (KE), sworn 3 December 1674. Inventory was exhibited.

6:336 Robertt Burle (g, AA) exhibited oath of Dr. William Jones & John Beamon, appraisers of estate of John Norwood (AA) & estate of Ann Boyd (AA, relict of said Norwood), sworn 26 November 1674. Inventories were exhibited.

Sarah Vaughan relict & administratrix of Richard Russell (SM) exhibited accounts.

William Chadborne (CE) who married relict of Richard Foxon (BA) exhibited accounts. Distribution to: widow (1/3rd), 3 sons.

6:337 Elisabeth Gardner (SM) widow of Capt. Luke Gardner (SM) exhibited an additional inventory.

William Robinson (DO) administrator of John Taylor (DO) exhibited accounts.

John Stone (g, CH) exhibited inventory of Joseph Harrison.

John Allen (CH) administrator of Nicholas Solsby (CH) exhibited accounts.

18 December. John Currer (KE)
administrator of John Currer, Sr.
(grocer, city of London, ENG) exhibited
accounts. Administrator to retain
residue for next of kin.

6:338   Michael Miller (KE) administrator of
Henry Lamb (KE) exhibited accounts.

Michael Miller (KE) administrator of
John Steevens (KE) exhibited accounts.

20 December. James Boyd (AA)
administrator of his wife Anne Boyd late
Anne Norwood relict & administratrix of
Capt. John Norwood (AA) exhibited
accounts. Distribution (Capt. Norwood)
to: accountant for widow (1/3rd),
orphans.

6:339   Tobias Wells (KE) executor of Mary Pine
(KE) exhibited accounts.

6:340   4 January. Mary Keely (AA) widow of
John Keely (AA) exhibited his will,
proved by William Currer & Robertt
Husbands. Will of John Keely (AA).
Bequests: wife Mary Keely 1/3rd.
Residue to: children. Plantation "My
Quarter" & 100 a. on Potapscoe River to
be sold.

6:341   Executrix: wife Mary Keely. Date: 25
November 1674. Witnesses: William
Currer, Robertt Husbands. Said Mary was
granted administration. Appraisers: Mr.
Richard Hill, John Beamon. Robertt
Burle to administer oath.

Elisabeth Preston (CV) widow of Thomas
Preston (CV) exhibited his will
(unsigned). Samuell Chew, Esq. (AA) to
prove said will.

6:342   8 January. Thomas Turner administrator
of Nathaniell Stinchecombe (AA) is
"paralitick". Continuance was granted.

11 January. Henry Sewell (AA) who
married Johanna Sewell sole daughter &
heir of James Warner (AA) exhibited the
commission to Nathaniell Heathcoate (g,
AA) to swear Elisabeth Warner widow &

executrix, but she didn't show. Date: 5 January 1674. She was found in contempt & refusal of executorship.

6:343   Administration is granted to next of kin: Johanna Sewell. She is unable to travel to the Office. Said Heathcoate to administer oath.

12 January. John Pile (p, Sarum, SM) was granted administration on estate of Thomas Stanley (Sarum, SM), who died died childless & unmarried. Appraisers (SM): James Boulin, Thomas Simpson. Capt. William Boreman to administer oath.

6:344   15 January. Marke Cordea (g, Crosse Mannor, SM) administrator of Thomas Covent (Britton's Bay, SM) exhibited accounts.

20 January. Stephen Murty (Newtowne, SM) exhibited will of Francis Selo (taylor, SM), proved by Morgan Jones. Will of Francis Selo. Bequests: Stephen Murty.

6:345   List of debts: Pope Alvin, Col. John Jarboe, John Warrick, James Pattison, John Angell, Daniell Hammon. Bequests: son in VA, Brien Daly & his son. Date: 7 January 1674. Witnesses: Morgan Jones, William Asbeston. Said Murty was granted administration.

23 January. Elisabeth Stappleford (TA) widow of Robertt Stappleford was granted administration on his estate,

6:346   who died leaving widow & 3 small children. Appraisers: Henry Alexander, Patrick Mullikin.

Elisabeth Gardner (SM) relict & administratrix of Capt. Luke Gardner was granted continuance.

6:347   Kenelm Cheseldyn attorney for Jonathon Squire (SM) administrator of Dr. John Morecroft (SM) was granted continuance.

6 February. Richard Rawlins (AA) was granted administration on estate of John Venals, who died childless & unmarried.

Security: Henry Pierpoint. Appraisers
(AA): Patrick Dunkin, William Frizell.
Richard Hill (g, AA) to administer oath.

6:348 8 February. John Laws (SO) who married
relict of John Nelson (SO) exhibited
accounts. Said Laws to pay orphans of
the dec'd.

6:349 9 February. Thomas Bland for Damorus
Bland (AA) relict & executrix of
Nicholas Wyatt (AA) was granted
continuance.

Richard Walters (TA) who married relict
of Richard Hacker (TA) exhibited his
will, proved by Thomas Sivell & Richard
Sexby. Will of Richard Hacker.
Bequests: wife Mary Hacker plantation
"Upper Power" 300 a.
6:350 Executrix: wife. Overseers: Thomas
Sivell, Richard Sexby. Date: 24 April
1674. Witnesses: Thomas Sivell, Richard
Sexby. Mary Walters, relict of said
dec'd, is lately dec'd. Said Richard
Walters was granted administration on
his estate. Security: John Edmonds.
Appraisers: John Standley, John
Whittington. Richard Gorsuch (g) to
administer oath.

6:351 Robertt Burle (g, AA) exhibited will of
John Browne (AA). Will of John Browne.
Bequests: wife Mary Browne. Executrix:
wife. Date: 17 November 1673.
Witnesses: John Lederer, Olliver
Stenson. Will proved by Olliver Stenson
on 29 June 1674. Said Lederer who "was
departed out of the County and suddenly
after out of the Province". Mary Browne
was granted administration.
6:352 Robertt Burle exhibited the oath of
William Hopkins & Mathew Howard
(gentlemen), appraisers of John Browne,
sworn 29 June 1674. Inventory was
exhibited.

William Burgesse (g, AA) exhibited oath
of John Beamon as administrator of
Arthur Briscoe (AA), sworn on 13 January
1674. Also oath of appraisers Mr.
Henry Stockett & Richard Tydings, sworn

Court Session: 1674

same day.

Robertt Henley (g, CH) exhibited oath of
John Douglas & William Winshaw,
appraisers of estate of John Harrington
6:353 (CH), sworn 4 January 1674.

Philemon Lloyd (g, TA) exhibited oath of
Andrew Skinner & Jonas Davis, appraisers
of Joseph de la Wood (TA) & William
Retchford (TA), sworn 16 January 1674/5.
Both inventories were exhibited.

William Lawrence (g, KE) exhibited will
of William Head (KE), with probate.
6:354 Also oath of appraisers Cristopher
Goodhand & Disboro Bennett, Sworn 29
October 1674. Executrix Elisabeth Head
was sworn 15 December 1674. Will of
William Head (KE). Bequests:
6:355 son William Head, son-in-law Edward
Kashey. Residue (in equal amounts): son
William (under age 21), daughter Jeane
Head (under age 21), wife Elisabeth.
Executrix: wife. Date: 16 June 1674.
Witnesses: Cristopher Goodhand, Disboro
Bennett. Will proved by Cristopher
Goodhand on 29 October 1674. Will
proved by Disboro Bennett on 2 November
1674.
6:356 Elisabeth Head (widow) was granted
administration.

Henry Sewell (AA) who married the sole
daughter & heir of James Warner (AA)
exhibited his inventory.

Thomas Bland for Damoras Bland (AA)
relict & executrix of Nicholas Wyatt
(AA) petitioned for new LoA, having lost
the previous ones. Granted.

William Coursey (g, TA) exhibited the
will of Sophia Beedle (AA) & petitioned
for Samuell Chew, Esq. (AA) to prove the
will, due to remoteness of habitation of
the witnesses.
6:357 Richard Ewen (g, AA) exhibited that
Sophia Beedle, widow & executrix of
Henry Beedle (AA), lately died, having
made her will, constituting William
Coursey & said Richard Ewen guardians to

her daughter & heir Sophia Beedle
(minor). Said Richard relinquished any
share of the estate.

- Mr. Henry Beedle left his daughter
  Sophia a legacy to be paid by her
  mother his executrix. The said
  executrix died before an inventory
  was made, leaving a will exhibited
  by Mr. Taylor. Mr. William Coursey
  is concerned with the orphan & the
  deponent is to go out of the
  country.

6:358 Signed: Richard Ewen. Date: 4 February
1674/5.

Said William Coursey (TA) was granted
administration on the estates of Henry
Beedle & Sophia Beedle, during the
minority of the orphan Sophia Beedle.

6:359 Will of Sophia Beedle (AA) widow & late
wife of Henry Beedle (g, AA). Bequests:
daughter Sophia Beedle land from her
father & "Beetle's Outlett" (TA) 400 a.
Should my daughter die before age 14 or
marriage, then land from her father to
go to William Coursey, Jr. & "Beetle's
Outlett" to my brother Richard Ewen.

6:360 Executrix: daughter Sophia Beedle.
Guardians & Overseers: my father-in-law
Mr. William Coursey, brother Richard
Ewens. My mother-in-law Mrs. Coursey
with my father-in-law to bring up my
daughter. Date: 30 December 1674.
Witnesses: Thomas Knighton, Benjamin
Lawrence, Hugh Connell, Henry Brady.

6:361 Said William Coursey was granted
administration on estate of Henry
Beedle. Appraisers (TA): Philip
Steevens, William Finny. Richard
Wollman (g, TA) to administer oath.
Appraisers (AA): Mr. Robertt Francklin,
Robertt Connogh. Samuell Chew, Esq. to
administer oath.

6:362 12 February. James Ringold now husband
of Mary Ringold (KE) relict &
administratrix of Edward Burton (KE) was
granted discharge.

James Ringold (KE) one of the executors
of John Ringold (KE) exhibited accounts
for self & Richard Hill. Discharge was

granted.

13 February. Robertt Procter (AA)
exhibited will of Joseph Morley (AA).
Richard Hill (g, AA) to prove will.
Said Proctor was granted administration.
Appraisers: Mr. Cornelius Howard,
Marin. duVall. Richard Hill to
administer oath.

6:363   Robertt Procter (AA) was granted
administration on estate of John Venall.
Appraisers: Cornelius Howard, Marin
duVall. Richard Hill (g, AA) to
administer oath.

Benjamin Rozer (CH) for Alice Walker
(CH) widow of James Walker (CH)
exhibited his will.
6:364   Robertt Henley (g, CH) to prove said
will.

Arthur Carleton brother of Thomas
Carleton (CE) was granted administration
on his estate, for benefit of his widow
& children. Security: Thomas Todd,
Charles James (gentlemen). Appraisers:
Thomas Salmon, John Cox. Capt. Thomas
Howell or John Vanheck (gentlemen) to
administer oath.

6:366   Based on the letter of John Vanheck
dated 6th instant, Elisabeth Waymoth
(CE) was granted administration on
estate of her husband Thomas Waymoth
(CE). Appraisers: Thomas Salmon, John
Cox. Thomas Howell (g, CE) to
administer oath.

Mathew Ward (g, TA) for Thomas Norris
(TA) was granted administration on
estate of John Martin, who died
childless & unmarried. Appraisers:
William Bishop, John Chese. Mathew Ward
(g, TA) to administer oath.

6:367   15 February. John Doxy (SM) was granted
administration on estate of Richard
Chapman (SM), who died childless &
unmarried. Security: Thomas Doxy.
Appraisers: Thomas Doxy, Henry Smith.
Thomas Dent (g, SM) to administer oath.

6:368 17 February. Lidia Solly (SM) widow & administratrix of Benjamin Solley (g, SM) was granted continuance.

Cornelius Howard (g, AA) for John Bruton, Jr. exhibited will of John Bruton, Sr. (AA). Richard Hill (g, AA) to prove the will. Appraisers: John Rockhoult, Henry Sewell. Richard Hill to administer oath.

6:369 Cornelius Howard (g, AA) for Edward Gardner (AA) exhibited will of Dorothy Bruton (AA). The witnesses are unable to travel so far as the Office. Richard Hill (g, AA) to prove the will. Appraisers: John Rockhoult, Henry Sewell. Richard Hill to administer oath.

Cornelius Howard (g, AA) for Elisabeth Sparrow & Salomon (AA) executors of Thomas Sparrow (AA) was granted administration on his estate. William Burgesse (g, AA) to prove the will. Appraisers: Thomas Francis, Nicholas Gassaway.

6:370 Sarah Thomas (AA) exhibited the will of Philip Thomas (AA). Richard Hill (g, AA) to prove the will. Appraisers: Jacob Harnes, John Taylor. Richard Hill to administer oath.

18 February. Richard Wollman (g, TA) executor of Charles Masters (TA) exhibited accounts. Discharge was granted.

6:371 David Browne (g, SO) exhibited the will of John Westlock (SO), proved by William Elgat & Thomas Gillis, on 26 December 1674. Magdalene Westlock was sworn on 19 November 1674. Appraisers James Weatherly & Henry Hayman were sworn 5 December 1674. Inventory was exhibited.

6:372 Samuell Cressy (CH) administrator of John Harrington (CH) exhibited inventory.

Nathaniell Heathcote (AA) exhibited oaths of appraisers of estate of James Warner (AA), sworn on 18 January 1674. Date of warrant: 10 January 1674. Johanna Sewell administratrix was sworn same day.

6:373 John Stansby (CV) one of the executors of Mary Peake (CV) was granted continuance.

Inventory of Dr. Robertt Bushby (AA) was exhibited, by appraisers Robertt Burle & Richard Hill (gentlemen, AA).

Thomas Howell (g, CE) exhibited oath of Mary Frisby widow & executrix of James Frisby, Sr. (CE), sworn 6 December. Also oath of appraisers John Gilbert & John Cox, sworn 20 January 1674. "The cause of the appraisers being so long before they were sworn, was the hardness of the winter." Date: 4 February 1674.

6:374 10 February. William Chadborne (CE) administrator of Richard Foxon (BA) exhibited accounts. Distribution: wife of accountant (her 1/3rd as relict of dec'd). Residue to: 3 sons. Said Chadborne to give security for orphan's estate.

6:375 Discharge was granted.

Robertt Franclin (g) for Susanna Waters (AA) relict & executrix of James White (AA) exhibited accounts. Said Susanna unable to travel to the Office. Said Franclin to obtain oath.

20 October. Elisabeth Foster (TA) widow & executrix of Seth Foster (TA) exhibited his will. Jonathon Sibrey (g, TA) to prove the will. Appraisers: Mr. John Anderton, Edmund Webb. Said Sibrey to administer oath.

6:376 22 February. Sarah Peirse (AA) was granted administration on estate of her husband William Peirse. Said Sarah is unable to travel so far as the Office. Robertt Franclin (g, AA) to take bond. Appraisers: Waller Carre, John Waters.

Said Franclin to administer oath.

6:377 Cornelius Howard (g, AA) administrator
of Robertt Good exhibited accounts.
Discharge was granted.

William Dare (merchant, County Dorset,
ENG, now CV) attorney of William Twisse,
John West, Philip Stansby, & Thomas
Brice (merchants, of afsd city)
creditors to estate of John Parker (CV)
& attorneys of Thomas Hyde (Waymouth,
ENG) & creditor to said estate, tendered
letters of administration proved before
John Wooder, Esq. (Mayor of Waymouth) &
justice of the peace. William Twisse is
merchant of Dorchester, County
Dorchester; John West is merchant of the
same place; Thomas Brice is clothier of
Sordington, County Dorchester;
6:378 Thomas Spicer (g) is from County
Dorchester. They all came & read
articles of agreement & deposed that
John Parker did execute them on 7
November 1670. Also, that Philip
Stansby in the presence of Thomas
Spicer, James Palfry, & William Bird
executed a PoA. Said Philip was very
sick on 24 September 1672. Articles by
John Parker
6:379 (merchant, Crewkhorne, County Somerset)
now living in MD or VA or West India to
William Dare (mercer, Dorchester, County
Dorchester).
6:380 Date: 7 September 1672.
6:381 Witnesses: George Perry, Richard Tucker,
Henry Smart. Said Twisse in the
presence of John Woder (mayor) & William
Bird. Said Stansby in the presence of
James Palfray, Thomas Spicer, & William
Byrd. Articles: mention: ship John of
Waymouth Theophilus Bigatt (commander),
6:382 ship William & John of London John Hoyle
(master).
6:383 Witnesses: Edward Hughe, Thomas Spicer.
6:384 Notice from John Woder, Esq. (Mayor of
Waymouth, Dorset, ENG) that afsd
William, John, & Thomas did deliver
their acts. William Waren (Dorchester),
servant of William Twisse, deposed.
Thomas Spicer (g, Dorset) & James
Palfrey (grocer, Dorset) deposed that

Philip Stansbie (merchant, Dorset) did execute said act. William Byrt also deposed.

6:385   Date: 24 September 1672. Notice by William Twisse (merchant, Dorchester, Dorset), John West (merchant, Dorchester, Dorset), Philip Stansby (merchant, Dorchester, Dorset), & Thomas Brice (clothier, Fordington, Dorset) that John Parker (merchant, Crewkheme, Somerset, now in MD or West India) was lately employed. They issued PoA to William Dare (mercer, Dorchester, Dorset).

6:386   ...

6:387   Date: 17 September 1672. Witnesses (to John West & Thomas Brice): John Woder (mayor), George Perry, Richard Tucker, Henry Smart. Witnesses (to William Twisse): John Woder (mayor), William Byrd. Witnesses (to Philip Stansbie): James Palfrey, Thomas Spicer, William Bird.

6:388   Inventory of Mr. John Parker. Date: October 1670.

6:389   ...

6:390   William Warren, age 21, of Dorchester, Dorset, deposed before John Woder, Esq. (mayor of Waymouth) on 23 September 1672 that, per the order of his master William Twisse (merchant, Dorchester) & his partner John West, in October 1670 the deponent delivered goods expressly for John Parker since gone to VA & shipped on the ship John of Waymouth to VA or MD.

6:391   Thomas Hide (merchant, Waymouth, Dorset) gave PoA to William Dare (merchant, Dorchester, Dorset) to demand of John Parker (merchant, Patuxent). Date: 24 September 1672. Witnesses: George Parrey, John Cox. Will proved 16 December 1672. Signed: C. Calvert.

6:392   William Dare was granted administration on said estate. Appraisers: George Beckwith, Richard Keene. Thomas Sprigg (g) to administer oath.

23 February. Samuell Gibbons (CE) relinquished his rights to estate of Capt. Nicholas Tovey (mariner, CE).

6:393   Witnesses to will of said Nicholas:

Henry Ward, John Moll, John Gilbertt.
Mentions: John Ward (neighbor of dec'd).
Said John Ward petitioned that the will
be proved by Henry Ward & John Moll.

6:394 Will of Nicholas Tovey (mariner, St.
George's Parish, Somersetshire, ENG).
Date: 9 January 1674. Bequests: brother
Robertt Whiting, brother George Whiting,
6:395 brother George Irish, wife Ann Tovey
then to cousin Robertt Whiting, Jr.
house in Bristoll on King St., Samuell
Gibings, wife Ann Tovey. Executrix:
wife. Written at house of Henry Ward
(Elke River, CE). Witnesses: Henry
Ward, John Gilbertt, John Moll.
6:396 Ann Tovey widow & executrix is in ENG.
John Ward was granted administration on
said estate for her. Appraisers: James
Frisby, Jr., John Cox. Capt. Thomas
Howell to administer oath.

James Frisby, Jr. (CE) one of executors
of James Frisby, Sr. (CE) exhibited his
inventory.

24 February. Francis Chissell (KE)
administrator of Richard Morris (KE)
exhibited accounts.

6:397 Nathaniell Heathcote exhibited bond of
Johanna Sewell, William Hopkins, & John
Beamon (AA) on administration of James
Warner (AA). Since said Johanna is a
"femme covert", the bond was returned.
Her husband Henry Sewell & 2 sureties to
provide bond. Thomas Taillor, Esq. to
take the bond. Said Thomas to divide
estate to: administratrix Johanna
Sewell, Elisabeth Warner (widow). Said
Elisabeth to receive per the will.

6:398 Samuell Chew, Esq. (AA) exhibited the
will of Thomas Preston (CV), with
probate. Will of Thomas Preston (CV).
Date: 8 November 1674. Executors: John
Steevens, William Steevens, Jr.
6:399 Bequests: wife Elisabeth Preston
(1/3rd). Residue to: children (1 son, 2
daughters). Will proved by Mr. Henry
Jowles, Richard Benger, & Susanna
Garnett on 8 February 1674.

Court Session: 1674

6:400 3 March. Joseph Tilly (CV) was granted
administration on estate of his wife
Mary Tilly late Mary Little relict &
executrix of John Little (CV) as well as
estate of said John. Appraisers: John
Leatch, John Cobbreth. Edward Keene (g)
to administer oath.

6:401 4 March. Zachary Wade (g, CH) exhibited
LoA of Jane Lee administratrix of her
husband James Lee. Appraisers:
Alexander White, Robertt Downes. Date:
26 February 1674.

John Moll (SM) for Mary Frisby & James
Frisby, Jr. (CE) executors of James
Frisby, Sr. (BA) exhibited that the
dec'd had no debts nor made any legacies
to be paid.
6:402 Capt. Thomas Howell to take oath.
Discharge was granted.

9 March. Mary widow of Lt. Col. John
Jarboe (SM) was granted administration
on his estate. Appraisers: Henry
Spinck, Peter Mills. John Jordain (g)
to administer oath.

10 March. John Smallpeece & William
Newport (SM) exhibited the will of
George Waker (SM) & petitioned to have
the will proved.
6:403 Will of George Waker (p, St. Jerome's,
SM). Bequests: Mr. Lucas, Mrs. Jane
Paine (widow), Isack Paine (eldest son
to Jane Paine (widow)), John Smallpeece,
William Newport.
6:404 Executors: John Smallpeece, William
Newport. Date: July 1674. Witnesses:
Richard Chapman, Robertt Ascoefield.
Will proved by Robertt Scoefield on 10
March 1674. William Newport was granted
administration. John Smallpeece
renounced executorship. Appraisers:
William Claw, Joseph Hackney. William
Calvert, Esq. to administer oath.
6:405 Renunciation by John Smalpeece. Date:
10 March 1674. Witnesses: Jean Jordain,
Michael Rochford.

13 March. John Paty (carpenter, Dublin,
Ireland) exhibited will of Henry

Page 157

6:406 Banister (St. George's River, SM), & petitioned that the will be proved by Thomas Dent (g) & Nicholas Rawlin. Will of Henry Banister (St. George's River, SM). Bequests: relation John Paty. Date: 18 February 1674. Signed: Henry Bannister. Witnesses: Thomas Dent, Nich. Rawlins. Will proved 13 March 1674.

6:407 15 March. Magdalene O'Bryan (CH) widow of Mathew O'Bryan (CH) exhibited his will, and was granted administration on his estate. Benjamin Rozer (g) to prove the will, & ensure that Benedict Marchegaiy (overseer) does not meddle. Appraisers: George Hinson, Richard Jones. John Stone (g) to administer oath.

6:408 16 March. Richard Whitton (CE) exhibited the will of Richard Leake (BA) & was granted administration on his estate. Abraham Wild (g) to prove the will. Appraisers: William Dunkerton, William Price. Said Abraham to administer oath.

17 March. Richard Tilghman (TA) was granted administration on estate of John Yates (TA). Appraisers: William Bishop, Richard Jones. Mathew Ward (g) to administer oath.

6:409 20 March. Joachim Guibert (SM) administrator of Dr. Luke Barbier (SM) exhibited accounts. Distribution: John Blomfeild who married the relict (1/3rd). Residue: 6 orphans.

John Clarke (CV) who married relict & executrix of John Elly (CV), & said executrix is dec'd, exhibited accounts. Discharge was granted.

6:410 23 March. Dr. John Stansby (CV) one of the executors of Mary Peake (CV) widow & executrix of George Peake (CV) exhibited accounts of said George. Continuance was granted.

Court Session: 1674

24 March. Thomas Waikfield (CH) executor of Jonathon Marler (CH) exhibited receipts, in accordance with accounts filed on 23 October last. Discharge was granted.

Court Session: 1675

6:411 25 March 1675. Thomas Armiger (BA) who married relict of Francis Trippos (BA) exhibited accounts. Discharge was granted.

Col. Nathaniell Uty (BA) exhibited the will of John Hall (BA), with probate. Will of John Hall (BA). Date: 21 August 1674. Executor: Bernard Uty. Bequests: said Bernard. List of debts: James Miles.

6:412 Said Bernard to pay Dr. John desJardins & Capt. George Wells. Witnesses: Thomas Greene, Elisabeth Bowden, Joanna Goldsmith. Will proved by Joanna Goldsmith on 3 January 1674. Signed: Johanna Goldsmith. Appraisers: George Wells, Samuell Boston (gentlemen, BA).

6:413 Col. Nathaniell Utie (BA) exhibited accounts of Henry Haslewood on estate of John Collett (BA).

27 March. John Paty (carpenter, Dublin, Ireland) executor of Henry Bannister (SM) was granted administration. Securities: Thomas Dent (g, SM), Henry Hull (g, SM). Thomas Dent (g, SM) exhibited oath of Patrick Forrest & John Macky, appraisers of Henry Bannister (SM), sworn 15 March 1674.

6:414 20 March. Robertt Henley (g) exhibited will of James Walker, with probate. Witnesses: John Allen, Thomas Lomax. The executrix Alce was granted administration. Date: 15 March 1674. Will of James Walker (CH).

6:415 Bequests: John Newby (in service of Mrs. Bridget Legate) his passage to ENG & to be conveyed to my cousin James Docker (Kendall, Westmoreland), Henry Randall (p, CH). Executrix: wife Alce Walker, provided my cousin James Docker does not

come to the Province within 10 years.
If he does, then he is co-executor with
wife. Further bequests: wife Alce &
next heir of her body "Docker's Delight"
100 a. in CH

6:416   should he not come or die with out
issue, then the land to go on behalf of
the Protestant Religion. Overseers:
Capt. Josias Fendall, Thomas Lomax.
Date: 31 October 1673. Witnesses: John
Allen, Thomas Lomax. Will proved by
John Allen on 10 March 1674. Will
proved by Thomas Lomax on 13 March 1674.
Said Alce Walker sworn on 13 March 1674.

6:417   last March. Michael Higguen (CV)
executor of William Diveare (CV)
exhibited accounts. Discharge was
granted.

8 April. Francis Wine (CH) executor of
William Marshall (CH) exhibited
accounts. Discharge was granted.

10 April. Henry Parker (TA)
administrator of John Barnes (TA)
exhibited accounts. Discharge was
granted.

12 April. Alice Solley (TA) widow of
George Solley (chirurgeon, TA) renounced
executorship.

6:418   John Pitt to be appointed. Date: 5
April 1674. Witnesses: Thomas Anderson,
Robert Mynott. Signed: Alice Soley.
Samuell Hatton (TA) was granted
administration on said estate.
Securities (TA): John Pitt, Henry
Parker. Appraisers: John Henrick,
Nicholas Bartlett. Richard Gorsuch (g)
to administer oath.

6:419   13 April. Thomas Dent (SM) exhibited
that William Dutton (merchant) was on a
voyage from ENG & fell sick & died
shortly after his arrival at Patuxent
River at the house of Richard Keene. He
declared his will before Capt. Leonard
Webber (commander of ship Golden Lyon):
- Made on 21 March 1674. Bequests:
  sister & 2 nieces (testator & a
  brother married 2 sisters. His own

wife died & left him no children.
His brother's wife died & left his
brother 2 daughters--the nieces.),
Mrs. Masters (his kinsman's wife)
that came in the said ship, Mr.
Edward Lascelles (merchant, London).

6:420 Date: 12 April 1674. Capt. Leonard
Webber swore to the validity on 5 May
1675. Thomas Dent was granted
administration on behalf of the sister &
nieces. Appraisers: George Mackall,
William Hatton. Henry Hide (g) to
administer oath.

Richard Gorsuch (g, TA) exhibited
inventory of Robertt Stapleford (TA) &
the bond of Elisabeth Stapleford the
widow & administratrix. Date: 8 March
1674.

6:421 Philip Lynes (CH) administrator of John
Place (CH) could not find the commission
to Thomas Mathews (g) to swear oath of
administration. Continuance was
granted.

19 April. Garrett Vansweringen (g, SM)
administrator of William Fellowell (also
William Felowell, CV) exhibited
inventory & accounts.

6:422 Thomas Knighton (AA) was granted
administration on estate of Ewen Davis
(AA), who died childless & unmarried.
Samuell Chew, Esq. (AA) to take the
bond. Appraisers: John Moonshott,
William Sivick.

Brian O'Daly & Constantine O'Kiefe (SM)
executors of Roger Shehee (SM) exhibited
accounts. Discharge was granted.

20 April. Thomas Dent (g, SM) exhibited
will of Jeremiah Dinkenson (CH).
Benjamin Rozer (g, CH) to prove.
6:423 Appraisers (CH): Mr. Zachary Wade, John
Warde. Benjamin Rozer to administer
oath.

John Larkin (inholder, the Ridge, AA)
exhibited the will of William Powell
(taylor, BA). Said William was a

batchelor & has no relations in the Province. He died last October. Said Larkin was granted administration.

6:424 Capt. William Burgesse (AA) to administer oath. Appraisers (BA): William Yorke, William Hollis. George Wells (g, BA) to administer oath.

Elisabeth relict of William Andrews (AA) exhibited his will. Robertt Franclin (g, AA) to prove it. Appraisers: John Waters, Thomas Pratt.

Nathaniell Stiles (high sheriff, CV) exhibited that Francis Barnes (CV) was killed by the fall of a tree. Charles James (coroner, CV) has seized the goods of said dec'd. John Coxe & Axell Still cited the contents of a chest.

6:425 21 April. Mathew Howard (g, AA) & Cornelius Howard (g, AA) exhibited that Thomas Turner (AA) is dec'd, & that they were bondsmen to him on the estate of Thomasin Stinchecomb widow & executrix of Nathaniell Stinchecomb (AA). Said Mathew & Cornelius were granted administration on said Turner's estate. Appraisers (AA): Ralph Hawkins, William Hawkins.

6:426 Patrick Dunkin & William Frizell (AA) appraisers of estate of John Venals (AA) exhibited inventory.

Nathaniell Heathcote (g, AA) exhibited that he had a commission to swear Joane Heliard widow of Daniell Heliard (AA). The oath was not effected due to bodily weakness of said Joane & her indisposition. Also, the appraisers & bondsmen were not available. Said Joane was granted continuance.

Edward Dorsey (AA) has "intermeddled" with the estate of Nicholas Wyatt (AA) &
6:427 Damoras Bland relict & executrix of said dec'd. Continuance was granted.

Thomas Howell (g, CE) exhibited 2 bonds of John Vanheck & one of widow Waymouth & Abraham Wilde (burgesse). Said Thomas

had a "sore distemper" since October &
was incapable of conducting business.
Abraham Wilde & John James were sworn on
16 March as appraisers of the estate of
John Allen. Thomas Salmon & John Coxe
were sworn on the same day as appraisers
of the estate of Capt. Thomas Carleton,
estate of Henry Knight, & estate of
Thomas Waymouth. Date: 6 April 1675.

6:428 Daniell Murphy (SM) exhibited that Peter
Robertts (SM) is dec'd. Anne Robertts
widow of said dec'd was granted
administration. Appraisers: Edward
Konnerie, William Sommerhill. William
Rosewell (g, SM) to administer oaths.

Thomas Hinson (g, TA) exhibited oath of
f William Bishop & John Chafe,
appraisers of the estate of Richard
Steevens (TA).

6:429 Securities: Richard Jones, Ralph
Blackhall. Date: 11 April 1675.
Inventory was exhibited.

Richard Tilghman (TA) one of the
executors of Thomas South (TA) exhibited
inventory.

John Philips (DO) who married relict of
John Felton (DO) exhibited accounts.
Discharge was granted.

Richard Owen (DO) one of the executors
of Samuel Spicer exhibited accounts.
John Raven (the other executor) was
unable to come.

6:430 Discharge was granted.

Nicholas Gassaway & Richard Tydings (AA)
appraisers of estate of John Shaw
exhibited inventory.

22 April. William Coursey (g, TA)
administrator of estates of Henry &
Sophia Beedle (AA) exhibited
inventories.

Elisabeth Foster (TA) widow & executrix
of Seth Foster (TA) exhibited that Mr.
John Anderton (one of the appraisers)
has gone to ENG. New appraisers: Mr.
William Hambleton, Edmund Webb.

6:431   Jonathon Sibrey (g) to administer oath.

24 April. Capt. Edward Tarleton (commander of the ship Dublin Merchant) exhibited that Robertt Barton (steward of said ship) is dec'd. Said Edward was granted administration.

William Hemsley (TA) administrator of William Bennett (TA) exhibited inventory & accounts.

6:432   Discharge was granted.

William Hemsley (TA) administrator of John Whaley exhibited accounts. Discharge was granted.

William Hemsley (TA) exhibited that John Drywood (TA) is dec'd. He was a batchelor & has no relation in the Province, & has been dec'd almost 1 year. Said Hemsley was granted administration. Appraisers: Andrew Skinner, William Jones. Richard Wollman (g, TA) to administer oath.

6:433   27 April. Mellow Claes Base (mariner, NY) exhibited that his father Clase Mellow Base drowned going to NY. Said Mellow was granted administration. Security: Garrett Vansweringen.

28 April. Roger Baker (CV) administrator of Henry Jubbar (Poole, Dorset, ENG) exhibited that Thomas Vaughan (TA) detains chattel belonging to said estate. Continuance was granted.

6:434   last April. Robertt Burle (g, AA) exhibited that John Bemon (AA), one of the appraisers of the estate of John Keely, is gone to ENG. New appraisers: William Slade, Richard Hill.

James Frisby & John Cox (CE) appraisers of estate of Nicholas Tovey (mariner, CE) exhibited inventory.

Dianna James (SM) exhibited will of Abell James. Witnesses: William Kennedy, John Powell.

6:435 Will of Abell James (SM). Date: 24
March 1674/5. Bequests: wife Dianna
James & son Charles James, Charles Mills
(servant). Executrix: wife. Patrick
Forrest to assist. Witnesses: William
Kennedy, John Powell.
6:436 Said Dianna was granted administration.
Appraisers: Patrick Forrest, William
Kennedy. Thomas Dent (g) to administer
oath.

1 May. Mary Oderon widow of Clory
Oderon (TA) exhibited his will.
Witnesses: Robertt Jenkenson, John Cox.
Will of Clory Oderon. Bequests:
son-in-law John Dill,
6:437 wife Mary Oderon. Date: 2 November
1674. Witnesses: Robertt Jenkenson,
John Cox. Said Mary was granted
administration. Appraisers: Robertt
Jenkenson, John Cox. Richard Gorsuch
(g) to administer oath.

3 May. Richard Moore (KE) for Johanna
Walton (KE) exhibited that her husband
John Walton is dec'd.
6:438 Said Johanna was granted administration.
Appraisers: Richard Moore, Isack
Winchester. Arthur Wright (g) to
administer oath.

Richard Moore (KE) administrator of John
Browne (KE) exhibited accounts.
Discharge granted.

John Wright (KE) executor of John
Lawrence (KE) exhibited accounts.
Discharge was granted.

6:439 Thomas Turner (AA, now dec'd) was coming
to exhibit accounts on estate of
Nathaniell & Thomasin Stinchecomb.
Mathew Howard & Cornelius Howard
(gentlemen, AA) to inventory estate of
said Turner, who was possessed of estate
of Paul Dorrell & his sister. Said
Mathew & Cornelius to view accounts of
said Nathaniell & Thomasin. Inventory
to be made in presence of Mr. Robertt
Burle or any other justice.

4 May. Clement Haly (SM) exhibited will of John Robertts (SM), proved by Edward Connerie.

6:440 Will of John Robertts (p SM). Bequests: Governor, Joshua Guibert, Mr. John Rolte, John Robertts (under age 16, son of Peter Robertts) to be kept by William Sommerhill & Clement Haly, Clement Haly.

6:441 Date: 9 April 1675. Witnesses: Edward Connerie, J. Guibertt. Said Haly was granted administration. Appraisers: Edward Connerie, Thomas Carvill. William Rosewell (g) to administer oath.

Margueritt Bird (CV) widow of Charles Bird (CV) was granted administration on his estate. Appraisers: Major Thomas Brooke, Raphael Haywood.

6:442 Baker Brooke, Esq. to administer oath. Security: Cuthbert Fenwick.

Margery Cooke (TA) widow of John Cooke (TA) was granted administration on his estate. Appraisers: Thomas Norris, John Broderiff. Jonathon Sibrey (g, TA) to administer oath.

6:443 Mary Maxwell (TA) widow of Alexander Maxwell (TA) was granted administration on his estate. Appraisers: Thomas Norris, John Broderiff. Jonathon Sibrey (g, TA) to administer oath.

Thomas Overton (BA) exhibited will of Bernard Utie (BA). Col. Nathaniell Utie to prove.

6:444 Will of Bernard Utie. Bequests: cousin Jeane Overton plantation & chattel with Mathew Sherisinton (?), Edward Jaxson, cousin John Overton, Henry Haslewood 125 a. the plantation he lives on, cousin Nathaniell Overton.

6:445 Executor: brother Thomas Overton. Date: 3 April 1675. Witnesses: Edward Jaxson, Richard Goodwine. Said Overton was granted administration. Appraisers: Henry Haslewood, John Jones. Col. Nathaniell Utie to administer oath.

6:446 Mary Harmer (BA) exhibited will of Johanna Spry (BA). Thomas Long (g) to prove will. Said Harmer was granted

administration. Appraisers: William
Hollis, William Yorke. Thomas Long (g)
to administer oath.

Sarah Hancock executrix of Benjamin
Hancock (TA) was granted administration
on his estate. Edward Roe (TA) to prove
the will. Witnesses: Thomas Vaughan,
William Smith. Said Roe to administer
oath.

6:447 Samuell Hatton (TA) administrator of
George Soley (TA) exhibited inventory.

Joseph Tilly (CV) administrator of John
Litle & Mary relict of said John Little
(CV) exhibited inventories of their
estates.

Richard Gorsuch (g, TA) exhibited oaths
of John Hendrick & Nicholas Bartlett,
appraisers of estate of George Soley
(TA), sworn 20 April 1675.

5 May. Samuell Boston (high sheriff,
BA) exhibited that Mary Boston his late
wife late Mary Goldsmith relict &
executrix of Capt. George Goldsmith

6:448 (BA), is dec'd. Said Samuell was
granted administration on both estates.
Security: Nathaniell Stiles (high
sheriff, CE). Appraisers (BA): Henry
Haslewood, John Ives. George Wells (g)
to administer oath.

6 May. Meverell Hulse (CH) was granted
administration on estate of Thomas
Greenfield (CH). Benjamin Rozer (CH) to
prove said will.

6:449 Appraisers: John Coutes, Alexander
Smith. Benjamin Rozer to administer
oath.

Edward Dorsey (AA) exhibited that the
warrant to sheriff (AA) to summon
Cornelius Howard, Richard & Waikfield,
Robertt Gudgeon, Nicholas Sheppard &
John Watkins, Morris Barker, & John
Browne to appear & testify regarding the
revocation of the will of Nicholas
Wyatt, arrived too late for the said
persons to appear. A commission is
granted to Nathaniell Heathcote (g) to

take their oaths.

6:450   Alice Walker (CH) widow & executrix of
James Walker (CH) was granted
administration on his estate.
Appraisers (CH): John Douglasse,
Humphrey Warren. Robertt Henley (g) to
administer oath.

Will of Mathew O'Brian (CH) was
exhibited.

7 May. William Slade (AA) exhibited the
will of Quenton Parker (BA), proved by
William Corum (witness).
6:451   Col. Nathaniell Utie to take oaths of
the other 2 witnesses. Will of Quenton
Parker (BA). Date: 16 January 1674.
Bequests: daughter Elisabeth Parker
(under age 13) 180 a. going to the
plantation of William Slead
6:452   on the Patapseco River & 130 a.
adjoining said land, Mrs. Margueritt
Penry, Anthony Henderick, James Smith,
William Corum. Executor: William Slade.
Witnesses: Anthony Henderick, Herman
Williams, William Corum.
6:453   William Slade was granted
administration. Appraisers (BA): Henry
Haslewood, James Ives. Said Utie to
administer oath. Appraisers (AA): Ralph
Hawkins, William Hawkins. Robertt Burle
(g) to administer oath.

Mary Norman (TA) widow of Edward Norman
(TA) renounced her portion of his
estate.
6:454   Date: 7 May 1675. Witness: Michael
Rochford. Ralph Blackhall (TA) was
granted administration on said estate.
Appraisers: Thomas Jones, Thomas Hinson.
Mathew Ward (g) to administer oath.
6:455   Hanna Sinkler (CV) widow & executrix of
John Sinkler (CV) was granted
administration on his estate. Edward
Keen (g) to prove will. Appraisers:
Mordecai Hunton, Thomas Bancks. Said
Keen to administer oath.

Richard Hill (g, AA) exhibited inventory
of Dorothy Bruton (AA).

6:456 10 May. Letter by Richard Flaws (chirurgeon) on the ship Dublin Merchant of Liverpoole (Capt. Edward Tarleton): To: Dr. James Fountaine. Date: 28 March 1675. Bequests: said Dr., his wife. Mentions: John Petty (carpenter), William Snallum (smith, Cooke St.), John Radmore (strongwaterman, Bredstreet, Toberbony). Bequests: Charles Tomson, Christofer (your servant). Will proved by Mary Cheverill, that she saw the dec'd deliver it to Henry Hull (g).

6:457 She also saw the dec'd give chattel to John Patty to be delivered to said Capt. Edward Tarleton for his wife, Thomas Godard, Mr. William Hays, William HoeRobbin (the cabin boy), Mr. Henry Hull, Clement Cheverill, Nicholas Rawlins. John Paty is to deliver chattel to: Mary Cheverill, Thomas Blount, Nicholas Rawlins.

6:458 An account of what was sold to: William Greene (of Pocamoke) on 31 December 1674, Dr. William Harper on 7 January, Thomas Bennett on 27 February 1674, Mr. Charles Hutchins (of Manticock).

6:459 John Paty gave oath on the accounts. Date: 10 May 1675. Capt. Edward Tarleton (of Liverpoole, commander of the Dublin Merchant) was granted administration on the estate. Appraisers: Thomas Goddard, John Anderton. Mentions: Mary Cheverill, John Paty, Dr. James Fountaine (Dublin, Ireland).

6:460 11 May. Samuell Chew, Esq. (AA) exhibited will of John Meers (AA). Maj. William Burgesse to prove said will.

6:461 James Lewis (SM) exhibited will of Benjamin Hunton (SM), proved by Thomas Potter & John Steevens. Will of Benjamin Hunton. Bequests: Thomas Vaughan & James Lewis (SM) to pay debts. Date: 1675. Witnesses: Thomas Potter, John Stevens. James Lewis was granted administration. Appraisers: Thomas Potter, John Stevens.

6:462 Thomas Vaughan renounced executorship. Date: 11 May 1675. Witnesses: Michael

Rochford, Thomas Potter.

12 May. Capt. Edward Tarleton (Liver
Poole, ENG) administrator of Richard
Flaws exhibited inventory.

14 May. Thomas Walker (SO) executor of
William Morgan (SO) was granted
administration on his estate. William
Stevens (SO) to prove the will.
6:463 Appraisers: William Planner, Charles
Hall. Said Stephens to administer oath.

William Steevens (g, SO) to prove will
of Patrick Robinson (SO). Executors:
Robertt Cattlin & Anne his wife.
Appraisers: William Planner, Charles
Hall. Said Stevens to administer oath.
Delivery to: Robertt Ridgely.
6:464 Richard Hill (AA) exhibited oath of
Thomas Watkins & John Grey (in place of
John Edwards), appraisers of estate of
William Pike (AA), sworn 25 February
1674. Administratrix Elisabeth Pike.
was sworn same day.

Emanuell Ratcliff (SM) executor of
Daniell Gover (SM) exhibited accounts.
Discharge was granted.

6:465 Henry Hide (g, SM) one of the
administrators of John Lawson (SM)
exhibited 2 general discharges: Jane
Ryder (widow, Poplar Hill, one of the
daughters), Peter Carwardin who married
Dorcas Lawson (the other daughter).
Randolph Hanson (the other
administrator) is unable to come.
6:466 Discharge by Jane Ryder. Date: 5
February 1670/1. Witnesses: Faith
Johnson, Richard Ryder, Sr. Discharge
by Peter Carwardin (p Poplar Hill).
6:467 Date: 22 November 1673. Witnesses:
Richard Hatton, Robertt Hatton, William
Harris.

Elisabeth Head (KE) widow & executrix of
William Head exhibited inventory.

19 May. Robertt Burle (g, AA) &
Cornelius Howard (g, AA) exhibited
inventories of

6:468 Nathaniell Stinchecomb & Thomasin Stinchecomb (AA) & inventory of Thomas Turner executor of said Thomasin.

6:469 Orphans of said Stinchcombe were remanded to his care. Date: 19 May 1675. Paul Dorrell has claim to estate of Thomas Turner as heir.

John Guilbert (CE) administrator of Roger Robertts (CE) was granted continuance.

6:470 Philemon Lloyd (TA) administrator of Henry Hawkins was granted continuance.

John Bowles & John Courte (CH) administrators of Thomas Bull exhibited accounts.

Nathaniell Heathcote (g, AA) exhibited will of Robertt Lusby (AA). Will of Robertt Lusby (AA). Date: 21 July 1673.

6:471 Bequests: son Jacob Lusby (under age 21) 50 a. on north side of Anne Arundel Creek near Ferry Creek, 2 sons Zachariah (under age 21) & Robertt (under age 21) plantation "George Towne" after the death of their mother my wife Dorothy Lusby,

6:472 daughter Sarah Lusby (under age),

6:473 wife Dorothy Lusby. Executors: wife, son Jacob. Witnesses: Phill. Thomas, Sr., Richard Hill. Dorothy Lusby was granted administration. Date: 4 December last. Will proved by Richard Hill (surviving witness) on 4 December last.

6:474 Appraisers: William Harnesse, Sr., William Ferguson sworn on 4 December last. Date: 26 February 1674/5

Thomas Dent (g, SM) administrator of William Ditton (merchant, ENG & Patuxent River, CV) exhibited inventory. Henry Hyde (g, SM) exhibited oaths of George Marshall & William Hutton, appraisers of said inventory, sworn 15 April 1675.

6:475 Thomas Dent (g, SM) exhibited oath of Thomas Doxey & Henry Smith, appraisers of Richard Chapman (SM), sworn 2 March 1674/5. Inventory was exhibited.

6:476 Robertt Burle (g, AA) exhibited oath of Ralph & William Hawkins, appraisers of Nath. & Thomasin Stinchecomb & of Thomas Turner executor of said Stinchecomb. Appraisers were sworn on 10 May 1675. Date: 12 May 1675. Inventories were exhibited.

Robertt Burle (g, AA) exhibited inventory of George Dorrell (AA). Also exhibited was the bond of Thomas Turner executor of said Dorrell.

Anne Arundel County Court. 8 November 1664. Present: Sam. Withers, Roger Grose, Richard Ewen, Francis Holland, Capt. John Norwood, Robertt Burle, Capt. Tho. Besson, George Puddington, Anthony Salway, Ralph Williams.

6:477 Court ordered that the estates be appraised & that Mr. Robertt Burle & Mr. George Puddington make a division of said estate on the 21st instant, & that Thomas Turner is to have tuition of the orphans & their estates until they come of age. Signed: Theo. Lewis.

Thomas Turner stood indebted to the Court. Date: 11 September 1666. Residue due to: Paul Dorrell & Sarah Dorrell (orphans of George Dorrell (dec'd)).

6:478 Signed: Thomas Turner. Witnesses: Nath. Heathcote, Rich. Boughton.

Thomas Taylor, Esq. (AA) exhibited a division of the estate of James Warner (AA): Elisabeth Warner (widow), Johanna Sewell (sole daughter) who married Henry Sewell.

6:479
6:480 ...
Date: 20 March 1674/5. Signed: Henry Sewell, Johanna Sewell. Witnesses: William Burgesse, Nathaniell Heathcote.

Mary Davis (AA) widow of Ewen Davis (AA) renounced administration on his estate. Date: 5 May. Witnesses: Alexander Humphrey, Charles Newman.

Samuell Chew, Esq. (AA) exhibited oath of John Moonshott & William Sineck, appraisers of estate of Ewen Davis (AA), sworn 7 May 1675.

6:481   Samuell Chew, Esq. (AA) exhibited oath of Thomas Knighton administrator of Ewen Davis, sworn 5 May 1675.

Thomas Salmon & John Cox (CE) administrators of Thomas Waymouth (CE) exhibited inventory.

Inventory of John Allen (CE) was exhibited, by appraisers Abraham Wilde (g, CE) & John James (g, CE).

6:482   Thomas Salmon & John Cox (CE) administrators of Henry Knight exhibited inventory.

Thomas Howell (g, CE) exhibited bond of the City of Bristoll by John Ward (CE) administrator of Nicholas Tovey. Said Ward was sworn on 16 March 1675. Date: 14 April 1675.

Samuell Chew, Esq. (AA) exhibited oath of Mr. Robertt Franclin & Robertt Connogh (AA) administrators of Henry & Sophia Beedle,

6:483   sworn on 18 March 1674/5. Benjamin Rozer (high sheriff, CH) administrator of Robertt Prouse (CH) exhibited inventory.

24 May. Examination of Capt. John Jordaine (SM) regarding the nuncupative will of Lt. Col. John Jarboe (SM) made on 9 March last. An earlier will has been found.

6:484   The judge ruled that the former will was revoked & Mary Jarboe (the widow) was granted administration on the estate. On 9 March last, John Jordain deposed that on 4 March instant, he went to the house of Lt. Col. John Jarboe & suggested that said Jarboe make his will. Jarboe sent for Mr. Edward Clarke, indicating that he intended to alter his earlier will because he had some children born since then. His daughter had some land to be made good by Marke Cordea & Walter Hall (gentlemen). Therefore, his own land

Page 173

was to be divided between his 3 sons:
John Jarboe the land where he then lived
& 150 a. where William Medley lived;

6:485 Peter Jarboe 300 a. bought of Henry
Aspinall by St. Lawrence's Creek on
Britton's Bay; to Henry Jarboe 500 a. on
the branches of St. Lawrence's Creek; to
Mary Jarboe (daughter) chattel; to Mary
Jarboe (wife) the old woman Cove &
plantation she lives on; to Edward
Barbier Mentions: Mr. Edward Clarke,
Mr. Foster.

6:486 Date: 11 March 1674. Since according to
the laws of ENG, the younger sons cannot
claim the lands given to them in the
nuncupative will & hold them against
their elder brother, the first will was
recorded, only to serve as an inducement
to his Lordship to provide in favor of
the younger sons. Will of John Jarbo
(Britton's Bay, SM). Date: 2 September
1671.

6:487 Bequests: son John Jarbo 150 a. land he
lives on Britton's Bay & "Mashes Hope"
150 a., daughter Mary Jarbo "St.
Lawrence's Freehold", unborn child "St.
Peter's Hill" 500 a. Residue: wife Mary
Jarbo, son John Jarboe, daughter Mary
Jarboe.

6:488 Mentions: father of St. Ignatius
Chappell for poor Catholiques, John
Jordaine, Walter Hall, Henry Neale.
Further bequests: Mr. Henry Warren.
Executrix: wife Mary Jarbo. Overseers:
John Jordaine, Walter Hall, Henry Neale.
Witnesses: Anne Neale, William Farding.

6:489 Sarah Harris (KE) widow of George Harris
(KE) renounced administration on his
estate & appointed her son John Ingram
as her attorney. Date: 8 April 1674.
Witnesses: Michael Miller, Thomas
Barnes.

6:490 Will of Henry Jubbar (mariner, master of
the ship Dorothy in the Choptank River,
Poole, Dorset, ENG). [Some of the
witnesses have runaway; some are dec'd.
The original will is to be sent to ENG
to the widow & executors.]

6:491 Executors: brother-in-law William Baker,
wife. Bequests: wife Rebecca Jubbar,
son Henry Jubbar (under age 14). Date:

27 August 1673. Witnesses: Richard
Girching, George Soley (chirurgeon),
Richard Barnes, John Barnes.

6:492 Philemon Lloyd (TA), weak from sickness,
took oath as administrator of Henry
Hawkins (TA).

26 May. Lidia Solley (SM) widow &
administratrix of Benjamin Solley (SM)
exhibited inventory.

28 May. Thomas Doxey (SM) who married
relict of Robertt Hooper (SM) exhibited
accounts.
6:493 Distribution: relict (1/3rd). Residue
to: orphan.

6:494 Discharge granted.

Richard Tilghman (TA) administrator of
John Barnes was granted continuance.

29 May. Thomas Knighton, at the request
of George Skipwith (AA), falsely
informed the court that Evan Davis (AA)
died childless & unmarried.
6:495 Said Evan left a wife & children. Mary
(widow) was granted administration on
his estate. Samuell Lane (g, AA) to
take bond. Said Knighton is to
relinquish the administration.

1 June. John Pile (g, SM) administrator
of Thomas Standley (SM) exhibited
inventory.
6:496 Robertt Burle (g, AA) & Thomas Marsh (g,
KE) executors of Ralph Williams (AA)
exhibited accounts. The 3rd executor is
living in ENG.

5 June. William Newport (SM) executor
of George Waker exhibited inventory.

9 June. Jane Paine (St. Jerom's, SM)
widow & administratrix of Thomas Paine
(SM) is lately dec'd & left 7 young
children (all under age). Dec'd has no
6:497 relations in the Province to whom
administration should be granted.
Appraisers: William Claw, Joseph
Hackney. Said appraisers to evaluation

estate of said Jane & estate of John
Smalpeece (brother of said Jane).

11 June. William Claw & Joseph Hackney
(St. Jerom's, SM) appraisers of Jane
Paine (SM) & John Smalpeece (brother of
said Jane) exhibited the inventories.

6:500 Robertt Franclin (g, AA) exhibited will
of William Andrews (AA). Will of
William Anderas (p, AA). Bequests: Anne
Anderas "The Greenwood" in the swamp of
Herring Creek then to my daughter
Elisabeth Anderas (under age 15).

6:501 Should my wife remarry, then Elisabeth
Parsons wife of Thomas Parsons (AA) is
be the guardian of my daughter.
Executrix: wife. Date: 3 December 1674.
Witnesses: William Parsons, William
Glover. Will proved 3 May 1675.

6:502 William Burgesse (g, AA) exhibited the
will of John Meers (AA). Will of John
Meers (AA). Date: 17 April 1675.
Bequests: daughter Sarah Meers (under
age 16) land on the north side of Severn
River given me by my father Thomas Meers
& reversion of land adjoining it which
was given by my father to my
mother-in-law, said daughter "Meeres" on
Clifts (CV) 400 a. (southern 200 a. now
belonging

6:503 to my brother-in-law John Homewood, said
daughter plantation on west side of said
land (CV) & 30 a. (CV) bought of Francis
Billingsly, said daughter 300 a. in
Trance Quaking (Eastern Shore). Should
said daughter die under age, then said
lands to go to my sister Sarah Homewood
wife of John Homewood (AA).

6:504 Should said sister die before said
daughter, then lands to my
brother-in-law John Homewood (AA) to be
sold & profits to the children of my
sister-in-law Elisabeth Cole wife of
William Cole (AA).

6:505 Further bequests: brother-in-law Samuell
Thomas chattel made by Richard Arnold,
Richard the carpenter (servant), Anne
Haile (servant), Samuell Underwood,
Quakers.

6:506 Should my daughter die under age, the

residue of my estate to: children of brother-in-law William Cole (West River), children of Thomas Homewood (Maggoty River).

6:507   Executors: Samuell Chew, Esq., Philip Thomas (brother-in-law), Samuell Thomas (brother-in-law), Richard Johns. Signed: John Meares. Witnesses: Edward Price, Tho. Mason, Edward Wood, Thomas Pazar, Thomas Lobla, Sarah Taly, Margueritt Stevens. Will proved by Thomas Peace & Edward Price on 25 May 1675.

6:508   Sarah Peirce (AA) widow & administratrix of William Peirce (AA) exhibited inventory.

Anne Dishoone (AA) relict & executrix of William Anderas (AA) exhibited inventory.

William Burgesse (g, AA) exhibited the will of Thomas Sparrow. Will of Thomas Sparrow (AA).

6:509   Bequests: son Thomas Sparrow (under age 21) plantation, wife Elisabeth Sparrow plantation at Potapscoe.

6:510   Residue to: wife Elisabeth Sparrow & son Thomas (under age 21) & daughter Elisabeth (under age 16) & brother Solomon Sparrow, sister Elisabeth Champ land she lives on.

6:511   Executors: wife Elisabeth Sparrow, brother Solomon Sparrow. Date: 1 January 1674. Witnesses: N. Heathcote, Richard Tydings. Will proved by Nathaniell Heathcote & Richard Tydeings on 5 June 1675.

Benjamin Rozer (high sheriff, CH) exhibited will of Jeremiah Dickeson (CH). Will of Jeremiah Dickeson (CH). Date: 29 September 1673.

6:512
6:513   Bequests: goddaughter Elisabeth Harrison, my servants, Mr. Nicholas Proddy, Luke Green. Residue: son Thomas Dickeson (age 17 at Easter next). Executors: MM Thomas Dent (SM), Nicholas Proddy (CH). Witnesses: John Gray, Walter Cooper.

6:514   Will proved by Walter Cooper & John Grey

on 14 May 1675. (Commission date: 20 April 1675.) Nicholas Proddy was granted administration on said estate. Appraisers: Zachariah Wade, John Ward.

6:515 Benjamin Rozer (high sheriff, CH) exhibited will of Thomas Greenfield (CH). Will of Thomas Greenfield. Bequests: Mr. John Baker. Residue: Meverill Hulse. Executor: said Hulse. Date: 18 April 1675. Witnesses: John Backer, William Mathews, Jone Baker. Commission date: 6 May 1675.

6:516 Will proved by John Baker & William Mathews on 16 May 1675. Meverill Hulse was granted administration. Appraisers: John Court, Alexander Smith.

Thomas Dent (g, SM) one of the executors of Jeremiah Dickeson (CH) exhibited inventory.

6:517 Jane Lee widow & administratrix of James Lee (CH) exhibited inventory.

Ignatius Causin (CH) & Thomas Hussy (CH) appraisers of estate of Joseph Peirse (CH) exhibited his inventory.

18 June. Samuell Chew, Esq. (AA) exhibited that Samuell & Philip Thomas 2 of the executors of John Meeres have renounced their executorships. Richard Johns was granted administration. Appraisers: Nathaniell Smith, John Sollers.

6:518 Major William Burgesse to administer oath.

Nathaniell Stiles (high sheriff, CE) exhibited will of Thomas Salmon (CE). Abraham Wilde (g) to prove will. Said Nathaniell Stiles & John Vanheck to be granted administration of the son & heir is under age 17. Appraisers: Mr. Joseph Hopkins, Nich. Allom.

GENERAL INDEX

(no surname)
  Beasely 83
  Christofer 169
  Clemment 55
  Cove 174
  Elisabeth 75
  Ellin 115
  Feago 116
  Francis 68
  Henry 68
  Isbell 103
  John 113
  Margarett 63
  Noel 103
  Richard 176
  Samuell 85, 92
  Sanders 68
  Tom 69
  William 103
  Witter 62

Abbenton 62
Abbington
  John 26
Abbot
  Michaell 28
Abbott
  Edward 71
Abell
  Lucus 15
Abington
  Mr. 41
Abinsts
  Pieter 41
Abott
  Geo. 37
Abraham
  Isaack 31
Abrahams
  William 74
Acton
  Katharin 36
  Richard 36, 51
Adams
  Elisabeth 4
  Francis 76, 77
  Georg 4

George 4, 81
Hen. 34
Henry 2, 3, 9, 10,
  11, 18, 21, 30,
  32, 82, 87, 88,
  101, 124, 130
Isabell 4
John 4
Margarett 4
Addams
  Fran. 64
  Henry 53, 63
Adwell
  John 71
Alcocke
  Samuell 37
Aldredge
  George 57
Aldridge
  George 7, 18
Aldwell
  John 114
Alexander
  Henry 147
Allanson
  Tho. 23
  Thomas 18
Allcocke
  Samuell 105
Allely
  Edward 65
Allen
  Elisabeth 17
  Jaspar 55
  Jesper 18, 77
  John 27, 73, 80,
    87, 88, 90, 109,
    131, 144, 145,
    159, 160, 163,
    173
  Martha 17
  Patrick 8, 12
  Pope 73
  Thomas 140
  William 17, 18, 23
Allenson
  Mary 17
  Thomas 23
Allerton
  Isaack 92

Ashcombe
    Charles 7
    John 22
    Nath. 18
Ashford
    Nathaniell 109
Asiter
    Will. 37
Askin
    John 82
Askwith
    John 88
Aspinall
    Henry 118, 174
Atchinson
    Vincent 20, 56
Atkins
    Robert 26
Attcheson
    Vincent 88, 98
Attlon
    Richard 108
Attwood
    Richard 83
Atwell
    John 101
Auborn
    John 115
Augustene
    Mr. 42
Auldwheele
    John 69
Axby
    Richard 84
Aylee
    Elisabeth 56
Ayres
    Elisabeth 108
Ayrs
    Edward 117

Backer
    John 178
Backstone
    Frances 6
Bailiffe
    Elisabeth 60
Baker
    Andrew 29
    Caleb 28, 29, 123,
        124
    Capt. 43
    Jacob 28

John 178
Jone 178
Morrice 2
Roger 18, 56, 92,
    94, 114, 164
Thomas 26, 64, 81,
    82, 112
Tomasine 29
William 78, 87, 89,
    174
Balderston
    James 53
Baley
    Richard 116
Ball
    Richard 8, 44, 45,
        62, 64, 65, 98,
        105, 117
    Tho. 28
    Walter 68
Balley
    John 44
Bally
    Godfry 61
    Mr. 61
Banckes
    Charles 115
    Nicho. 16
Bancks
    Thomas 113, 168
Band
    Peter 2
Banister
    Henry 158
Bankes
    George 27
    Richard 72
    Thomas 44
Bannister
    Henry 158, 159
Barber
    Edward 72
    Elisabeth 27, 72
    Luke 72, 120
    Mary 72
    Thomas 72
Barberton Mannor 128
Barbier
    Ann 95
    Edward 95, 174
    Elisabeth 95
    Luke 72, 95, 106,
        158
    Mary 95

Thomas 95
Barbour
   Tho. 69
Barclett
   Sarah 57
Barker
   John 42
   Morris 167
Barkhurst
   James 136
Barnard
   Robert 37
Barnes
   Christop 79
   Elisabeth 48
   Francis 162
   Grace 48
   John 8, 14, 20, 22,
      48, 56, 68, 125,
      142, 160, 175
   Joshua 139
   Richard 175
   Thomas 174
Barns
   John 123
Barnwell
   Charles 52
Barret
   William 67
Barrett
   William 66
Bartlett
   Nicholas 160, 167
Bartley
   Ralfe 62
Barton
   Edward 40
   Mr. 103
   Robertt 164
   William 27, 87, 90,
      130
Base
   Clase Mellow 164
   Mellow Claes 164
Bassell
   Mary 47
   Ralph 45, 46
   Richard 43
Basset
   Thomas 21
Bastfoord Mannor 92
Batchelor's Range 22
Battee
   Fardinando 93, 95

Batten
   William 74
Battens Clift 30
Battin
   Margary 87, 88
   William 87, 88
Battle Creek Neck 23
Bayard
   Peter 18, 43
Bayle
   John 44
   Tho. 44
   Thomas 44
Bayley
   Godfrey 1, 57
   Rich. 77
   Richard 9, 91, 93,
      94, 106, 114
Baylie
   Richard 52, 56
Bayly
   Elisabeth 19
   John 30
   Mr. 19, 57
   Richard 7, 43, 46,
      124
   Rosamond 19
Baynard
   John 52
Beale
   Ninian 72
Beaman
   John 105
Beamon
   John 36, 46, 59,
      63, 145, 146,
      148, 156
Beamont
   John 44
   Tho. 26
Beane
   Elinor 1
   Ellinor 26, 51
   Walter 103
Beanen
   Charles 11
Beard
   Mr. 109
   Richard 36, 51, 133
   Robert 21
Beason
   Steephen 92, 93
Beck
   Richard 24

Becker
  Thomas 3
Beckwith
  Geo. 18, 21
  Georg 85
  George 8, 10, 37,
    72, 89, 94, 155
Bedloe
  Isaack 27
Beedle
  Henry 50, 127, 149,
    150, 163, 173
  Sophia 127, 149,
    150, 163, 173
Beedles Outlett 127
Beeson
  Stephen 36
  Tho. 51
  Thomas 36
Beetle's Outlett 150
Beetle
  Edward 17, 20
Beeven
  Charles 40
Bell
  Ed. 42
  Richard 1
  William 69
Bellerbe
  Tho. 27
Bellers
  Francis 60
Bellingham
  Richard 75
Bellocs
  Francis 90
Bellowes
  Francis 74
Bemon
  John 164
Bemont
  John 140
Benen
  Charles 11
Benet
  Thomas 23
Benett
  Henry 19
Benger
  Richard 156
Benitt
  Henry 11
Bennet
  Richard 21, 105

Thomas 21
William 7
Bennett
  Disboro 114, 149
  Fran. 18
  Henry 19
  R. 138
  Robert 93
  Susanna Maria 83
  Thomas 103, 134,
    169
  William 164
Bennit
  Disburough 78
Bennitt
  John 93
  Richard 102
Benson
  Elisabeth 8
  Stephen 6, 8, 12,
    14, 15
Bentall
  Edward 95
Berkely
  William 82
Berry
  John 28
  William 35, 42, 54,
    76, 77
Bersheba 11
Beson
  Thomas 10
  William 1
Besson
  Tho. 10, 172
Best
  Edward 32, 47
Bicknall
  John 46
Bigatt
  Theophilus 154
Biger
  John 2
Bigger
  (N) 76
  John 39, 55, 56,
    65, 69, 71, 76,
    77, 104, 113,
    121, 125
Billingsley Chance 106
Billingsley's Folly
  106
Billingsley
  Elisabeth 106

Francis 106
Mary 106
Sarah 106
Thomas 21, 45, 56,
  106, 107
Billingsly
Francis 176
Tho. 30
Bineham
Anne 117
James 117
Binehames
Hanna 117
Birckett
Richard 79
Bird
Charles 166
Margueritt 166
William 154, 155
Birkhead
Christopher 63
Birknall
John 107
Birknell
John 106
Bise
William 57
Bishop
Abraham 57, 61
William 8, 98, 151,
  158, 163
Bishopp
Abraham 14
Bisse
William 61
Blackhall
Ralph 136, 139,
  163, 168
Blackiston
Ebenezar 6, 26
John 6, 7
Nehemiah 6, 7, 25
Blackistone
John 27
Nehemiah 27
Blackleach
Solomon 2
Blackleeth
Elisabeth 75
John 75
Blackstone
(N) 92
Nehemiah 87
Blade

Daniell 50
Blakistone
Nehemiah 106
Bland
Damoras 149, 162
Damorus 148
Thomas 148, 149
Blanford
Tho. 72
Thomas 69
Blangy
Louis 131
Block
Hans 41
Blomfeild
John 46, 60, 79,
  158
Mr. 52
Blount
Thomas 169
Bluff Point 48
Boarman
William 116
Bodkin
Dominicke 88
Body
John 93
Bold
William 4
Bone
Edward 83
Boner
Mr. 59
Bonner
Henery 115
Henry 20, 27
Mr. 71
Booker
Thomas 121
Boone
John 109
Thomas 73, 81
Booth
John 24, 89, 107
Thomas 53
Boothe
John 14
Boreman
William 82, 112,
  119, 139, 144,
  147
Borne
Samuell 86, 87
Borter

Mr. 116
Boston
    Mary 167
    Samuell 139, 159,
        167
Boswell
    John 1
    William 21
Boteler
    C. 18
    Charles 12, 14, 24,
        33, 43, 64
    P. 123
Botler
    Charles 8
Boudell
    Thomas 111
Boughen
    David 3
Boughton
    Rich. 172
    Richard 26
Boulden
    William 48
Boulding
    William 48, 58
Boules
    John 68, 82, 114,
        115
Boulin
    Elisabeth 117
    James 147
    John 117
Boulton
    John 3, 86, 105,
        137
Boume
    Samuell 116
Bovill 17
Bowdell
    Thomas 4
Bowden
    Elisabeth 159
Bowdle
    Thomas 4, 19, 31
Bowen
    Sa. 16
    Samuell 16, 33
Bowles
    John 34, 56, 85,
        87, 88, 98, 116,
        171
    Margary 87, 88
Bowling

James 26
Bowth
    Mary 38
    Thomas 38
Boyce
    Cornel. 50
Boyd
    Ann 145
    Anne 140, 146
    James 140, 143, 146
Boyden
    William 64, 112
Bradley
    Henery 113
    Henry 113
    Samuel 113
Bradly
    Roger 39
Bradnox
    Thomas 110
Bradshaw
    Thomas 32, 47
Brady
    Henry 150
Bramble
    Mary 13, 19
    Thomas 13, 19
Brannack
    Edmund 128
    Jane 128
Brannock
    Edmund 128
Brawsgrove
    John 62
Bredborne
    John 15, 34
Breedon
    Gerard 27
Brent
    Margaret 12
Breton
    William 26
Bretton
    Temperance 11
    Will. 10, 11
    William 10, 11
Brewer
    (N) 86
    Thomas 28
Brice
    Thomas 154, 155
Bridges
    Will. 57
Brien

Lewis 117
Bright
    Thomas 8, 40, 51,
        102, 105, 115
Brinnell
    Falck 115
Brisco
    John 18
Briscoe
    Arthur 145, 148
Brittaine
    Mr. 102
Broadwater
    (N) 5
    Henry 1
    Hugh 5
Brobant
    John 31
Broccas
    George 48, 58
    William 58
Brockas
    Samuell 104
Brockhouse
    Sam. 106
    Samuel 68
    Samuell 82
Broderiff
    John 166
Brokes
    William 48
Bromfeild
    John 18, 19
Broock
    John 124
Brooke Place 23
Brooke Ridge 23
Brooke
    Ann 23, 24
    Baker 23, 24, 33,
        65, 166
    Charles 8, 23, 32,
        43
    Elisabeth 23
    Francis 8, 140
    Henry 23, 64, 84
    John 23, 24, 52,
        55, 60, 79
    Mary 23, 129
    Mathew 141
    Robert 23
    Roger 23, 24, 29,
        64
    Thomas 8, 129, 141,

        166
    William 23
Brookes
    Francis 1, 140
    John 82, 89, 91,
        104, 106
    Tho. 2
    Thomas 29, 129
Brooks
    John 139
    Mathew 139
Broomdoun
    Tho. 71
Broome
    John 133
Brosty Hall 13
Brough 111
    Joseph 70, 83
Brougham
    William 113
Browne
    David 138, 152
    Gerrard 17
    John 5, 7, 12, 15,
        60, 93, 94, 100,
        110, 111, 115,
        132, 148, 165,
        167
    Mary 148
    Mr. 109
    Philip 109
    Robert 26, 112
    Tho. 46, 65
    Thomas 36, 65, 95
    William 28
Browning
    John 36, 37
Bruff
    Joseph 132
Bruton
    Dorothy 152, 168
    John 152
Bryan's Clift 30
Bryan
    Lewis 98
Bryant
    Margarett 86
Brymington
    Jacob 60
Buckingham
    Tho. 101
    Thomas 84
Budden
    Elisabeth 96, 97

Bull
    John 139
    Thomas 171
Bullock
    John 25, 139
Bullocke
    John 7
Burford
    Samuell 20, 88, 90,
        109
Burger
    Ann 118
    Daniell 118
    Isack 114, 118
    Jeremiah 118
    John 110
    Joseph 118
    Mary 118
    Samuell 118
    William 118
Burges
    Amy 19
    John 20, 92
    William 12, 31, 67,
        73, 84, 93, 127
Burgess
    George 127
    William 10, 71,
        127, 132, 134
Burgesse
    Edward 133
    George 133
    James 132
    Susanna 133
    William 128, 132,
        133, 137, 145,
        148, 152, 162,
        169, 172, 176,
        177, 178
Burggess
    William 13
Burket
    Richard 60
Burkitt
    Abraham 93
Burkley
    Blansh 99
Burl
    Robert 12
Burle
    Robert 3, 16, 31,
        36, 44, 46, 53,
        63, 83, 87, 94,
        105, 107

Robertt 120, 129,
    130, 131, 138,
    140, 141, 142,
    145, 146, 148,
    153, 164, 165,
    168, 170, 172,
    175
    Steephen 105
Burlt
    Robert 12
Burly
    Robert 50
Burnit
    John 42
Burras
    John 71
Burridge
    John 78
Burrows
    John 60
Burston
    Thomas 20
Burton
    Edward 5, 15, 78,
        150
    Mary 5
    William 65
Bury
    William 116
Bushby
    Margueritt 131, 143
    Richard 143
    Robertt 131, 142,
        143, 153
    Thomas 143
Bussy
    Paule 93
Butten
    John 128
Buttolph
    Thomas 75
Button
    Nathaniell 115
Buttow
    Thomas 75
Buttram
    Nicholas 38
Byard
    Peter 33
Byrd
    William 154, 155
Byrt
    William 155

Cable
  John 9
Cadge
  John 34
Cafford
  Tho. 59
  Thomas 59
Cage
  John 51
Cager
  Robertt 142
  Thomas 27
Calvert
  C. 155
  Charles 54, 55, 74,
    77
  Col. 82
  Philip 26, 66
  Will. 70
  William 20, 78, 83,
    84, 114, 122,
    132, 138, 157
Camell
  John 27
Cammel
  Mary 24
Cammell
  Patrick 1
Canadee
  William 107
Cannady
  Jeremiah 71
Cantabell
  Ed. 41
Cantwell
  Edward 48, 49
Carcu
  Mr. 128
Carew
  Henry 94
Carey
  Robert 27
Caricio
  Evan 22
Carleton
  Arthur 151
  Capt. 77
  Thomas 4, 21, 118,
    125, 151, 163
Carnell
  John 134
Carpenter
  Charles 60, 73, 79

  Simon 15, 79
  Symon 126
Carr
  John 41
  Peeter 96
  Walter 40, 47
Carraway
  John 98, 117
Carre
  Waller 153
Carroway
  John 117
Cartwright
  Demetrius 31, 43,
    52, 55, 77
Carver
  Richard 40
Carvile
  Robert 52, 62, 104
  Robertt 122, 128,
    129, 130
  Thomas 26
Carvill
  John 112
  Ro. 57
  Thomas 111, 112,
    118, 166
Carward
  Peter 73
Carwardin
  Peeter 120
  Peter 170
Carwardine
  Peter 105, 107, 110
Cary
  John 4
Casey
  Tho. 27
Cassell
  Ralph 19
Catterton
  Michaell 43
Cattlin
  Anne 170
Catton
  Jerome 15
Causeene
  Ignatius 18
Causin
  Ignatius 2, 136,
    178
Causine
  Ignatius 142
Caussin

Ignatius 140
Cawdry
  Edward 38
Chadborne
  William 132, 145,
    153
Chafe
  John 163
Chaffe
  John 98
Chagreman
  Elisabeth 21
  John 21
Champ
  Elisabeth 177
Champe
  Elisabeth 65
Chandborne
  Susanna 80
  William 80, 87
Chandler
  Thomas 40, 52
  William 78
Chapman
  Daniell 65
  Richard 56, 84,
    151, 157, 171
Charlseworth
  Georg 68
Charnam
  John 28
Cherman
  John 10
Chese
  John 151
Cheseldine
  Kenhelm 68
Cheseldyn
  Kenelm 147
Cheshire
  William 27
Chesledyn
  Kenelm 125, 130,
    131, 133, 142
Cheslidyne
  Kenelme 122, 124
Cheverill
  Clement 169
  Mary 169
Chevirall
  Clement 29
Chew
  Joseph 93, 95, 100,
    105

Margarett 93
Margrett 95
Sam. 34, 79
Samuel 10, 76
Samuell 11, 13, 22,
  29, 32, 39, 43,
  47, 50, 56, 79,
  93, 127, 130,
  131, 132, 142,
  146, 149, 150,
  156, 161, 169,
  172, 173, 177,
  178
Chilcott
  James 93
Child
  Abraham 119, 120
  Francis 80
Childe
  Abraham 138
Chille
  Abraham 107
Chilsott
  James 133
Chissell
  Francis 86, 97,
    102, 105, 156
Chiverell
  Clement 56
Chivrall
  Clement 29
  John 29
Christeson
  Winlock 42
Christison
  Wenlock 131
Clabone
  Thomas 29
Clagett
  Mary 134
Clarcke
  Daniell 113
Clare
  Marck 127
  Mark 112
  Marke 9, 59, 86,
    100
Clark
  Abraham 93
  Daniel 67
  Joane 81
  Thomas 55
Clarke
  Daniell 67, 72, 108

Page 189

Edward 2, 37, 73,
    173, 174
Jo. 11
John 38, 81, 89,
    158
Thomas 56
Clarkson
    Robert 108
Claw
    William 78, 82, 84,
        134, 137, 142,
        157, 175, 176
Clay
    Henry 60
Clayland
    James 90, 120
Cleare 6
Cleaver
    John 122
Clement
    John 55
Clements
    Nicholas 115
Clemons
    John 80, 85
Clenck
    Conrad 46
Clerck
    Mr. 116
Clerk
    John 12
    Neale 133
Clerke
    Abraham 30
    Daniel 13
    Daniell 17, 58, 60,
        61
    Edward 26, 58
    George 32
    James 99
    John 12
Cleverly
    Thomas 100
Clifford
    John 95
Clocker
    Daniell 68
Cloister
    Benjamin 113
Cloyster
    Benjamin 50, 92
Coarles
    John 130
Coates

Bartholomew 3, 10
Bartholos 28
John 3, 87, 90, 130
Ralph 17, 49, 59,
    80, 85, 96
Cobbreth
    John 157
Coberthwayt
    Robert 13, 65
Cobham
    Tho. 65
    Thomas 65
Coboren
    William 99
Cobreth
    John 9, 59, 60, 63,
        86, 100
Cock
    John 27
Cockey
    William 143
Cocks
    John 60
Coffens
    Abraham 57
Coffin
    Abraham 61
Cofile
    Robert 78
Colchester
    Richard 61
Cole
    Bettee 103
    Betty 103, 104
    Edward 28, 103, 104
    Elisabeth 176
    Eliz. 103
    Fran. 103
    Frances 103
    Gyles 27
    Hen. 41
    Henry 41
    Mary 73, 81, 85,
        102, 103
    Mr. 92
    Mrs. 103
    Presella 44
    Richard 27
    Robert 52, 53, 73,
        77, 81, 85, 97,
        102, 103, 104
    Robertt 110
    Tho. 93
    Thomas 44, 51

William 42, 78, 93,
    103, 104, 176,
    177
Coleman
    Sara 70
Colins
    Thomas 40
Colle
    Sarah 44
Colleck
    Joane 139
Collet
    Elisabeth 76
    Nicholas 76
Colleton 75
Collett's Point 76
Collett
    John 75, 80, 137,
        159
    Mr. 79
Collier
    Ann 40, 104, 108,
        109
    Eliza. 104
    James 104, 108, 117
    Jane 104
    John 1, 5, 14, 16,
        40, 51, 104,
        108, 109
    Philip 104
    Sarah 104
    William 104
Colling
    John 17
Collings
    Francis 36
    Geo. 36
    George 12, 13
Collins
    Francis 21, 37, 47
Collison
    George 60
Collman
    John 9
Comander
    Hercules 61
Comes
    Abraham 27
Common
    Bryant 109
Compton
    John 26
Connaway
    James 105

Connell
    Hugh 150
Connerie
    Edward 166
Connitt
    Robert 40
Connogh
    Robertt 150, 173
Connore
    Edward 27
Constable
    Henry 106
Consturier
    Hendrick 41
Conyer
    Philip 18
Coock
    John 110
Cook
    Edward 130
Cooke
    And. 5
    Andrew 92
    Barbara 3
    Capt. 103
    Edward 33, 36, 60,
        79
    Elisabeth 42, 53
    Henry 3
    John 105, 107, 166
    Margery 166
    Mary 48
    Thomas 51, 109
Cookeman
    Richard 15
Cookesey
    Philip 43, 101
Cooksey
    Samuell 112
Coony
    Philip 116
Cooper
    Benjamin 25, 27
    John 40
    Judith 9
    Robert 27
    Thomas 6, 45, 67
    Timothy 6
    Walter 17, 177
Coouper
    John 92, 93
Coperthwayte
    Ann 7
    Robert 7

Cordea
    Hester 113, 140
    Marck 19, 121
    Mark 124, 130, 140
    Marke 73, 79, 82,
        94, 147, 173
Cormiell
    Elisabeth 64
Cormihill
    Elisabeth 64
Cornelius
    Morene 49
Cornellis
    Hugh 49, 63
Cornellison
    Hugh 48, 60
Cornwallis
    Tho. 26
Corseliss
    (N) 92
Corthes
    John 112
Corum
    William 168
Cosden
    Mr. 71
    Thomas 23, 27
Cosman
    Thomas 71
Cossins
    William 92
Costin
    Henry 83
    Robert 90
Cottell
    William 123
Cotton
    William 96, 124
Coudere
    Edward 47
Cougdon
    James 27
Coulson
    William 28
Courseene
    Ignatius 11, 64
Coursey
    Henry 15, 126
    Mrs. 150
    William 25, 79, 94,
        97, 100, 127,
        149, 150, 163
Court
    John 115, 178

Courte
    John 26, 171
Courts
    Ralph 10
Cousens
    Ignatius 62
Coutes
    John 167
Covant
    Tho. 27
Covent
    Thomas 37, 147
Covington
    Nehemiah 92
Cowdrey
    Edward 96
Cowdries
    Edward 1
Cowell
    Benjamin 142
    Joane 142
Cox
    George 31
    Henry 77, 130
    John 71, 116, 151,
        153, 155, 156,
        164, 165, 173
    Philip 30
Coxe
    John 135, 162, 163
Coysh
    George 74
Cozens
    Richard 42
Crawly
    John 65
Craxon
    Thomas 88
Crayly
    John 36
Credwell
    George 34, 51
Cremmin
    Dennis 128
Cressey
    Sa. 82
    Samuel 82
    Samuell 26, 71, 82,
        107, 137
    Susanna 82
Cressy
    Samuell 2, 62, 152
    Susanna 2
    Susannah 81

Criss
  Oliver 78
Cropper
  Gilbert 26
Cross
  William 71
Crosscomb
  Capt. 79
Crosse
  William 52
Crossman
  Robert 73
Crossy
  Samuell 60
Crouch
  Jeffryas 140
Crouche
  Joshua 140
Crump
  William 52
Crumpp
  Jarvis 80
Cumber
  John 127, 133
Cumfrey
  Robert 108
Cummin
  Bryan 27
Cuningham
  Dan. 77
  Daniel 71
  David 69
Cuninham
  Daniel 69
Curre
  William 83, 131
Currer
  John 8, 136, 146
  William 131, 146
Currie
  Thomas 115
Curvell
  John 105
Cussam
  Francis 88
  Mary 88
Cutts
  Mr. 108, 109
Cydings
  Richard 65

Dabridge
  Robert 3, 6

Daly
  Brien 147
Damells
  Leonard 74
Damering
  John 47
Damrell
  John 11, 36, 37
Danborne
  Thomas 78
Daniell's Denn 18
Daniell's Hope 18
Daniell
  Constant 37, 68
  Constantyne 121,
    122
Dare
  William 5, 18, 91,
    154, 155
Darnall
  Hen. 18
Dauson
  Anthony 108
  Henry 123
  Rebecca 108
Davidg
  Robert 12, 13
Davidge
  Robert 16
Davidson
  William 46
Davigi
  Robert 15
Davis
  Elisabeth 15, 19,
    118, 127, 135
  Ewen 161, 172, 173
  Henry 14
  Hopkin 2, 15, 19
  Joannas 119
  John 85
  Jonas 74, 107, 118,
    127, 140, 149
  Mary 172, 175
  Thomas 42
  Walter 139, 141
  William 46
Davisson
  Robert 28
Davonport
  Humphry 129
Dawbone
  Thomas 47
Dawkins

Joseph 43, 55
Dawson
  Abraham 12, 36
  Anthony 79
  Richard 60
Day
  Edward 95
  George 49
  Thomas 107
Dayly
  Bryan 37
Dayne
  John 55
de la Roch
  Charles 51, 70, 96,
    97
de la Roche
  Charles 121
de la Wood
  Joseph 149
de Ring
  Hance 50
de Ringe
  Aemilius 41
  Hans 41
  Mathias 41
  Mattheus 41
de Wogolaen
  Jacob 46
de Young
  Jacob Claus 50
Deale
  William 51
Deane
  Edward 17
  John 21
Deaner
  Richard 106
Deanie
  Daniel 68
Deareing Gallyer 62
Deareing's Gallier 77
Deareing
  Alce 62
  John 62, 77
Deareings Increase 62
Dearing
  John 64, 121, 125
Deavor
  Grace 11
  Richard 11
DeCosta
  Mathias 44
Degdby

Francis 143
Delap
  Abraham 7
  Adam 7
  Ann 7
  Deborah 7
  John 7
  Mathew 7
  Sarah 7
Delaroch
  Charles 12, 40, 66,
    78
Dellawood
  John 140
  Joseph 140
Dennis
  John 92
Denny
  Robert 79
Dent
  John 1, 115
  Tho. 37, 48, 59,
    123
  Thomas 20, 22, 73,
    96, 97, 100,
    121, 131, 151,
    158, 159, 160,
    161, 165, 171,
    177, 178
Depee
  John 80
Descura
  Martin 91
desJardins
  John 159
Devall
  Mr. 59
Dewall
  Mary 38
Dewberry
  Tho. 26
Dhynoyossa
  Alexander 66
Diacosta
  Mathias 68
Diamond
  George 27
Diar
  John 81
Dickenson
  Edward 64
Dickeson
  Edward 49
  Jeremiah 177, 178

Thomas 177
Dickinson
  Jonathon 15
Dickison
  Jeremiah 87, 100
  Jeremias 109
  Roger 17
Dill
  John 165
Dillaroch
  Peter 49
Dinkenson
  Jeremiah 161
Dishoone
  Anne 177
Ditton
  William 171
Diveare
  William 160
Divine
  Daniell 121, 122
Dixon
  Jane 126
  John 5, 14, 126
Dobbs
  John 27
Dobson
  John 100
  Mr. 92
  Samuell 26, 112,
    116
Docker's Delight 160
Docker
  James 159
Docksie
  Thomas 122
Dod
  Richard 71
Dodd
  Richard 3, 26
Dogget
  Benjamin 100
Dolby
  John 22, 42
Donning
  William 123, 124
Donnman
  Edw. 26
Dorell
  Nicholas 135
Dorington
  Dorothy 86, 134
  Francis 99
Dorman

Will. 59
Dorrell
  George 172
  Nicholas 135
  Paul 165, 171, 172
  Sarah 172
Dorrington
  Francis 52
Dorsey
  Edward 105, 162,
    167
Dosson
  Peter 18
Douglas
  John 55, 68, 85,
    96, 137, 149
Douglasse
  John 139, 141, 168
Doulan
  Elisabeth 117
Doulin
  John 117
Dove
  Robert 29, 39
Dowdle
  Honour 4
Dowglas
  John 30
Dowlin
  John 98
Downes
  Robert 27
  Robertt 157
Downs
  Robertt 144
Doxe
  Thomas 1
Doxey
  Thomas 68, 171, 175
Doxsy
  Thomas 125, 132
Doxy
  John 151
  Thomas 151
Doyne
  Robert 80, 88
Drady
  (N) 52
Draper
  Alexander 23, 38
Dring
  Mathias 39
Drue
  Samuell 37

Drury
　　Robert 21, 55
Drywood
　　John 164
Duberg
　　Edward 71
Dubery
　　Edward 73, 89
Dubrey
　　Edward 123
Ducres
　　Charles 27
Dugins
　　John 89
Duglass
　　John 116
Dulap
　　Ann 7
Dumberton
　　William 18
Dunberton
　　William 19
Duncan
　　David 134
Dundas
　　Geo. 29
　　George 29
Dunkerton
　　William 16, 19, 41,
　　　51, 158
Dunkin
　　Mary 127
　　Patrick 127, 148,
　　　162
Dunn
　　Robert 8, 40, 45,
　　　69, 78, 88
Dunning
　　William 28
Durand
　　Elisabeth 57, 71,
　　　118, 127
　　William 56, 57, 71,
　　　118, 127, 135
Dutton
　　William 160
DuVall
　　Marin 137, 144, 151
　　Marin. 151
　　Martin 132
Dweare
　　William 81, 89
Dwiggen
　　Roger 27

Dyer
　　John 38, 89, 113
Dyne
　　John 28
Dynoyossa
　　Allexander 69

Eason
　　John 57, 61, 90,
　　　100
Eaton
　　Jer. 24
　　Jeremie 115
　　Jeremy 109
　　Nathaniell 90
Eaves
　　George 49, 64
Edelen
　　Richard 27, 49, 62
Edlin
　　Richard 144
Edloe
　　Joseph 82
Edmond
　　John 57
　　Robert 82
Edmonds
　　John 148
Edmondson
　　John 36, 52
Edmunds
　　Joseph 28
　　Richard 125, 137
Edwards
　　John 60, 145, 170
Edwyn
　　Miles 133
Egelstone
　　Bernard 143
Eglestone
　　Barnard 46
Eglington 79
Eke
　　M. 59
Elck Neck 76
Elgat
　　William 152
Elgett
　　William 138
Elinge
　　Mary 34, 126
Elinor
　　Andrew 57

Elior
    Thomas 6
Elles
    William 118
Ellgate
    Edward 74
Ellinor
    Andrew 61
Elliott
    Edward 88, 129
    Thomas 25
    William 123
Ellis
    Peter 75, 76
    Thomas 1, 79, 93
    William 93
Ellton
    John 103
Ellwood
    Richard 139
Elly
    Joane 38
    John 53, 92, 158
Elmes
    John 21
Elstone
    Ralph 15
Elton's Plantation 5
Elton
    James 50, 92
    John 102, 103
Emanson
    Elisabeth 18, 24,
        35, 49
    Mary 18, 49
    Nicholas 49
    Phebe 18
Emerson
    Thomas 8, 66, 73,
        74
Emerton
    Humphry 39, 93
Emet
    John 34
Emett
    William 117
Emory
    Ann 25
Endecott
    John 74
Englesby
    Robert 26
Enloes
    Hendrick 5

Ereckson
    Eliz. 102
    John 15, 105
Erickson
    John 102
    Mathew 102
Erreckson
    John 34
Essex
    John 131
Eure
    Peter 78, 82, 94,
        95
Eurickson
    John 115
Eurrson
    Marcus 135
Evans
    Col. 102
    Mary 107
    Obadiah 52
    Peeter 111
    Pet. 115
    Thomas 26
    William 5, 136
Evars
    Peter 28
Evatt
    Nathaniell 70
Even
    Richard 132
Evens
    Richard 118, 127
Every
    John 40
Evet
    Nathaniell 43
Evett
    Nathaniel 73
    Nathaniell 81
Ewen
    Richard 13, 51, 90,
        149, 150, 172
Ewens
    Richard 13, 45, 150
Exon
    Henry 58, 59
Exons
    Elisabeth 121
    Henry 121
Exton
    Catherin 143
Eyles
    William 101

Page 197

Eyres
   Thomas 132

Faning
   John 55
Fanning
   John 80
Farding
   William 58, 174
Faredall
   Richard 81
Fargison
   Ellenor 144
Farguson
   Ellnor 132
   William 132, 144
Farlo
   Ambroze 71, 93
Farmer
   Elisabeth 143
   Mary 39, 143
   Michael 13, 143
   Michaell 7, 39, 50
Farra
   Robert 26
Farrell
   John 27, 71
Farrendell
   Richard 80
Farsen
   John 26
Fellowell
   William 161
Felowell
   William 161
Felstead
   William 27
Felsted
   William 139
Felsteed
   William 103
Felton
   John 57, 65, 67,
      73, 163
   Katherine 57
   Kathrine 57
Fendall
   Josias 8, 26, 160
Fenix
   George 121
Fenwick
   Cuthbert 24, 33,
      166

Ferguson
   William 171
Fernly
   Francis 64
   John 64
Fidoe
   John 42
Finney
   William 94, 107
Finny
   William 119, 150
Fish
   Jeffery 28
Fishborne
   Ralph 60
Fishbourne
   Ralph 60
Fitzharbert
   Edward 12
   John 12
Fitzherbert
   Edward 28, 29, 123,
      124
   Francis 31, 103
   Maier 29
   Maj. 59, 68
   Mr. 103, 104
Flaws
   Richard 169, 170
Fletcher
   Curtis 20, 29, 68
Foat
   Robertt 130
Foote
   James 78
Ford
   Robert 27
   Sarah 95
   Thomas 93
   William 86, 95
Forrest
   Eliz. 29
   Ellinor 29
   Patrick 29, 46, 54,
      159, 165
   Patricke 73, 89, 91
Foster
   Elisabeth 153, 163
   John 1, 112
   Michaell 11, 38
   Mr. 23, 122, 174
   Richard 27, 36, 37,
      103
   Seth 21, 22, 42,

57, 61, 129,
153, 163
Seth, 112
Seth. 42
Fouch
Hugh 58
Foun
Julian 42
Fountaine
James 169
Founteine
Richard 39
Fowck
Hugh 48
Fowke
Ann 88, 109
Gerard 26
Foxall
John 26
Foxhould
Mr. 102
Foxon
Richard 80, 87, 89,
132, 145, 153
Susanna 80
Foxwell
George 9, 10, 82
Mr. 103
Francis
Thomas 93, 133,
137, 152
Franckes
Richard 42
Francklin
John 33, 130
Robert 22, 32, 34,
40, 84
Robertt 137, 150
Franckling
Robert 62
Francklyn
Robert 32
Franclin
Robertt 133, 153,
162, 173, 176
Frankes
Thomas 96
Franklin
Ro. 90
Robert 13, 51, 76,
79, 93
Robertt 133
Franklyn
John 49

Robert 10, 45, 56
Fraye
Edward 39
Freeman's Fancy 62
Freeman
John 88
Fresh Ponneck 114
Fretwell
Roger 48
Frippos
Francis 137
Frisby
James 41, 122, 125,
135, 137, 153,
156, 157, 164
Mary 135, 153, 157
Thomas 135
William 135
Frith
Elisabeth 112, 129
Henry 112, 129
Frizell
William 148, 162
Frodshall
John 27
Fry
David 93
Fuller
Mr. 109
Nathaniel 114
Robert 60
William 104
Fullinggam
Richard 70
Funnis
Justinian 144

Gant
Jone 4
Thomas 4, 114
Gantt
Thomas 4
Gardiner
Christopher 84
Gardner's Landing 128
Gardner
Ann 56
Capt. 58, 68
Christopher 56
Edward 152
Elisabeth 128, 129,
141, 145, 147
John 48, 58, 128

Luke 27, 58, 73,
77, 81, 85, 97,
102, 104, 128,
141, 145, 147
Richard 58, 128,
141
Thomas 128, 129
Garett
James 113
Garge
William 65
Garnett
Susanna 156
Garret
James 113
Garrett
Nathaniell 70
Gary
Alce 42
Alice 42
John 42, 100
Richard 73
Steeven 109
William 84
Gasaway
Nicholas 7
Gascoway
Nicholas 134
Gaseway
Nicholas 127
Gaslings
William 129
Gassaway
Nicholas 152, 163
Gater
Will. 56
Gates
Robert 102, 103
Gather
John 131
Gaudy
William 27
Geater
William 40
Gee
John 27
George Towne 171
Georgoe
William 89
Gerard
John 6, 92, 106
Justinan 7
Justinian 6, 25,
27, 92

Justinian. 28
Mary 6, 7, 92
Rose 92
Susanna 92
Thomas 6, 27, 28,
106
Gerrard's Reserve 92
Gerrard
(N) 103
John 87, 92, 93
Justinian 110, 124
Mr. 104
Tho. 48
Thomas 48, 87, 92,
112
Gervis
Thomas 101
Gibbens
widow 102
Gibbon
Philip 109, 126,
140, 142
Gibbons
Samuell 155
Gibbs
Elisabeth 74
Robert 74, 75
Gibings
Samuell 156
Gibson
Miles 99, 136
Robert 115
Thomas 27, 96, 124
Gilbert
John 36, 37, 47,
118, 125, 153
Gilbertt
John 156
Giles
Thomas 138
Gillam
John 27
Zachary 27
Gillis
Thomas 152
Gimbo
John 85
Ginnet
Elisabeth 60
Girching
Richard 175
Gittings
John 44, 133, 138
Glover

Isack 55, 56
John 74, 124
William 176
Godard
Thomas 169
Goddard
Elias 42
Thomas 169
William 27
Godfrey
Geo. 71
George 49, 53, 80, 90
James 78
John 44, 51
Godscrose
Alice 39
James 39
Godscrosse
James 50, 143
Godsgrace
James 55
Goffe
Edward 76
Goldbery
Margarett 57
Nicholas 57
Goldhawke
George 51
Mary 51, 121
Goldsmith
George 167
Joanna 159
Johanna 122, 159
Maior 122
Mary 167
Samuell 125, 138
Gooch
John 27
Good
Georg 96
Richard 96
Robertt 154
Goodgin
Robert 102
Goodhand
Cristopher 149
Goods
Edward 113
Goodwin
George 58
Goodwine
Richard 166
Gooldhawke

George 40
Goosey
Margarett 9
Samuell 29, 39, 50
Gorsuch
Charles 45
John 62
Richard 15, 31, 148, 160, 161, 165, 167
Goshum
Heaster 109
Gott
Elisabeth 98
Henry 98, 115
Gough
Robert 118
Gould
Daniel 42
John 115
Richard 1
Gouldhawke
George 24
Mary 24
Gouldsmith
Elisabeth 76
Georg 16
Johann 16
Johanna 16
John 27, 110, 111, 112
Mary 16, 75
Mathew 76
Samuell 16, 35
Goulson
Alice 143
Gover
Daniell 121, 131, 170
Grace
John 27, 62, 64, 106, 111, 112
William 15
Gramm
John 4
Grammer
John 29, 92
Granger
William 40, 105
Grannt
William 32, 34
Grant
William 47
Gray

Francis 28
John 93, 132, 137,
144, 177
Green
John 113
Luke 177
Walter 21
Greene
Elisabeth 68
James 26, 48, 105
John 37
Leonard 73
Luke 17, 100
Thomas 20, 159
William 24, 91,
141, 169
Greeneaway
James 2
Greenewood
Arinegill 40
James 31
Greenfield
Thomas 167, 178
Greengoe
William 133
Greenwell
James 73
Grenlaw
Jeane 112
Grey
John 74, 170, 177
Griffett
Even 119
Griffin
John 68
Richard 115
Tho. 59
Thomas 59
Griggs
John 31, 59, 64
Grimsditch 128
Groome
John 7
William 7, 33, 35,
39, 43, 44, 53,
55, 56, 60, 65,
77, 96, 101, 113
Grose
Roger 172
Grosse
William 69
Grunby
John 80
Gudgeon

Robertt 167
Gugen
Robert 102
Guibert
Elisabeth 95
Joachim 95, 106,
158
Joshua 26, 166
Guibertt
J. 166
Guift 49
Guilbert
John 125, 171
Guilbertt
John 135
Guin
John 115
Guither
Nicholas 84
William 11
Gundry
Ben. 33
Benj. 19
Gidion 19
Gunnill
William 93
Guthery
James 65
Gutrick
Henry 14
Gutterick
Henry 13
Katherine 13
Guyther
William 11, 64
Gwinn
Richard 44
Gwyn
Richard 51

Hacker
Mary 148
Rachell 22
Richard 22, 148
Hackett
Nicholas 74
Hackney
John 82
Joseph 68, 70, 78,
82, 157, 175,
176
Thomas 82
Hacksby

Richard 65
Haile
    Anne 176
Hailes
    Spencer 144
Haines
    Bernard 11
Haisiney
    Joseph 142
Hales
    John 111
    Spencer 100
Haley
    Clement 26
Halfhead
    John 67, 71, 73,
        131
Halkins
    Ralph 84, 101
Hall
    Charles 38, 170
    Edward 40, 111
    Henry 93
    John 138, 159
    Josias 106
    Mr. 122
    Walter 2, 29, 60,
        72, 84, 91, 94,
        114, 173, 174
Hallet
    Lancellot 18
    Lanncelot 41
    Richard 41
Hallett
    Lancelott 50
Hallwell
    James 49
Haly
    Clement 166
Hambleton
    Will. 56
    William 55, 89,
        112, 113, 119,
        129, 163
Hammon
    Daniell 147
Hamon
    Daniell 31
    Margaret 30
    Mordecay 30
Hamond
    Daniel 31
    Margaret 31
    Mordecay 31

Hance
    John 116, 127
Hancock
    Benjamin 167
    Rebecca 99
    Sarah 167
Handcock
    Rebecca 99
Hanson
    John 32, 49
    Randall 95, 129,
        141
    Randolph 170
    Robert 118
Haper
    Xopo 115
Hapwale
    William 132
Hapwate
    William 137, 144
Harbert
    William 3, 8
Hard
    Edward 68
Harden
    Math. 36
    Mathew 46
Harding
    Math. 63
    Mathew 63
    Robert 22, 42
Hardy
    Henry 27, 51, 85,
        89
    Jemima 85, 89
Harison
    Joseph 87
Hariste
    Henry 38
Harman
    Augustine 100
    Godfrey 57
    Godrey 14
    Mr. 36, 37
Harmer's Mount 57
Harmer
    Elisabeth 117
    Godfrey 58, 81
    Godfry 117, 126
    Gothofrid 57
    Mary 117, 166
    Sarah 117
Harmon
    Henry 49

Harnes
  Jacob 152
Harnesse
  William 171
Harniss
  Issack 80
Harper
  Robert 37
  Thomas 28
  William 65, 121,
    123, 124, 131,
    169
Harpin
  Thomas 113
Harrington
  John 61, 82, 137,
    149, 152
Harris
  George 104, 137,
    138, 145, 174
  John 3, 63
  Moses 65
  Mr. 78
  Samuell 26
  Sarah 104, 114,
    137, 138, 174
  Simon 74
  Tho. 57
  Thomas 30, 63
  William 14, 54,
    107, 144, 170
Harrison
  Benjamin 100
  Elisabeth 100, 177
  Francis 100
  John 27
  Joseph 17, 100, 145
  Katherine 100
  Mary 17, 100
  Peter 51
  Richard 100
  Sarah 89
Harrwood
  Phillip 35
Hartwell
  John 140
Harvey
  Ellinor 2
  John 27
Harwood
  Elisabeth 42
  Judith 42
  Philip 84
  Phillip 64

Robert 42
Thomas 42
Hasellwood
  Henry 75, 76
Haselwood
  Henry 16, 35, 75
Haslewood
  Henry 122, 137,
    159, 166, 167,
    168
Hatch
  John 27
Hatoft
  William 123
Hattoft
  Richard 29
  William 28, 123,
    124, 125
Hatton
  Hanna 61
  Henry 61
  John 57, 61, 77, 86
  Margret 54
  Mr. 61, 108, 109
  Richard 107, 170
  Robertt 170
  Samuel 77
  Samuell 61, 86,
    160, 167
  Sara 61
  Susann 61
  Thomas 46, 54, 61,
    77
  William 96, 97,
    129, 141, 161
Hause
  John 9
Hauskins
  John 26
Haward
  Cornelius 94
  Mathew 94
Hawes
  George 116
  John 9
Hawkins
  Elisabeth 131
  Henry 67, 83, 119,
    171, 175
  John 11, 21, 36,
    37, 47, 93
  Ralph 37, 105, 106,
    162, 168, 172
  Ralphs 105

Richard 119
Robert 37, 80
Sarah 11
Thomas 66, 69
Will. 37
William 106, 131,
    162, 168, 172
Hawse
  John 9
Hawton
  William 27
Hayes
  James 27
Hayles
  John 68
Hayman
  Henry 138, 152
Haynes
  Charles 3
  Georg 68
Hays
  William 169
Hayse
  James 71
Haywood
  Raphael 166
Head
  Elisabeth 136, 149,
    170
  Jeane 149
  William 13, 84, 86,
    89, 105, 110,
    115, 136, 149,
    170
Heaman
  Abra. 78
Heard
  John 26
Heath
  Thomas 126
  William 34
Heathcoate
  Nan. 93
  Nath. 133
  Nathaniell 77, 86,
    127, 133, 137,
    143, 146
Heathcote
  N. 177
  Nath. 172
  Nathaniell 143,
    153, 156, 162,
    167, 171, 172,
    177

Hebb
  Thomas 53
Hedge
  John 70
  Tho. 10
  Thomas 10
Heigh
  Robert 8, 12, 21,
    29, 30, 45
Heighe
  Robert 9
Heliard
  Daniell 143, 162
  Jane 143
  Joane 162
Hemen
  Henry 54
Hemfreys
  Thomas 140
Hemsley
  Mr. 15, 74
  Will. 57
  William 7, 14, 56,
    57, 61, 71, 83,
    119, 120, 137,
    164
Hemsly
  William 83, 90
Henderick
  Anthony 168
Hendeson
  Andrew 47
Hendrick
  John 167
Henfry
  Thomas 83
Henley
  Robert 61, 85, 88,
    101
  Robertt 137, 149,
    151, 159, 168
  William 82
Henly
  Robert 9, 30, 68,
    71, 82, 91, 96,
    116
Henrick
  John 160
Herbert
  Clement 65, 84
  Elisabeth 65
  Philip 85
  William 4
Herman's Mount 61

Herman
  Augustin 49
  Godfry 61
  Gothofred 61
  Mr. 36
Herne
  Thomas 93
Herring
  Bartholomew 35, 43,
    44
  Margarett 35
  widow 35
Herrmen
  Augustine 63
Hett
  Elliphellet 27
Hewbery
  William 83
Hewes
  Samuell 16, 33
Hews
  Samuell 33
Hewson
  Samuell 103
Hide
  Edward 36
  Henry 161, 170
  Thomas 54, 91, 155
Higgen
  Mic. 97
  Michael 81
  Michaell 53, 81, 97
Higgins
  Michael 5
  Michaell 38
Higgs
  Andrew 113
Higguen
  Michael 114, 160
Hill
  Clement 128, 129,
    141
  John 4, 40, 51
  Margueritt 114
  Marke 92
  Mathew 26, 91
  Mr. 71
  Penelope 3
  Richard 12, 13, 24,
    27, 31, 43, 50,
    119, 130, 131,
    132, 138, 142,
    143, 144, 145,
    146, 148, 150,

    151, 152, 153,
    164, 168, 170,
    171
Hillen
  John 93
Hilliard
  John 49
  Thomas 49
Hillilce 128
Hillton
  John 103
Hilton
  John 27, 103
Hinksman
  George 27
Hinley
  Robert 55
Hinsey
  William 61
Hinsley
  William 15
Hinson
  Charles 79
  George 1, 158
  John 43, 70, 73, 78
  Randall 72, 95, 100
  Thomas 16, 78, 98,
    105, 163, 168
Hiscox
  Joseph 63
Hitchcock
  Christop 85
  Christopher 85
  Heugh 93
Hitchcox
  Joseph 63
Hittson
  Richard 100
Hobbs
  Thomas 39
Hobson
  John 93
  Thomas 88
Hocker
  Thomas 62
Hodgson
  John 24, 32
HoeRobbin
  William 169
Holis
  William 81
Holland
  Anthony 22
  Daniell 88, 89

Hynson
Tho. 33

Inch
James 76, 80
Incon
John 44
Ingolsby
Robert 20
Ingram
(N) 52
John 15, 24, 45,
51, 80, 89, 90,
110, 137, 138,
174
Maier 15
Thomas 40, 45
Inloes
Henry 5
Innes
William 4, 7
Inness
William 55
Innis
Thomas 29
Irelire
John 28
Irish
George 156
Isaacks
Edward 111
Island Creek Neck 23
Ives
James 168
John 167

Jackson
John 74
Richard 90
Thomas 25
William 79, 80, 87,
113, 130, 144
Jacob
John 138
Jacobe
John 119
James
Abell 3, 29, 56,
71, 73, 107,
123, 164, 165
Charles 6, 47, 80,
91, 151, 162,

165
Diana 73
Dianna 164, 165
Elisabeth 6
John 1, 144, 163,
173
Richard 39, 80
Tho. 68
Thomas 28, 42, 84
William 18, 71
Jansen
Henrich 41
Jarbo
John 26, 174
Mary 174
Jarboe
Henry 174
John 147, 157, 173,
174
Mary 157, 173, 174
Peter 174
Jardins
John des 159
Jaxson
Edward 166
Jeamoth 106
Jefferson
Michaell 2
Jeffryes
John 13
Jeffs
John 2
Jenckins
John 61
Jenifer
Daniel 78
Daniell 1, 2
Mary 1
Mr. 71, 78
Jenkens
John 57
Jenkenson
Robertt 165
Jenkins
Francis 34, 51
Heaster 114
Jers
John 73
Joannes
Jenken 26
Johns
Rich. 6
Richard 6, 9, 177,
178

Johnson
  (N) 103
  Christopher 115
  Daniel 81
  Daniell 3, 71
  David 119
  Elisabeth 3
  Eliz. 27
  Faith 170
  Frances 7
  Francis 7, 90
  Jacob 28
  James 27
  Jane 4
  John 102, 103, 112
  Judeth 4
  Richard 21
  William 19
Jollee
  Edward 68
Jolley
  James 35
  Storn. 40
Jolly
  Edward 84
Jones
  Ann 16
  Charles 117
  Cornelius 113
  David 93
  Dr. 92
  Edward 105, 114
  Francis 143
  Henry 16, 33, 50
  Humphry 27, 127
  Isbell 102
  John 136, 142, 143,
    166
  Mary 16
  Morgan 126, 138,
    139, 147
  Owen 32, 47, 71
  Philip 14, 24, 105
  Richard 15, 114,
    139, 158, 163
  Robert 89
  Ruth 114
  Sarah 16
  Thomas 2, 20, 117,
    168
  William 36, 46, 52,
    58, 65, 73, 77,
    89, 105, 138,
    140, 145, 164

  Winifred 20
Jordain
  Jean 157
  John 157, 173
Jordaine
  John 7, 27, 173,
    174
  Thomas 93
Jordeene
  John 59
Joules
  Dr. 92
Jourdaine
  John 95
  Thomas 26
Jourdin
  Dr. 105
Jowles
  Henry 105, 156
Joyner
  Cathrine 55
  Mary 55
  Robert 26, 55
Jubbar
  Henry 87, 94, 114,
    116, 164, 174
  Rebecca 174
Juell
  William 93

Kane
  Edward 29
Kanedy
  James 69
Karkhick
  John 78
Kashey
  Edward 149
Keef
  Constantine 122
Keele
  John 100
Keeley
  John 105
Keely
  John 139, 146, 164
  Mary 146
Keen
  Edward 124, 168
  Richard 4
Keene
  Ed. 96
  Edw. 92, 113

Edward 8, 9, 12,
    21, 30, 33, 38,
    39, 41, 50, 60,
    77, 86, 97, 107,
    112, 157
Henry 9, 31, 85, 89
Ric. 21
Richard 10, 21, 31,
    52, 65, 79, 105,
    125, 155, 160
Kemp
    John 44
    Thomas 76
    William 93
Kendall
    Thomas 17
Kene
    Edw. 30
    Richard 44
Kenedy
    Will. 105
Kennedy
    William 110, 164,
        165
Kennimont
    (N) 120
    John 113
Kent
    Robert 15
    William 100
Kershaw
    James 25
Keynes
    John 118
Kilborn
    Elisabeth 71
    Fran. 71
Kilborne
    Elisabeth 71
Kileley
    Humphry 100
King
    Elisabeth 25
    Margrett 107
    Robert 20, 25
    Susanna 20
    Thomas 35, 62
    William 7, 9, 18,
        52, 55, 77, 126
Kinge
    Elisabeth 25
    John 25, 29
    Marck 25
    Thomas 24

Kingly
    John 26
Kingsbury
    Robert 11, 32
Kingsland
    Anthony 39, 40, 45
Kinseys Cheird 14
Kirkley
    Thomas 28
Kirum
    William 52
Knap
    Elisabeth 30
    Henry 54
    John 30, 43
    Mary 54
Knapp
    John 43
    Robert 1
Knight
    George 71
    Henry 163, 173
    Thomas 78
Knighton
    Tho. 52
    Thomas 47, 150,
        161, 173, 175
Knott
    Ann 103
    Fran. 104
    Francis 26, 103,
        104, 119
Konnerie
    Edward 163
Koyd
    Mr. 109
Kyley
    James 105

Lad
    Richard 92, 124,
        136
Ladd
    Richard 38, 53
    William 90
Lake
    Edward 93
Lakeby
    Edward 15
Lamb
    Henry 16, 33, 146
    Susanna 16
    widow 33

Tho. 51
Lookwood
 Robert 56
Louder
 Edward 73
Lovelace
 Francis 11, 109
Low
 Vincent 105
Lower Bennett 9
Loyd
 Phil. 15
 Philemon 15
Luan
 James 112
Lucas
 Mr. 157
 William 82, 84,
  111, 114
Ludford
 Arthur 35, 39, 44,
  50, 53, 60
Lugor
 John 4
 Martha 4
Luke Land 72
Lumbrozio
 Dr. 102
Lumer
 Dr. 59
Lune
 Edward 37
Lunford
 John 81
Lunn
 Edward 100, 105
 Robert 28
Lupton
 William 42
Lusbe
 Robert 12
Lusbie
 Robert 13, 16
Lusby
 Dorothy 143, 171
 Jacob 143, 171
 Robert 3, 6, 12, 13
 Robertt 143, 171
 Sarah 171
 Zachariah 171
Lynes
 Phil. 126
 Philip 144, 161

Macall
 George 3
Macane
 Patrick 4
Macary
 Daniell 47
Mackall
 Georg 91
 George 161
Mackary
 Daniel 49
Mackeand
 Patricke 69
Mackell
 John 128
Mackey
 Richard 49
Mackloglin
 Kallom 59
 Mary 59
Mackloughlyn
 Kenelm 21
Macknemarry
 Hugh 26
Mackunna
 Dennis 93
Macky
 John 121, 131, 159
Madbery
 John 15
Maddox
 Samuell 27, 111
 William 1
Magrah
 William 90
Magreger
 James 49
Magrooder
 Alexander 9
Magrowgh
 Dormand 65
Magruder
 Alexander 69, 72
 Allexander 77
Mahaun
 Timothy 103
Mailum
 John 44
Makriger
 James 63
Malam
 John 44
Male

Thomas 73
Mosely
    Thomas 73
Moss
    Richard 87, 99, 105
Mosse
    Richard 36, 46
Mountagne
    Steephen 90
    William 90
Mountagu
    Steeven 18
Mountague's Addition
    59
Mountague's Mountayne
    59
Mountague
    Steephen 80
    Stephen 21, 28, 49,
        58, 59, 80
Mountgue
    Steeven 18
Moy
    Mr. 107
    Rich. 68, 84
    Richard 2, 20, 30,
        80
Mucert
    Nathaniell 28
Much Haddum 31
Mudd
    Strangwaies 6
Muffet
    William 33, 35, 43,
        44
Muffett
    William 46
Muffitt
    William 35
Muginbrug
    Martin 75
Mullikin
    Patrick 147
Munday
    Elisabeth 1
Mungomery
    Ann 42
Munkister
    Elisabeth 21
Munn
    John 17
Murphey
    Owen 128
Murphy

Daniell 163
    Owen 135
Murty
    Stephen 147
My Quarter 146
Mynott
    Robert 160

Nash
    Alexander 24
    Richard 14, 15
    Sarah 24
Neale
    Ann 58, 73
    Anne 58, 121, 122,
        123, 174
    Henry 2, 31, 46,
        58, 73, 121,
        122, 123, 174
    Jacob 45, 50, 65,
        97, 105, 143
    James 26, 62
    Margret 22
    Rebecka 22
    Samell 56
    Samuell 22, 40, 125
    Susanna 99
    William 46, 105
Neall
    Henry 26
Neave
    Robert 3, 47
Neavill
    John 21
Needles
    James 25
Negroes
    Alce 26
    Anthony 111
    Bambo 26
    Bess 26
    Caffee 28
    Clare 53
    Clauser 26
    Cloise 103
    Dockay 26
    Hannah 26
    Joane 26
    John 115
    Love 26
    Margueritt 135
    Maria 26
    Mingo 26

Constantine 122
Love 122
O'Keefe
Constant 37
O'Keel
Constantyn 125
O'Kiefe
Constantine 161
Oakely
Thomas 27
Oakley
John 63
Oataway
Thomas 139
Obryan
Mathias 64
Obryand
Mathias 76
Odally
Bryen 122
Odaly
Brien 132, 139
Brine 121
Bryen 121, 122
Oddonell
Thomas 61
Oderon
Clory 165
Mary 165
Odonnel
Tho. 57
Ogdon
James 40
Okeef
Constantine 121
Constantyne 122
Okieffe
Constantyne 122
Oling
Moses 65
Oliver
Nicholas 42
Samuel 75
Oneal
Hugh 26
Oneale
Hugh 101
Orsborne
Henry 123
Orum
Elisabeth 75
Francis 75
John 75
Osberne

Tho. 97
Osbeston
Will. 68
Osborne
Henry 108
Katherine 108
Samuell 28
Sara 108
Sarah 108
Tho. 40
Thomas 57, 110,
131, 136
William 126
Osbourne
William 35
Oswolivant
Denis 59
Otame
Richard 26
Outgers
Henry 46
Overton
Jeane 166
John 166
Nathaniell 166
Tho. 19
Thomas 33, 166
Owen
John 17
Richard 60, 163
Timothy 93
Owing
John 59

Padget
Thomas 30
Padison
James 120
Paget
Thomas 11, 19
Pagett
Thomas 113
Paine's Lott 70
Paine
Elisabeth 70
Hannah 70
Isaack 70
Isaacke 84
Isack 130, 157
Jane 70, 78, 112,
118, 124, 130,
157, 175, 176
John 31, 32, 34

Phillpott
  Edward 101
Philpot
  Tho. 28
Phinney
  William 90
Phipps
  Henry 2, 46, 77
Pickard
  Nicholas 57, 61
Pickering
  Mr. 65
Pickquascoe 101
Picks
  William 80
Piera
  Pier 34, 98
Pierpoint
  Henry 148
Pike
  Elisabeth 170
  William 170
Pile
  John 26, 147, 175
Piles
  Mr. 103
Pinckney
  Christopher 53
Pine
  Francis 15, 33, 36,
    42, 110
  John 37
  Mary 36, 110, 115,
    131, 146
  Mr. 59
Piper
  John 53, 111, 112,
    116
  Marguerit 112
Pitt
  Edward 34, 98
  John 15, 52, 160
Place
  John 73, 144, 161
  Thomas 92
Planner
  William 38, 170
Plat
  Thomas 19
Plumer
  Thomas 78
Polinger
  Mary 143
Pollard

(N), 77
  John 52, 77, 91
  Will. 14
Pomffrett
  Edward 99
Pomfret
  Edward 3
Pomfrett
  Edward 105
Poole
  David 78
Pooly
  John 71
Poore
  John 60
  William 73
Pope
  Francis 20, 26, 30,
    55, 81, 82
  John 30
  Richard 30
  Thomas 30, 91, 96
Poppin
  John 27
Portwood
  John 112
Poteete
  Francis 78
Pott
  John 35
Potter
  Cuthbert 42
  Richard 40
  Thomas 169, 170
Powell
  Henry 23, 38
  John 56, 164, 165
  Mr. 75
  Roger 53
  William 63, 161
Power
  William 56, 66,
    110, 120
Powill
  John 55
Powre
  William 92
Powstney
  William 105
Pramch
  Morgin 78
Prater
  Jonathon 4
Pratt

Nath. 83
Nathaniel 67
William 100
Reade
Ellen 20
George 125, 126
Mathew 8
Nath. 83
Nathaniell 74
William 20
Readway
John 131
Reannalls
John 114
Red
Mathias 40
Reddor
Symon 26
Reed
William 43
Reeves
Thomas 48
Refue
Henry 124
Regan
Cornelius 86, 99, 134
Regann
Cornelius 99
Relisford
William 140
Resfne
Ann 77
Mary 77
Newill 77
Thomas 77
Retchford
Mary 140
William 140, 149
Retisford
William 140
Reves
Thomas 26
Rey
John 103
Reynolds
John 68, 70, 78, 84, 134, 137
Thomas 107
Rhoads
John 98
Rhodes
John 34
Rich Neck 6, 14

Richardson
John 19, 20, 33, 100
Marke 91
William 93
Richeson
William 40
Rickston
Nicholas 51
Rider
Henry 44, 68
Richard 14, 24
Robert 41
Ridgely
Henry 32, 47, 132, 144
Robert 2, 16, 20, 54, 55, 62, 64, 70, 123
Robertt 122, 123, 124, 170
Ridgley
Henry 84, 100
Ridor
Richard 134
Riede
Mathew 136
Rigbey
James 105, 106
Rigbie
James 57, 61
Rigby
James 3, 57, 61
Rigell
Hannah 68
Riggs
Francis 6
Jane 9, 21
Joseph 9, 21, 45, 63
Rigold
John 73
Ring
Hance de 50
Ringall
James 139
Ringe
Aemilius de 41
Hans de 41
Mathias de 41
Mattheus de 41
Ringgold
James 47, 126
Ringold

Rosewell
  William 139, 163, 166
Roswell
  Eme 52
  Emma 52
  Mr. 71
  William 26, 52, 110
Rotton
  William 90
Rouell
  George 116
Rousby
  Christop 92
  Christopher 39, 65, 77
  Mr. 52, 67
Rouse
  Mr. 102
  Robert 30
Rowell
  George 113
Rowland
  Okey 84, 100, 132
  Robert 26
Rowlant
  Robertt 139
Rowlants
  Robertt 141
Rowles
  Christopher 131
  Gerratt 96
Rowlin
  Ebrius 21
Rowsby
  Christopher 5, 144
  John 144
Rowse
  Gregory 2, 26
  Mathew 28, 102
Rowsell
  William 55
Royden
  John 23
  William 49
Royston
  (N) 52
  Richard 1, 21, 36
Rozer
  Benj. 26, 49
  Benjamin 11, 20, 24, 35, 49, 53, 59, 64, 76, 80, 87, 88, 89, 90,

98, 109, 112, 116, 118, 126, 136, 140, 142, 144, 151, 158, 161, 167, 173, 177, 178
  Mr. 63, 71, 80
Ruckston
  Nicholas 45
Ruckstone
  Richard 106
Rudd
  Nathaniell 28
Rugsten
  Nicholas 98
Russel
  Richard 111
  Sara 111
Russell's Plantation 70
Russell
  Elisabeth 6, 70
  John 30, 56
  Mary 70
  Peter 51
  Richard 68, 69, 70, 82, 83, 144, 145
  Sara 68, 69
  William 40
Ruxston
  Nicholas 117
Ruxton
  Nicholas 117
Ryder
  Elisabeth 129
  Henry 68
  Jane 141, 142, 170
  Richard 170
Ryely
  John 80
Ryland
  John 18

Sale
  Clement 31
Salisbury
  William 1, 17, 21
Saller
  John 40
Salley
  Mr. 102
Salloway
  Anthony 13

Sally
    Benjamin 48
Salman
    Thomas 109
Salmon
    T. 21, 35
    Tho. 50
    Thomas 1, 11, 16,
       19, 36, 37, 41,
       76, 80, 151,
       163, 173, 178
Saloway
    Anthony 40
Salsbury
    William 19, 36, 37,
       109
Salway
    Anthony 172
Sampson
    Robert 27, 106
Sanders
    Mary 46, 140
    Mr. 107
Sandry
    Francis 45
Sanford
    Elisabeth 75
    John 75
    Samuel 75
Sangoe
    John 131
Sarall
    William 100
Sargent
    Joseph 19
Saucall
    William 83
Saughier
    Geo. 57
    George 61
Saunders
    Robert 19
Saunderson
    Richard 27
Sauvage
    Edward 76
Savage
    Edward 61
    William 73
Sawyer
    Peter 40
Sayer
    Peter 94
Scoefield

Robertt 157
Scot
    James 8
    Thomas 17
Scotland 55
Scott
    James 14
    John 109, 117
    Tho. 17
Scottow
    Thomas 75
Seaell
    William 128
Seager
    James 27
Seale
    William 135
Sealeing
    George 81
Sealer
    Edmond 53
Sealing
    George 38
Sealling
    George 38
Sealy
    George 4
Sean
    James 27
Sedgewick
    Tho. 4
    Thomas 3, 8
Sedwell
    Roger 62, 64
Seekings
    Thomas 22
Segivant
    John 14
Selby
    James 13, 17, 19,
       35
    John 28
Selo
    Francis 147
Selog
    Georg 92
Sempler
    William 69
Seth
    Jacob 86
Sewall
    Henry 105
    Johanna 143
Sewell

Barbary 75
David 75
Henry 37, 119, 143,
    146, 149, 152,
    156, 172
Johanna 119, 146,
    147, 153, 156,
    172
Reynold 75
Sexby
    Richard 148
Shackerly
    John 50
Shadock
    Henry 27
Shadwell
    John 5
    Michael 5
    Michaell 5
Shanker
    John 27
Shankes
    John 102
Shanks
    John 92
Shapleigh
    Joyce 88
    Philip 16, 43, 78,
        90, 93
Sharpe
    Mary 42
    Peter 92
    William 42
Shaw
    Gervas 96
    John 127, 134, 163
    Sara 127
    Sarah 134
Shawe
    Gervas 96
Sheafe
    Elisabeth 74
    Jacob 74
    Margaret 74
    Margarett 74
    Mehittabell 74
    Mehittable 74
Sheaffe
    Elisabeth 74, 75
    Jacob 74
    Margarett 75
    Mehittabell 75
Sheehee
    Roger 121

Shehee
    Edmond 122
    Roger 68, 70, 111,
        122, 125, 161
Sheires
    Will. 22
Shelton
    Tho. 40
Sheppard
    John 27
    Nicholas 167
Sheppey
    Mary 102
Sheppy
    Richard 102, 103
Sheradon
    Thomas 116
Sherisinton
    Mathew 166
Sherman
    John 10
Sherrington
    Richard 129
Sherwood
    Hugh 2, 15, 60, 129
Shippey
    Richard 26
Shipppoint 114
Shirt
    Katherine 107
    William 94, 119
Shirtclife
    Ann 26
Shirtliffe
    widow 62
Short
    Amos 3
Shrewes
    William 28
Shudall
    Warner 7
Shuttleworth
    Thomas 100
Sibrey
    Jonathon 119, 153,
        164, 166
Silvaine
    Daniell 18, 33
Silvane
    Danyell 33
    Jeremiah 18
Simons
    Lawrence 98
Simpson

Marmaduke 27
Thomas 27, 147
William 27
Sinckler
John 43, 69, 71
William 60
Sincler
John 43
William 49
Sineck
William 172
Singleton
William 11, 32, 97, 114
Sinker
John 30
Sinkler
Hanna 168
John 116, 168
Sittwell
Dorithy 103
Sivell
Thomas 148
Sivick
William 161
Skillton
Thomas 4
Skinner
A. 14
Andrew 8, 14, 113, 119, 140, 149, 164
Augustin 133
Tho. 36
Thom. 72
Thomas 17, 67, 86, 91, 128, 135
Skipwith
George 175
Sam. 57
Samuell 61
Slade
Will. 37
William 14, 36, 46, 164, 168
Slater
Richard 73
Slaughter
Bartholomew 27
Slead
William 168
Sleydon
Samuell 8, 14
Sluilivant

Jeremiah 45
Sly
Gerrard 87, 90
Mr. 104
Robert 89
Slye
Elisabeth 6
Frances 6
Gerard 6, 7, 25, 106
Gerrard 48
John 25
Mr. 102, 103
Robert 6, 7, 25
Susanna 6
Smallhope 76
Smallpeece
John 78, 84, 157
Smallpeese
John 137
Smallpeice
John 70
Smallspeece
John 134
Smallwood
James 71
Smalpeece
John 157, 176
Smalpeice
John 70
Smart
Henry 54, 154, 155
Mrs. 29
Nicholas 54
Thomas 28, 29, 123, 124
Smethwick
Thomas 127
Smicke
William 90
Smith
Alexander 167, 178
Allexander 26
Elisabeth 15, 19
Francis 37, 71, 105
George 127
Grace 139
Henry 22, 48, 78, 151, 171
James 132, 168
John 26, 68, 69, 71, 76, 79, 114
Mary 1, 28
Mathias 78

Thomas 51
Taly
    Sarah 177
Tarleton
    Edward 164, 169,
        170
Tassell
    John 15, 89
Tasterling
    Henry 21
Taunt
    Ann 56
    Thomas 56
Tawney
    John 9
    Michaell 9
Taylor
    Fran. 71
    Francis 36
    Henry 14, 26, 73
    John 65, 66, 67,
        70, 73, 99, 121,
        145, 152
    Joseph 93
    Miles 42
    Morgan 120, 129,
        131
    Mr. 150
    Robertt 111, 125
    Samuell 111
    Tho. 40, 61, 63,
        87, 91, 105
    Thomas 31, 36, 50,
        60, 62, 65, 70,
        79, 81, 87, 89,
        93, 94, 96, 118,
        172
Taylour
    John 66
    Thomas 45, 46
Teagle
    Elisabeth 22
    Eliz. 42
    Nathaniell 22
Tenahill
    Alice 134
    William 134
Tenahills
    William 134
Teneson
    John 105
Tennahill
    Alice 134
    John 134

Mary 134
William 134
Tennison
    John 48
    Justinian 26
Tennisson
    John 26
Territ
    Nicholas 40
Tetershall
    Lawrence 122
    Mary 122
    William 122
Tettershall
    William 2
Thatcher
    Thomas 74, 75
The Greenwood 176
The Quarter 102
The Range 14
The Vineyard 119
Theabush 5
Theobalds
    Clement 109
Thimbleby
    John 102
Thomas
    Dorothy 17
    Evan 66, 74, 110,
        120
    Hew 87
    Hugh 115
    John 27, 90, 116,
        127
    Mary 90, 116
    Mr. 108, 109, 119
    Phebe 127
    Philip 40, 93, 152,
        177, 178
    Phill. 171
    Robert 107
    Samuell 176, 177,
        178
    Sarah 152
    Thomas 21
    Tristram 119
    Trusram 101
    Truston 100
    Trustram 25, 94,
        107
    Walter 45
    William 13, 19, 67,
        72, 125, 138,
        139

Thompson
    Arthur 26
    George 27
    James 15, 91, 141
    John 29, 68, 70, 82
    Michaell 26
    William 7, 55, 67,
      72
Thompton
    William 111
Thomson
    Arthur 21
    John 56
Thorneton
    Ann 103
Thornton
    Ann 103
    Fran. 64
    Francis 76
Throster
    John 6, 8, 60
Thurston
    (N) 109
Thussell
    Richard 20
Thwayte
    Mary 48
    Thomas 48
    William 48
Tier
    James 30
Tilghman
    Dr. 15, 79
    Richard 139, 142,
      158, 163, 175
Tilley
    J. 47
Tillman
    Richard 136
Tilly
    Joseph 29, 30, 41,
      99, 157, 167
    Mary 41, 157
Tinker
    John 19
Tittmarsh
    John 77
Tod
    Capt. 117
Todd
    Elisabeth 22
    Tho. 100
    Thomas 151
Tollard

    William 65, 84
Tolley
    Tho. 57
Tolly
    Thomas 61
Tomkins
    Gyles 26
    William 49, 64
Tomlim
    Edward 25
Tompkinson
    Giles 68
Tomson
    Charles 169
Tossey
    Martha 31
Toulson
    Alexander 2
    William 43, 50, 80
Tovey
    Ann 156
    Nicholas 155, 156,
      164, 173
Towerson
    Alexander 89
    Sander 57
    Saunder 61
Towlson
    William 89
Tranes
    William 93
Traske
    James 27
Trip
    Nicholas 86
Tripp
    Henry 91
Trippe
    Henry 61, 79
Tripper
    Francis 81
Trippos
    Francis 159
Trippus
    Anne 58
    Francis 58
Troster
    John 9, 12, 30, 63,
      106, 107, 127
Trueman
    Ann 53
    Anne 116
    Elisabeth 53
    James 33, 60, 116

Vahan
John 6
Vandenan
William 50
Vanderminen
Amedes 41
Vanhak
John 144
Vanhake
John 122
Vanheck
John 1, 151, 162,
178
Vanswaringen
Garret 19, 20, 29,
41
Garrett 26
Vanswearingen
Garrett 123
Vanswering
Garret 61
Garrett 73
Vansweringen
Gar. 94
Garet 94
Garett 106
Garret 125
Garrett 69, 91,
161, 164
Mr. 68, 78
Varnell
Capt. 108
Vaughan
Sara 68, 69, 111,
144
Sarah 145
Tho. 2, 43
Thomas 20, 68, 69,
74, 80, 85, 111,
124, 164, 167,
169
Vaughen
Thomas 15
Vawghan
Bru. 20
Veitch
James 6
Vellmead 62
Velmeade 77
Venall
John 151
Venals

John 147, 162
Vicaris
Mr. 45
Viccerous
John 49
Vizard
Henry 24

Wade
John 107
Zacharia 101
Zachariah 178
Zachary 100, 101,
128, 129, 144,
157, 161
Wadsworth
Richard 25
Waghob
John 3
Wahob
Archibald 47
Archiball 32
John 3
Wahobb
Archibold 26
Waikfield
Richard & 167
Thomas 139, 159
Wakefeild
Thomas 85, 88
Waker
George 157, 175
Wale
Edward 97
Walker
Alce 159, 160
Alice 151, 168
Daniell 7
George 78
James 1, 8, 27, 34,
51, 151, 159,
168
Thomas 170
Wall
Richard 17
Walley
Thomas 4
widow 43
Wallop
John 23, 38
Walrave
Matheus Garardi Van
Alren 94

Walston
    Jobe 59
Walter
    James 68
Walterlin
    Mary 48
    Walter 142
Walterling
    Grace 48
    Patience 48
    Walter 68
Walterlyn
    Mary 47
    Walter 48, 123
Walters
    Ann 25
    Christopher 25
    Mary 148
    Richard 148
    Robert 25
    Susanna 136
Walton
    Elisabeth 114
    Johanna 165
    John 27, 110, 114,
      165
    Jone 114
    Mary 114
Wamsley
    Thomas 47
Wanhap
    Achiball 115
Wany
    Teigue 122
Ward
    Andrew 26
    Henry 36, 37, 47,
      98, 156
    John 62, 76, 87,
      156, 173, 178
    Mathew 123, 136,
      137, 151, 158,
      168
    Mr. 36
    Thomas 26, 44
Warde
    John 161
Warder
    John 91
    Margery 91
    William 91
Ware
    John 28
    Robert 71

Wareing
    Bassill 5
    Samson 5
    Sarah 5
Waren
    William 154
Warne
    Tho. 26
Warner
    Elisabeth 119, 138,
      143, 146, 156,
      172
    James 119, 129,
      138, 143, 146,
      149, 153, 156,
      172
    John 7
Warreck
    John 55
Warren 11
    Ellinor 8, 26, 67,
      68
    Henry 3, 11, 58,
      59, 62, 63, 64,
      174
    Humphrey 8, 168
    Humphry 66, 67, 68,
      71, 116, 120,
      124, 129
    Ignatious 102
    Ignatius 73, 81,
      85, 102, 104
    John 14, 26, 31,
      46, 60, 105
    Mary 73, 85, 102
    Mr. 23, 58, 62
    William 155
Warrick
    John 147
Warring
    Samson 6, 8
    Sarah 6, 8
Warwick 49
Washington
    John 27, 28
Waterlin
    Mary 25
    Walter 37, 40
Waterling
    Walter 20, 22, 25,
      29, 40
Waterman
    Ellinor 22
    Nicholas 22, 32

Waters
  John 153, 162
  Susanna 153
Waterton
  John 117
Watkins
  John 62, 167
  Thomas 45, 145, 170
Watson
  William 33, 130
Wattkins
  John 77, 90, 93, 95
  Thomas 93
  Walter 106
Watts
  Anthony 27
  William 73, 89
Wattson
  Richard 91, 96
Wauge
  John 92
Waugh
  John 92, 93
Waymack
  Jacob 125
Waymacke
  Jacob 72
Waymoth
  Elisabeth 151
  Thomas 151
Waymouth
  Thomas 163, 173
  widow 162
Weatherly
  James 138, 152
Webb
  Edmond 60
  Edmund 71, 129,
    153, 163
  Henry 74
  Jane 75
  John 75, 86
  Margarett 74
  Mehittabell 75
Webbe
  Edm. 112
Webber
  Leonard 160, 161
Webster
  John 21, 40
Wedge
  John 81
Weeden
  James 49, 97

Luce 49
Weedon
  Ann 34, 98
  James 34
  Luce 34, 98
  William 34, 98
Weedone
  Lucee 98
Weekes
  John 61
  Joseph 15, 24, 79
Weeks
  John 57
  Joseph 3
Welch
  John 10, 76, 79, 93
Wells Cont 13
Wells Hills 13
Wells
  Benjamin 13, 45,
    50, 51
  Edward 113
  Georg 16
  George 13, 16, 41,
    76, 122, 125,
    138, 139, 159,
    162, 167
  Hannah 16
  James 37
  John 137
  Richard 10, 40, 41,
    50
  Robert 45
  Sophia 13
  Thobyas 110
  Tobias 12, 15, 45,
    49, 78, 89, 105,
    110, 131, 137,
    145, 146
  Toby 33, 36
  Tobyas 47
Welsh
  John 51, 90, 93,
    95, 105
West Humphreiss 14
West
  Ann 16
  John 16, 91, 154,
    155
  Richard 55
  Thomas 29
  William 27
Westlock
  John 138, 152

Magdalena 138
Magdalene 152
Westwood Lodge 92
Whaley
  Edward 34
  John 14, 164
Wharton
  Hanry 15
  Jesse 7, 64, 76
  Joseph 80
  Walter 41
Wheatland 64
Wheatly
  Capt. 66
  William 67
Wheeler
  John 15, 17
Whips
  John 40
White Clifts 57, 61
White
  Alexander 144, 157
  Ann 44
  Dennis 27
  Elisabeth 79
  Ellinor 119
  Guy 18, 52, 56
  Henry 10
  James 22, 76, 79,
    90, 93, 136, 153
  Margarett 79
  Mistress 92
  Richard 2
  Rowland 27
  Steeven 109
  Stephen 37
  Susanna 79, 136
  William 19, 77
Whiting
  George 156
  Robertt 156
Whittey
  Richard 16, 43
Whittington
  John 148
Whittle
  Anne 120
  Catherin 120
  Catherine 110
  James 119
  John 110, 120
  Katherine 104
  Thomas 110, 120
  William 105, 107,

    110, 120
Whitton
  Richard 158
Whyte
  James 32
Wickes
  Joseph 24, 121, 126
  Josh. 15
  Rachell 24
Wild
  Abraham 125, 137,
    144, 158
Wilde
  Abraham 11, 21,
    137, 162, 163,
    173, 178
Wilkenson
  Ralph 25
Wilkeson
  William 40
Wilkinson
  William 96
Willard's Purchase 54
Willard
  Daniell 54
  George 54
Willbery
  Paule 88
Willcocks
  John 107
Willey
  Humphrey 25
Williams
  Amy 24
  Frances 19
  Henry 15
  Herman 168
  James 18, 19, 52,
    85, 89
  Lodowick 51, 109,
    117
  Lodowicke 104, 108,
    109
  Lodowike 58
  Mary 104, 108, 109
  Michael 23
  Morgan 57, 61, 138
  Mr. 37
  Ralph 46, 50, 87,
    105, 107, 120,
    130, 141, 172,
    175
  Rebecca 107
  Robert 37

Thomas 113
Willmer
Thomas 124, 133
Willoby
William 72
Willoughby
William 67, 86
Willson
William 92
Wilson
Jam. 41
James 41, 47
John 41, 75
Joseph 41
Margaret 41
Robert 63
William 45
Wimbery
Paule 88
Winchester
Isaack 4, 15, 40,
145
Isaacke 86, 89
Isack 114, 115,
131, 137, 165
Issaace 102
Issaacke 105
Issacke 110
John 4, 24, 33, 40,
47, 51, 57, 61,
100
Winckles
Edward 66, 90, 119,
120
Wincles
Edward 57, 66
Windley
Richard 5
Wine
Francis 160
Winfeild
John 133, 138
Winfield
John 126
Winkels
Edward 110
Winsemore
Robertt 135
Winshaw
William 149
Winslow
Samuell 8, 74, 75,
89
Winsmer

Robertt 128
Winsmore
Richard 113
Robertt 135
Witham
Cuthbert 51
Withers
Elisabeth 12, 13,
31, 53
Sam. 172
Samuell 3, 6, 12,
13, 53, 56
Witter
Thomas 109
Wlate
Richard 105
Woder
John 154, 155
Wogolaen
Jacob de 46
Wolderton
Micaell 22
Wollman
Elisabeth 119
Mary 119
Rebecca 119
Richard 56, 84,
119, 120, 124,
150, 152, 164
Wolman
Richard 107, 135
Wood
Edward 177
James 120, 138
John 80
Joseph de la 149
Mathew 85
William 18, 31
Woode
James 113
Wooder
John 154
Woodfine
John 78
Woods
Marthew 51
Woolchurch
Henry 100
Woolderton
Micaell 22
Michaell 22
Woolen
Charles 17
Wooley

Index to Equity Cases

www.ingramcontent.com/pod-product-compliance
Lightning Source LLC
Chambersburg PA
CBHW061007280326
41935CB00009B/865